Content

Acknowledgement 9

Foreword 11

I. Introductions
Dr Abdul Waheed Khan
Media Education, a Crucial Issue in the Building
of an Inclusive Knowledge Society 15

*Geneviève Jacquinot-Delaunay, Ulla Carlsson,
Samy Tayie & José Manuel Pérez Tornero*
Empowerment Through Media Education. An Intercultural Approach 19

II. Why Media Education? The Grünwald Anniversary
*Evelyne Bevort, Divina Frau-Meigs, Geneviève Jacquinot-Delaunay
& Catherine Souyri*
From Grünwald to Paris. Towards A Scale Change? 37

The Paris Agenda. 12 Recommendations for Media Education 49

Grünwald Declaration on Media Education 57

Geneviève Jacquinot-Delaunay
Media Education: quand il n'est plus temps d'attendre…
Media Education: When the Waiting is Over 59

III. Young People's Media Culture in the Digital Age
Samy Tayie
Children and Mass Media in the Arab World. A Second Level Analysis 67

Evelyne Bevort & Patrick Verniers
The Appropriation of New Media and Communication Tools
by Young People Aged 12-18 in Europe. New Trends for Media Education 89

IV. Education and Media Culture in the Context of Media Literacy

José Manuel Pérez Tornero
Media Literacy. New Conceptualisation, New Approach 103

Matteo Zacchetti & Philippos Vardakas
A European Approach to Media Literacy 117

Saeed Abdallah Hareb
Educational and Mass-Media Cultures: Integration or Contradiction 125

Essmat Sweedan
I, Myself and The Other. In the Light of Educational Culture
and the Media Culture: Integration or Contradiction? 135

Sanjay Asthana
Young People, Media Education and Civic Engagement
in the Postcolonial World 145

Vítor Reia-Baptista
Multidimensional and Multicultural Media Literacy.
Social Challenges and Communicational Risks on the Edge
between Cultural Heritage and Technological Development 155

V. Media Education in the Digital Age

Divina Frau-Meigs
Media Education. Crossing a Mental Rubicon 169

Muhammed El-Khateeb
The Role of School Media Education 181

Susanne Krucsay
Media Education and School Curriculum 193

Pier Cesare Rivoltella
Introducing Multimedia in the Classroom 201

Hanan Ashi
Developing Skills of Interaction with the Screen in Saudi Families 211

Fathia Al Qurashy
Role of the Family in Forming the Rational Interaction with Mass Media.
A Case Study of a Saudi Family 225

Cary Bazalgette
Media Education. International Strategies 235

ORDINARY LOAN

This book should be returned or renewed by the date below. Failure to return books promptly will result in fines and affect your borrowing rights.

LIBRARY
T 020 7919 7150
lending@gold.ac.uk

Goldsmiths
UNIVERSITY OF LONDON

EMPOWERMENT

THROUGH

MEDIA
EDUCATION

An Intercultural Dialogue

EMPOWERMENT
THROUGH
MEDIA
EDUCATION

An Intercultural Dialogue

Ulla Carlsson, Samy Tayie,
Geneviève Jacquinot-Delaunay
and José Manuel Pérez Tornero (Eds.)

**The International Clearinghouse
on Children, Youth and Media**

NORDICOM at Göteborg University

302.2307 EMP

10/10

Empowerment Through Media Education
An Intercultural Dialogue

Editors:
Ulla Carlsson, Samy Tayie, Geneviève Jacquinot-Delaunay
and José Manuel Pérez Tornero

We would like to acknowledge the support of UNESCO in producing this publication

ISBN 978-91-89471-56-6

Published by:
The International Clearinghouse on Children, Youth and Media
in co-operation with UNESCO, Dar Graphit and the Mentor Association

Nordicom
Göteborg University
Box 713
SE 405 30 GÖTEBORG
Sweden

Cover by:
Karin Persson
Printed by:
Livréna AB, Kungälv, Sweden, 2008
Environmental certification according to ISO 14001

VI. Media Literacy in Practice

Cary Bazalgette
Transforming Literacy   245

Sanjay Asthana
Teaching about Media. Media Education, Learning, and Literacy:
Sketching a Dialogic Process   251

Susanne Krucsay
Educational Television and School   259

Geneviève Jacquinot-Delaunay
New Educational Needs. Distance Training and Life-long
Learning for Teachers   265

The Authors   269

Acknowledgement

We would like to acknowledge the support
of UNESCO in producing this publication.

Foreword

Although media, digital and information divides certainly do exist in the world, more and more people have access to a steadily swelling flow of material through many new channels. An interactive and mobile media society has grown up alongside the traditional mass media society. More and more, media use is media activity – passive media consumers are becoming active media producers. In the midst of these developments are children and youth.

The medialized symbolic environment we live in today largely shapes the choices, values and knowledge that determine our everyday lives. Many parents, teachers and policy-makers are concerned about the negative influence they believe media exert on young people. Yet from a historical perspective, such concerns have been voiced as long as mass media have existed. The media, however, are also valued as social and cultural resources. It is in this complex context that we must see the importance of media literacy.

When discussing issues regarding democracy and development we often forget that media literate citizens are a precondition. An important prerequisite for the empowerment of citizens is a concerted effort to improve media and information literacy – skills that help to strengthen the critical abilities and communicative skills that enable the individual to use media and communication both as tools and as a way of articulating processes of development and social change, improving everyday lives and empowering people to influence their own lives. Media and information literacy is needed for all citizens, but is of decisive importance to the younger generation – in both their role as citizens and their participation in society, and their learning, cultural expression and personal fulfilment. A fundamental element of efforts to realize a media and information literate society is media education.

But when issues such as these are discussed, all too often the frame of reference is the media culture of the Western world. There is an urgent need for the agenda to become open to non-Western thoughts and intercultural approaches to a much higher degree than is the case at present. Internationalization is both enriching and necessary with regard to our common interest in broader, more all-inclusive paradigms. Against this background, basing a book on the *First International Conference on Media Education* in Riyadh, March 2007, which was filled with cross-cultural dialogues, and on the *International Meeting on Media Education: Progress, Obstacles, New Trends since Grünwald: Towards New Assessment Criteria?* in Paris, June 2007, seemed to be an excellent idea.

The very preparation of the book is the result of cross-cultural cooperation between organizations such as the Mentor Association, Dar Graphit for Media Services, UNESCO, the European Commission, the French National Commission for UNESCO and the Clearinghouse on Children, Youth and Media at Nordicom, Göteborg University. It is our hope that the articles included here will stimulate further multicultural and intercultural dialogues, and inspire new research initiatives and policy approaches. We are pleased to have been able to gather a good number of scholars and other experts, who presented conclusions from experiences and research to date on media education at the conferences in Riyadh and Paris. They did so from a variety of perspectives and different cultures, contributing their most valuable reflections. We are deeply indebted to all the contributors all around the world who have made this publication possible. We also wish to express our great appreciation of the support provided by UNESCO and Dar Graphit for Media Services in Saudi Arabia, without which this publication could never have come into being.

Göteborg, Cairo, Paris and Barcelona in December 2007

Ulla Carlsson   *Geneviève Jacquinot-Delaunay*

Samy Tayie   *José Manuel Pérez Tornero*

I. Introductions

Media Education, a Crucial Issue in the Building of an Inclusive Knowledge Society

Dr Abdul Waheed Khan

Assistant Director-General for Communication and Information, UNESCO

We live in an era in which mediated forms of communication not only have become the primary means of delivering information and knowledge but also create essential frameworks for hosting and fostering dialogue and exchange across cultures. Media are increasingly accessible at home and in public spaces providing diverse types of information and entertainment that attract young people everywhere. As a matter of fact, media have become part and parcel of the upbringing and socialization processes of all girls and boys and therefore need to be considered by parents, educators, and media professionals as seriously as formal education

Ultimately, media education provides the critical knowledge and the analytical tools that will empower media consumers to function as autonomous and rational citizens, enabling them to critically make use of the media. Media education helps to make people well-informed and responsible citizens, who will be able to take a certain distance towards the immediate pleasures that media can provide.

Numerous studies in the last three decades have demonstrated that young people are spending more and more time interacting with media. Increasingly, media are shaping the meanings and practices of their daily lives based on the information they receive through print media, radio, television, and the Internet.

As we all know, young people are among the most significant consumers of new technologies and delivery formats. Moreover, young people today can and do gain access to media aimed at adults via cable TV, video, or the Internet much more readily than their parents did as children. This development has resulted in a sometimes desperate search for new means of asserting parental control.

Yet, the notion of the vulnerable child in need of protection from the dangers of the media is steadily giving way to the notion of the child as a sovereign consumer. On the one hand, children are being much more intensively targeted by commercial interests; on the other hand, contemporary media culture offers enormous diversity, learning tools and interactivity. Young people are increasingly addressed, not as delicate young minds in need of careful nurture, but as lively, street-wise and self-confident people.

Indeed the media increasingly offer children an experience of autonomy and freedom.

As a matter of fact, young people themselves point out that media can unlock gateways to social mobility, economic improvement, prosperity and creativity. As radio, television, film, and the Internet increasingly reach young people around the world, these media take on power to initiate social change by acting as a motivating and mobilizing force.

Today, many young people take advantage of opportunities presented by media to participate actively in democracy. Online discussion forums act as a neutral ground where they can connect with others, exchange ideas and work together for change. These forums test their opinions, introduce new ones, and expand their ideological horizons, increasing the potential of young people as facilitators in the free exchange of diverse information and knowledge.

But what are the implications of these developments for education? Most obviously, they seem to widen the gap between young people's experiences outside school and their experience in the classroom. While the social and cultural experiences of young people have been dramatically transformed over the past fifty years, schools have not always kept pace with change.

The ways in which teaching and learning are organized, the kinds of skills and knowledge that are valued in assessment, have changed only superficially over time. Yet, much of our learning about important social issues, such as global warning or poverty, have not emanated from school. Rather, much of the knowledge that we gather on these and other global issues come from the media.

Schools need to make much stronger attempts to address and build connections with young people's media cultures.

And this makes the case of media education all the more important.

Some countries have recognized this importance. Media education curricula are used effectively in Canada and North America, Europe, in some countries in the Mediterranean and Asia.

However, much needs to be done before media education is accepted globally. Already overburdened curriculum and the cost of training teachers are two of the many obstacles that prevent media education from being integrated into school programmes.

Many efforts must be undertaken for school teachers to obtain basic qualifications in media education. A secondary school teacher who has been trained in the subject will have a better understanding about the factors contributing to young people's socialization, the culture of media and the power relations it promotes, the use of semiotics and how semiotic references compare to natural languages, the relationship between fiction and non-fiction productions, the notion of genre and the hybridization of genres and so forth.

Schematically, we observe two schools of thought on media education. The first claims the use of media as a teaching tool incorporated within a particular teaching methodology and subject. The second that is more important yet less prevalent, is to ensure that media consumers are well informed about media ethics so that they can deconstruct media products and judge the value of the content with some objectivity.

UNESCO has worked on both approaches. For many years, it has supported initiatives aiming at introducing media literacy in the classrooms.

At the same time, we have produced self-training tools providing an insight on how reality is documented, how certain truths are created and legitimized and how a camera's viewpoint may become the viewer's version of reality. Another example of UNESCO's action is the production of a model curriculum that aims to provide skills to develop young people's access to, and understanding of, the media, or of a media education kit for teachers, parents and professionals.

Let me introduce here the concept of Information Literacy that complements in a certain way the notion of media education and which has become another area of UNESCO's priorities in the past years.

Information literacy is the skill to use information and communication technologies and their applications to access and create information. It extends from knowing how to use computers and access information to critical reflection on the nature of information itself, its technical infrastructure and its social, cultural and philosophical context and impact. It empowers people to seek, evaluate, use and create information effectively to achieve their personal, social, and educational goals.

For example, the ability to navigate in cyberspace and negotiate hypertext multimedia documents requires both the technical skills to use the Internet as well as the literacy skills to interpret the information.

Media education comes within reach of Information Literacy as we are facing a *"convergence culture"*, which according to Henry Jenkins, is *"where old and new media collide, where grassroots and corporate media intersect, where the power of the media producer and the power of the media consumer interact in unpredictable ways."*[1] Blogging, YouTube, Wikipedia, and other social networking sites are all examples of how this convergence culture is playing out in the networked world.

Media pluralism is a prerequisite for development and therefore crucial for young people's participation in social life. Media pluralism permits the expression of diverse opinions, cultures, languages and groups in any society. Diversity of cultures and expressions, tolerance of different opinions, transparency and equity in the management of public resources and services are challenges, which require informed decision-making by governments and communities. It is obvious that an appropriate media environment is a prerequisite for the successful implementation of any media education programme.

Young people today are faced with a vast proliferation of media options, many of which may be unavailable or at least incomprehensible to many adults. We can no longer assume that students will be sharing similar experiences with each other, let alone that they might do so with us. And we can no longer trust in a simplistic account of the impact of the media on identity, where media images are seen to have singular and predictable consequences in terms of our students' perceptions of their place in the world.

Media education can foster new educational practices and pedagogies, especially related to collaborative work, project-oriented productions and new forms of evaluation.

Today, teachers and students are being provided with the tools that can help them design courses and material that are based on their own local needs and productions. Hence, project management skills are developed along with competencies that guide and assess young people's projects. At the same time local content courses are designed and evaluations are undertaken individually or collectively.

The knowledge and awareness nurtured through media education points to a common ground between communication and education. I hope that this book will provide useful guidelines and recommendations that may guide our concrete action in this area in the years to come.

Note

1. Jenkins, H. (2006). *Convergence Culture*. New York: New York University Press. "Introduction," pp.1-24.

Introduction
Empowerment Through Media Education.
An Intercultural Approach

*Geneviève Jacquinot-Delaunay, Ulla Carlsson,
Samy Tayie & José Manuel Pérez Tornero*

Modern information technology has transformed the media landscape and the media culture dramatically over the past decade. Without media and modern information technologies the globalization we speak of would not be possible. Access to a variety of media, telephony and online services is increasingly recognized as a vital factor for political, economic, social and cultural development. At the same time media – especially new media technologies – arouse fears as to the influence they may have on young people.

Although there are media, digital and information divides in the world, more and more people have access to an enormous array of knowledge and diversions of many kinds – on television, on the Internet, and in mobile telephones. Our perceptions of time and space, of the bounds between private and public, central and peripheral, have changed. Convergence, fragmentation, diversification and individualization are characteristics that are frequently in the focus of debate on media culture.

An interactive and mobile media society has grown up alongside the traditional mass media society. Media use is less a matter of exposure or consumption, but more and more an activity. Passive media consumers are becoming active media producers. Young people around the world have already opted in to the new regime.

The technological changes – communications satellites, digitalization and advances in online services, especially the Internet – have made truly global flows of information possible, while they have also opened up transnational markets for global media companies. The categories information, entertainment and advertising are no longer clear-cut; neither are the bounds between hardware and software, and between product and distribution. The media market is heavily concentrated, with respect to both ownership and content.

Young people have increasingly attracted media industries' interest, both because they are major consumers of the media and because they hold the key to future markets, as well. Children and youth represent more than one-third of the world population. With the changes in the media landscape, media producers have focused their energies on 'winning' youthful audiences.

How to bridge the digital or, rather, the knowledge divide has been the topic of considerable attention and effort. The main question is the gap between north and south. The gap between the rich and poor still prevails as a result of disparities in access to resources, knowledge and technology, especially in rural areas. But, the divide is also reproduced within virtually every country of the world and often reflects other gaps – those between income groups, the sexes and ethnic groups. A significant generational gap is also involved. The younger generation today have a command of new media technologies that far surpasses the knowledge and skills the rest of us have managed to develop. Much of the content that is accessible via, for example, the web and mobile telephones remains terra incognita to many adults.

Many parents, teachers and policy-makers are concerned about the negative influence they believe media exert on children and adolescents. Such concerns have been voiced as long as mass media have existed, but the concern has grown in pace with developments in media technology. There is particular concern about what we call 'harmful media content' or 'harm and offence in media content' distributed more widely via satellite/cable television, the Internet, computer games and mobile telephones. The content takes the form of violent and pornographic fiction and non-fiction, offensive advertisements, stereotypical and disrespectful depictions of young people, women and minorities, hate-mongering messages, and so forth. Interactive media like the Internet also imply invitations to risky behaviour in real life in connection with media use. With the Internet and other online technology we cannot see or be seen by the person at the other end of the communication. As a consequence, simple media effects approaches no longer suffice. Instead, the issues of media content and media use need to be contextualised in a multifactor, risk-based framework (Hargrave and Livingstone 2006).

If we are to be able to take care of our young, the level of public understanding and awareness of the media must be raised – among children and youth, among parents and teachers, and among political decision-makers and media professionals.

Protect or Promote?

Some decades ago, the protection of minors was often discussed in terms of government regulation and prohibitions. In today's complex society in an era of successive deregulation and globalisation, the role and powers of government have changed. The dispersion of authority, both vertically to supranational and subnational institutions and horizontally to non-state actors, has challenged the structure and capacity of national governments. We live in an era of multilevel governance; there are many actors in this field, within public as well as in private sectors including the civil society, and on all levels: local, national, regional and international. Multi-level governance relies on networks, mutual trust and confidence, i.e., on collaboration and partnership. In recent decades, this overall trend in political steering, together with the rapid pace of development in the communications sector have shifted the approach to protecting young people from harmful media content from legislation toward a focus on the responsibilities of the parents and other adults and, especially, the interaction between parents and children. But the adults need help in the form of both political decisions and initiatives on the part of the media industry, e.g., codes of ethics and rules that require the industry to assume its share of responsibility vis-â-vis young people.

The approaches to protecting minors from harm and offence in media content largely boil down to three kinds: law and regulation, self-regulation and co-regulation of the media. No one instrument of regulation is sufficient; today and in the future some form of effective interaction between all three kinds of media regulation – that is, between government, the media and civil society – will be required to reach satisfactory results. Stakeholders need to develop effective means by which to collaborate.

But, viewers' and users' perspectives must also be included. Only then will an essential piece of the puzzle fall into place, namely, the necessity of more widespread media and information literacy and awareness in society at large. Children and youth, parents, teachers, media professionals and other adults – all are equally important in this regard. Proponents of media literacy see increased media knowledge in society as contributing to participation, active citizenship, competence development and life long learning. In this way universal, or at least widespread, media literacy becomes crucial to ensuring a democratic society.

Empowerment and Awareness.
The Need for Media and Information Literacy

While the media and new information technologies are believed to cause some problems, they are also valued as social and cultural resources. An often raised question is whether children are helpless victims or are actually capable of meeting the challenges contemporary media present. In this context, the importance of media literacy is often mentioned. Consequently, 'protection' is no longer viewed exclusively in terms of keeping young people away from certain content, or vice versa. The importance of strengthening young people in their role as media consumers is recognized.

Media literacy means understanding how mass media work, how they construct reality and produce meaning, how the media are organized, and knowing

21

how to use them wisely. In short, it is seen to empower people to be both critical thinkers and creative producers of an increasingly wide range of messages using images, sound and language. The medialized symbolic environment we live in today largely shapes the choices, values and knowledge that determine our everyday lives. Media literacy helps, therefore, to strengthen the critical abilities and communicative skills that give human existence meaning and enables the individual to use communication for change.

In the span of a single decade new media like the Internet and mobile telephones have revolutionized media cultures around the world. With the growing convergence of radio, TV and computer solutions, including the emergence of various hybrids and specializations, we see how a variety of electronic media, information and communication is gradually becoming common goods. But with interactivity follows what have come to be known as 'safety risks', which have to do with the fact that we cannot see the person at the other end of the communication. As Insafe puts it: "The problem is further complicated because many people act irresponsibly and feel less accountable when they believe they are acting anonymously… " (Insafe, EU 2006). Another new feature of the media culture is computer games (Media Morphoses 2001, 2008). Traditional media literacy is no longer sufficient. *There is a need to develop new skills and competencies that render users and consumers 'information literate'.*

Media literacy has tended to focus on cultural expression and has a critical dimension that information literacy lacks. Recently, however, information literacy is increasingly connected to issues of democracy and active citizenship. There is a need to bring the two forms of literacy together (Livingstone, van Couvering and Thumim 2007).

The young need these skills, but so do parents and other adults around them. It is essentially a question of awareness. Research has found that many parents have no idea how their children use the media, or of what the new media make available to their children. Furthermore, young people interpret the content of the media in frames of reference that differ more from adults' experience more than ever before (SAFT 2003, 2005).

The Concept of Media and Information Literacy

Naturally some scopes and objectives linked with media literacy are not news. The concept of literacy was traditionally linked to mastery of an alphabet or a language code, that is, through reading, writing and understanding of print media and, subsequently, to television. Today, however, the term literacy has been extended to cover the skills and competencies involved in finding, selecting, analysing, evaluating and storing information, in dealing with and using information, independent of the codes or techniques involved.

The emergence of digital media, which have expanded at a speed and to an extent never before seen, has led to a new intellectual, semiotic, communicative and cultural climate, which has had a marked effect on both personal, work-related and social development. This new climate has led to a qualitative leap, and to a certain extent a rupture, in the systems of mass communications that dominated almost the entire second half of the 20th century (Buckingham 2003, 2005).

Nevertheless, mass media have not been replaced by multimedia and digital media, at least not yet. This means that within the information society, the systems of mass communication and the new digital multimedia environment currently exist side by side. It is important that the survival of the literacy framework built up over the centuries with regard to reading and writing not be ignored; it still forms the basis of much personal and social activity, the system of mass communication, and the systems of multimedia and digital communication.

Meanwhile, multimedia society has brought media convergence. This has led to an increase in communication platforms made up of various media – e.g., computers that also receive TV and radio – and content crossover, such as that of the press and Internet. The concept of WEB 2.0 clearly represents radical changes, which are currently taking place in the field of communications (Rivoltella 2006, *MediaMorphoses* 2007). Changes, past and present, include opportunities to self-edit, publish, access sources, interact, search, etc. Net users have within their reach a complete system of appropriation in a new informative and creative environment: blog and video blog networks, RSS and related services, podcasting systems, news sources in which users participate in classification and circulation, specialized search engines and alert systems for information published on the Internet, wiki systems, new image and audiovisual banks, professional networks, social networks, homepages and personalized desktops, social makers, etc. All of these features favour a new kind of media production, a social kind of production in which citizens cooperate with each other to weave and distribute a new fabric of information and knowledge.

Media literacy must respond to these new challenges in the communicative environment, which require new creative and critical approaches and which highlight the need for media appropriation by individuals, groups and society as a whole: That is to say, *Media Education,* as an educational process, is needed to improve media literacy, as a result.

Media Education: A Fundamental Element in Media and Information Literacy

The answer to the question, 'Promote or protect?' is that it is hardly a question of either-or, but a combination of both – different kinds of regulations and a higher degree of media and information literacy among both youth and adults are necessary ingredients in the work to reduce harm and offence in media content, and to strengthen young people as media consumers and media producers.

Given the increasing convergence of radio, television, and computer technology, media and information literacy is increasingly linked up with issues of democracy and active, participatory citizenship. Media and Information Literacy has come to the fore, and *media education is a fundamental element in the efforts to realize a media and information literate society* in order to promote a well-oriented, democratic, sustainable society.

How to Define the Scope of Media Education?

The answer to this question is complex, as 'layers' of answers have accumulated over the years. The diversity of terms used has often been stressed: image education, audiovisual education, media education, digital education, etc. – and the lack of any definition of the scope of media education has been seen as one of the major obstacles to its spread.

To understand the situation, we should bear in mind that the design of education has changed in step with the evolution of the media (print press, radio, cinema, television), with worldwide social developments, with cultural change and local educational reform, and with the media theories that spur such practices. The content and aim of media education will be different, depending on the ultimate objective: if you are seeking to protect young people from what you see as the manipulative side of the media; if you adopt a more reflexive approach based on personal motivations and preferences; if you are trying to elicit critical analysis of the representations conveyed by the media of a given society; or, if you intend to study language and the use of images and sound as means of expression. In fact, all these approaches have been and are asserted in the work being implemented.

For a few years now, both in school and outside the school setting, emphasis has been laid on learning by doing. This takes place via workshops in which the pupils produce the outputs: newspapers, newscasts, radio slots, video programmes, Internet spaces, and now blogs. Nonetheless, it is still necessary to examine the assumptions that govern such production workshops. Under the same name and with the same eagerness everywhere, activities such as video production call upon quite different notions. Sometimes the emphasis lies on the semiological analysis of the message produced, sometimes on the communication circuit and the response of the receivers, or yet again on the aesthetics of the images and sounds used to create the message (hence on the gratification felt by the creators). Emphasis is seldom placed on work that has a genuinely social aim.

Many initiatives have been undertaken, especially since the 1960s, in various countries and regions of the world. They have been driven by different players – teachers, trainers and leaders of educational communities, theorists, researchers, activist groups or associations, parents, religious communities, even the media themselves (both public and private), and regulatory agencies (where such bodies existed). One might cite any number of ground-breaking experiments in many different settings: an initiation to the audiovisual culture conducted in 1965-66 in the Bordeaux education area in France and, later, the interministerial 'Jeunes Tétéspectateurs Actifs' operation; or the production of radio programmes 'by and for' young Cubans to engage them in their country's economic drive in 1971; or the "press at school" operation conducted in 1972 by the education department of the *Jornal do Brasil,* to mention but a few (Morsy 1984). More broadly, educational interest in the media, which has centred on media education has had different stages or origins which we will describe below.

Stages of Media Education

It should be noted that the phases discussed here are evolutionary and often correspond to specific focuses and models of media literacy models and which, therefore, can coexist at the same time and in the same setting. Still, we will present the phases in stages for the sake of comprehension and to explain the dynamic orientation of the phenomenon.

During the 1960s and a large part of the 1970s, film captured the attention of European teachers. Its rising influence and the emergence of new aesthetic and cultural trends boosted the interest in bringing film into schools. In France, this orientation coincided with the promotion of the 'nouvelle vague', a trend in which film makers themselves became concerned with theoretical discussion, pedagogy and the spread of aesthetics; in the United Kingdom, with the free cinema (albeit the British Film Institute had done a lot for media education ever since 1933); in Italy, with the emergence of cinematographic neo-realism; and in Germany and Poland, in relation to the cinematographic trends of the time.

Film club activities, education in film image and evaluation of the aesthetic and linguistic opportunities in film were all parts of the model approach to media studies. Initiatives were few and far between and on a voluntary basis, but they did succeed in promoting a group of teachers who were dedicated to the field, many of whom became influential.

In the 1970s and early 1980s, interest shifted to television, discussions about the emerging consumer society and, in particular, criticism of advertising. Media education became more critical and took advantage of the critical experience of French semiology (based on Barthes and the magazine, *Communications*), as well as the suggestions of critical ideology derived from the movements of May 1968 – in particular those related to criticism of the consumer society – and proposals made in British cultural research (Hoggart, Williams, Stuart Hall).

During the 1980s, media education was enriched by a quest for alternatives to mass communication. It was during this time that the video appeared – and with it many types of popular content and the development of local or close communication began. This trend was particularly strong in France, Italy, Spain, etc.

The end of the 1980s the beginning of the 1990s saw the deregulation of broadcasting and the appearance of private television channels – i.e., the end of the monopoly of public television channels – and the focus of media education and media literacy turned to the impact of the media and its contents. Concerns were raised about violence, the influence on young people, consumerism, the influence of advertising on values, etc. Discussions and debates began on public service and independent regulatory authorities started to appear. Regulation and self-regulation codes were proposed, and citizens were invited to participate in the configuration of the new electronic media services. The unprecedented strength of electronic media and the need to connect schools with current information led to the first systematic links between schools and the media.

In the mid-1990s, the arrival of digital media had a huge impact on communication systems, in particular Internet and the web. The need for digital literacy became very apparent. The novelty of these new media, and the need for digitalisation that they brought, changed the focus of literacy to the need to acquire instrumental skills, and above all to combat the digital divide, which developed into serious levels of inequality in access to new media.

As a result of all these factors, the beginnings of digital literacy in Europe were distanced from the focus and style that media literacy had had until then. A very European tradition, based on critique, was thus abandoned, and all eyes turned to the United States, which presented itself as a model for the introduction of an information society, and which accentuated an instrumental focus.

At the beginning of the 2000s, media began to converge with force, and there was a call for a synthesis of digital literacy and the tradition of audiovisual literacy (media education), which came to be known as *media literacy*. During the first few years of the 21st century, the barriers between conventional and electronic media and digital media began to disappear. Firstly, this was because all media started to be affected by digitalisation in at least some of their processes. Secondly, it was because new media, the new communication platforms, develop and promote media convergence and multimedia language; convergence and multimedialization based on digitalisation and the development of new mobile communication technologies.

Basic and Mixed Trends

Decisive steps forward have been made since then, at school (from the lower to the higher academic level) and outside the school: media and journalists, editors-in-chief, programme makers, producers, schools of journalism, media associations, local or community media and even regulatory authorities have a role in media education. In fact, we can make a relatively positive inventory of media education practices, even if it is generally on a small scale (a class or a region); another problem is to widen media education to include all the new digital technologies: we can now speak of 'media and information literacy'. The convergence of audiovisual, IT, and telecommunications is now a fact, and media education has to introduce new knowledge and skills to allow critical and creative use of digital and mobile technologies. For example, there is a major difference between knowing how to use a computer to query a search engine or a databank and 'come up with something' – something most young people know how to do – and mastering the requisite skills to retrieve targeted information and verify the sources – which have to be learned. And, for both the mass media and ICTs, we still need a deeper goal of mastery because there is a great difference between being able to analyse television messages as an academic exercise to change one's viewing behaviour and being able to participate as a citizen with the new means of expression, so as not to be merely a consumer but also a 'producer' of information.

There are a number of tendencies in the conceptions of media education as praxis that we should bear in mind: Critical reading, related to semiotics and critique, and with cultural studies; Creative production, related to active pedagogy, alternative communication theories and the establishment of communication policies; and Cooperative production, which is related to policies promoting information society and communication theories in cooperative and community work.

Media Education: Progression and Obstacles

The relationships between the media and society are becoming more complex; hence, the design of media education has become more intricate and fuller. Beginning with the analysis of media messages, it proceeded to analyse the conditions under which all media were produced and disseminated, and to examine the political and economic forces at work – aspects that are too often overlooked in teaching – and the current transcultural implications running through them. Therefore, "media education", reflects an attempt to include all these dimensions for both the media and information technology.

In several academic authorities in Russia, in a women's association in Japan, through citizens' groupings in the USA and Canada, in a department of the national education ministries in Mexico, France, and Belgium, to mention but a few, innovative practices and didactic resources (teachers' notes, guides, manuals, programmes, etc.) have been developed, often supported by European and international agencies (Frau-Meigs 2006). In recent years, research has made headway by involving more and more teachers in projects that enable them to better understand the relationships between young people and their media – a prerequisite for any teaching.

At national and international levels, an active network of specialists has developed by way of meetings, symposia, and seminars – especially those supported by UNESCO, the European Commission, and the Council of Europe. Without doubt, all this has contributed steadily to recognition of media education – to varying degrees in different countries and settings – by education authorities. However, it is regrettable that policies and support agencies still often prefer to fund the acquisition of equipment, believing that this promotes pedagogic innovation!

Consequently, although a positive assessment of the quantitative and qualitative development in all types of media education initiatives can be made, in the final analysis the work done has not reached all education systems, the media world, or even public opinion.

The obstacles identified are still the same structural, pedagogical, and socio-cultural impediments. How can new interdisciplinary and changing content be injected into highly structured, subject-organised education systems based on definite curricula in ways that do not relegate media education to the status of add-on or optional courses? Various responses have been made in different countries and contexts: optional "club-centred" activities or training included in coursework; activities included in a particular subject or across all subjects; education given in the early years of schooling or, alternatively, only to senior pupils.

Undeniably, sociocultural obstacles are the most recalcitrant. These may include the still negative representations held by teachers – and parents – of the mass media and even more so of the new "*net-generation*" culture. Also, the notion or principle of media education as a fundamental right in a democratic society presupposes the defence of values that are not equally shared by all countries.

Two Conferences and One Book

When media literacy and media education are discussed, all too often the frame of reference is the media landscape of the Western world, even though we know there are major differences among cultures, political systems and faiths, and that all these factors influence media culture. Several countries of the South and Eastern Europe still lack adequate infrastructure for modern mass media and ICT – the differences between town and country are huge – whereas the flow of media content is infinite for those who have access to it. And it remains a fact in many countries that those who can change the situation are not always motivated to do so; those who want to change the situation are not always in a position to.

Empowerment through media and communication – by using traditional media and/or new information technology – can contribute to good governance by identifying corruption and holding leaders to account, and it can assist sustainable development by enabling people to take control over their own livelihood by identifying their needs and problems and by providing access to knowledge and information to enable informed choices – to use communication for change. A most important prerequisite for the empowerment of citizens is a concerted effort to improve media and information literacy.

Information and communication technology has the potential to be a useful tool in the effort to realise an inclusive knowledge society, but it is not a goal in itself. Content is more important than technology. Developing countries face numerous problems regarding ICT and capacity-building. As the prime tool for development, it is vital that the distribution of knowledge does not reinforce existing disparities and disempower. Instead, assistance to infrastructural development and new paradigms of ICT and traditional media, and learning should open up a variety of opportunities, with particular attention to children and youth. We should recall that about 87 per cent of the young people of the world live in what we call developing countries, and 13 per cent in what we term wealthy countries. And we should bear in mind the fact that there is a clear link between ICT and gender equality, that modern communications technology can facilitate the integration of girls and women into society – economically, politically, socially and culturally. Properly designed, a Knowledge Society – with its starting point in the Declaration of the Human Rights and the principle on Freedom of Expression – has a great potential to support more democratic, just and developed societies. The context of media and information literacy, and media education should inform these efforts.

We are all parts of a global system with its transnational flows of information, and we agree on the value of multi-cultural societies, of diversity and pluralism in media culture. National solutions alone cannot solve the problems we face. We need to learn from one another, to share our knowledge and insights. This is particularly true of the issues relating to young people and media. In this context two conferences arranged on a global scale during 2007 are of special importance: the *First International Conference on Media Education* in Riyadh, Saudi Arabia, and the *International Meeting on Media Education: Progress, Obstacles, New Trends* Since *Grünwald: Towards New Assessment Criteria?* in Paris, France.

The First International Conference on Media Education
in Saudi Arabia, Spring 2007

The Mentor Association, together with the Ministry of Education in Saudi Arabia, and with support from UNESCO and the European Union, initiated the *First International Conference on Media Education* in Riyadh, March 4-7, 2007.

The Mentor International Media Education Association was formed in May 2004 to offer media education services to all members, both associations and individuals. The Mentor Association reinforces media education strategies promoted by UNESCO and strives to strengthen an agenda which upholds media education initiatives, first and foremost, in Latin America, Europe, North Africa, and the Middle East and throughout the rest of the world.

This was the first international conference on media education to be held in the Middle East. It was convened under the auspices of H.R.H. King Abdullah, who charged the Minister of Education to open the conference and welcome the participants on his behalf. Among those attending the conference were 1 500 researchers, teachers and policy-makers within the media and communication field from countries of the Arab World, the Middle East, Europe and North and South America. With its wide range of intercultural dialogues the conference was a most important step in the exchange of knowledge between researchers and experts in the field of media education from different parts of the world. The focus on media education in the Arab World was of vital importance.

Before 2002, there were no real workshops or conferences on media education. The first workshop was organized by UNESCO in Cairo in December 2002, which was preceded by another workshop in Tunisia. The situation of media education in the Arab World differs to a great extent from that in Europe or in North America. In most Arab countries, the media education at schools is narrowed to the level of media use in the educational process. Consequently, it mainly has to do with media literacy.

There is a real need for media education in most Arab countries. Most studies have shown that mass media have numerous negative influences on children. Children need to be taught how to deal with mass media. Families also, especially mothers, need to be advised on how to help their children in dealing with mass media.

There is also an obvious need for some kind of collaboration between different organizations, such as educational and mass media organizations. This will help significantly to improve the conditions of children's use of media and consequently the media effects on young audiences. The media education at schools was narrowed to the level of media use in the educational process.

As of today, the situation of media education has witnessed some slight progress that may be seen in the number of studies, especially at doctoral level, which are being carried out on media education. This trend has started very recently.

The objectives of the conference were to support and coordinate current and future research and other efforts in the field of media education, serving people from developing countries through raising awareness about currently available research; identifying critical problems that must be addressed in order for the field of media education to move forward; promoting new collaborative efforts between researchers and other experts; and discussing potentially beneficial international initiatives.

It was recommended to encourage initiatives for joint research projects among scholars of different countries. It was also recommended to sustain this kind of interactions and to organize this kind of meeting every year, although the initial proposal was every two years. Requests were made from some countries to host the next conferences. The United Arab Emirates was selected to host next year's conference in March 2008.

The International Meeting on Media Education: Progress, Obstacles,
New Trends Since Grünwald: Towards New Assessment Criteria?
in France, Summer 2007

A second important conference was the *International Meeting on Media Education: Progress, Obstacles, New Trends Since Grünwald: Towards New Assessment Criteria?* held in Paris 21-22 June 2007. On the occasion of the 25th anniversary of the UNESCO Grünwald Declaration, which paved the way for media education at the international level, the meeting aimed at taking stock of the advances and obstacles met in developing media education through the implementation of education policies or practical experiences.

Initiated by UNESCO and the French national commission for UNESCO, with the support of the Council of Europe and the French Ministry of National Education, this international meeting brought together experts (many of whom had attended the conference in Riyadh), education-policy authorities, teachers-cum-researchers, representatives of associations, and media professionals from different parts of the world. They noted the continued validity of the Grünwald Declaration and the relevance of the analysis made in 1982. They also noted the lack of recognition given the Declaration twenty-five years later, whereas the context described makes the principles set out in it even more pressing. Media education activities in school and outside the school setting are not getting enough attention.

Despite some genuine progress, as mentioned by some participants, media education has remained experimental and not gone to the necessary scale (French National Commission for Unesco 2007).

Furthermore, the education that *is* being provided needs to evolve in order:

- to respond to the major changes in society and take account of new directions of research into the media and information and communication technologies; and,

- to adapt to different political, cultural, and social circumstances so that models established in developed countries are not merely transferred everywhere else.

The true challenge of this new international meeting stems from the variety of situations obtaining in the countries represented. Some, such as Turkey, had just launched a pilot experiment in five primary schools, while others in Europe or Canada have been working with pupils, teachers, and parents some forty years.

It is even more difficult to compare developed countries, with high enrolment rates and a democratic tradition (albeit democracy needs always to be safeguarded everywhere), and developing countries, where the drawback of illiteracy is compounded by diverse religious sensitivities and areas where human rights have yet to be won everywhere and for everyone. Interested readers can refer to the bilingual summary of presentations and the full record of the proceedings published by the National French Commission for UNESCO. The debates, issues covered, and final recommendations drafted with the input of all participants complement the presentations of the Riyadh Congress.

31

The Book: A Cross-cultural Project

From time to time the Clearinghouse on Children, Youth and Media at Nordicom, Göteborg University in Sweden, brings together scholars and experts from all around the world to highlight the main conclusions that can be drawn from the research and other experiences relating to media and information literacy and media education – with the future in mind. Indeed, these issues form a pivotal theme in the work of the Clearinghouse. We survey various efforts to raise media and information literacy, offering examples of activities and projects with a focus on children's and young people's own media production as one of the more effective means to raise their level of knowledge and awareness. Against this background a book based on these two conferences was an excellent idea for the Clearinghouse' publishing activities.

There is a need for international cooperation with a view to achieving broader and more all-inclusive paradigms regarding media and information literacy and media education. We have to build on past work but break new ground. There is a need for fresh insights, innovative approaches, and new comparative questions, and we need to develop analytical frameworks that will guide comparative analysis. Without comparative perspectives we run an obvious risk that certain factors will grow out of proportion. The work of supranational organisations is therefore of crucial importance today.

But, we also have to maintain and further develop national and regional collaboration, not least as a means to ensure that internationalization does not take place at the expense of knowledge about, and reflection on, our own societies and cultures. Fruitful national and regional dialogues are a great boon in international exchanges, and vice versa.

Meaningful media literacy and media education programs need to be based on knowledge from both research and experience. It is our hope that such a cooperation between organisations as the Mentor Association, Dar Graphit for Media Services, UNESCO, the European Commission, the French National Commission for UNESCO, and the Clearinghouse on Children, Youth and Media, will contribute to generating the kind of knowledge that the media culture and information society of today calls for – to strengthen the quality and value of media education activities in different parts of the world. In the landscape of global media and communication we have to move towards an innovative and international agenda for media and information literacy, and media education that cuts across ethnic, cultural, religious and political boundaries.

Against this background it is our hope that the articles in this book will stimulate further intercultural dialogues, and inspire new research initiatives and policy approaches, all in constructive co-operation and a creative spirit.

References

Buckingham, David: *Media Education, Learning and Contemporary Culture*. Cambridge Polity Press, 2003

Buckingham, David: *The Media Literacy of Children and Young People. A review of the research literature on behalf of Ofcom*. Centre for the Study of Children, Youth and Media Institute of Education, University of London, London 2005 (www.ofcom.org.uk/advice/media_literacy/medlitpub/medlitpubrss/ml_children.pdf)

Carlsson, Ulla (ed.): *Regulation, Awareness, Empowerment. Young People and Harmful Media Content in the Digital Age*. International Clearinghouse on Children, Youth and Media, Nordicom, Göteborg University 2006 (www.nordicom.gu.se/common/publ_pdf/232_Regulation_Awareness_Empowerment.pdf)

Current Trends and Approaches to Media Literacy in Europe, carried out for the European Commission by the Universidad Autonoma de Barcelona, 2007 (http://ec.europa.eu/avpolicy/media_literacy/studies/index_en.htm)

von Feilitzen, Cecilia and Carlsson, Ulla (eds.): *Promote or Protect. Yearbook 2003*. International Clearinghouse on Children, Youth and Media, Nordicom, Göteborg University 2004

Frau-Meigs, Divina (ed.): *Media Education: A Kit for Teachers, Students, Parents and Professionals*. UNESCO, Paris 2006

Insafe. Europe's Internet Safety Portal (www.saferinternet.org)

Livingstone, Sonia., van Couvering, Elisabeth and Thumim, Nancy.: "Converging traditions of research on media and information literacies: Disciplinary, critical and methodological issues". In D.J. Leu, J. Coiro, M. Knobel and C. Lankshear (Eds.) *Handbook of Research on New Literacies*. Mahwah, NJ: Lawrence Erlbaum Associates (forthcoming)

Mediappro: the Appropriation of new media by the youth, CLEMI, 2006 (http://www.mediappro.org/publications/finalreport.pdf)

Media Education, Advances, Obstacles, and New Trends Since Grünwald:Ttowards a Scale Change? Proceedings, Synthesis and Recommandations. International Meeting, 21-22 june, 2007, Paris. French National Commission for Unesco, October 2007

MediaMorphoses, n° 3: 'Qui a encore peur des jeux vidéos?', INA/A Colin, 2001

MediaMorphoses, n° 21: 'Web2.0, Culture numériques, cultures expressives', INA/A.Colin, 2007

MediaMorphoses, n° 22: 'Les jeux vidéo: un "bien" culturel?', INA/A.Colin, 2008

Millwood Hargrave, Andrea and Livingstone, Sonia: *Harm and Offence in Media Content. A Review of the Evidence*. Intellect, Bristol 2006

Morsy, Zaghloul: *Media Education* (ss dir). UNESCO, Paris 1984

Rivoltella, Pier Cesare: *Screen Generation.Gli adolescenti e le prospettive dell'educazioneeta dei media digitali*. Vita en pensiero, Milano, 2006

SAFT – Safety, Awareness, Facts and Tools (www.saftonline.org)

II. Why Media Education?
The Grünwald Anniversary

From Grünwald to Paris
Towards A Scale Change?

Evelyne Bevort, Divina Frau-Meigs,
Geneviève Jacquinot-Delaunay & Catherine Souyri

In June 2007, the Paris international meeting on media education went back over 25 years of media education through four main issues that organized the diversity of the experiences and analysis presented by the participants coming from all the regions of the world.

The objective of the first working session was to come back to the question of the basic principles of media education as they were appropriately formulated in the Grünwald Declaration, whilst at the same time trying to situate the major changes which have come about over the last 25 years. Why then media education?

- Because we live in a world where the medias are omnipresent and we have to take into consideration their increasing importance in social life, in particular as concerns the younger generation.

- Because, rather than condemn or commend the power of the medias, it is better to admit that they constitute an important element of contemporary culture and can be oriented towards encouraging citizens' active participation in society;

- Because the differences, which often separate education systems and the world which surrounds us, impair preparations for the adult life of the younger generation.

David Buckingham, from the London University Institute of Education, the first observer invited to give his views, recalled the major changes, as much technological as economic and social, which have taken place since the Grünwald Declaration, which render forever more urgent this mobilisation in favour of media education; acceleration of technological evolutions for an interactive communication offering possibilities of democratisation; simultaneously, emerging liberal economies oriented towards consumer logic which increasingly perplex relations between the public and private sectors and make governmental control over the medias more difficult; profound changes in contemporary society inciting more individualism, mobility and flexibility, the reverse of what could have been the culture of mass medias; increasing complexity of media relations between the local, national and global levels to preserve identities and the building of a trans-national culture.

He underlined the current paradoxical situation whereby new means of information and communication offer the possibility to reduce certain inequalities between members of a society and the people whilst yet creating others: hence the increasing importance of media education to combat unequal access to different medias and training for the necessary skills to master them in order to develop a critical understanding, not only of the messages they deliver but also the politico-economic forces which structure them, and to encourage the active participation of the younger generation based on an acknowledgement of their cultural and characteristic diversity. The Convention of Children's Rights – right to freedom of expression, access to information sources and to participation in cultural life – adopted by UNESCO in 1989, enables us *to make media education a basic human right.* This point having been made – incidentally, underlined several times by David Buckingham in his conclusions – it remains to pass from recommendations to actions and not to "reinvent the wheel", hence a reminder from several participants as to the agenda priorities which will be taken up again in the final recommendations.

But we, of course, know that the political, economic, social, cultural and educational situations are very different according to the regions, countries and continents and that media education is, by this very fact, a territory which must be put into context. Such were the observations in the name of India by the second speaker, Professor Keval J. Kumar, Director of the Centre for Education and Research for the Medias in Pune.

After having given a wide panoramic view of the current media situation on the Indian scale and underlined the difficulties, nigh impossibilities, of public control in the absence of a unique and powerful regulating organisation, Keval J. Kumar insisted on the difficult situation for media education in such a context. Tackled in the 1980s by some pioneers, mostly members of the Catholic Church, and largely influenced by Australia and the United States with the backing of UNDA[1], media education in India was also propped up, as in other countries, by the nationalist and anti-imperialist claims, the Southern Regions of India being opposed to the domination of the Hindu language and the culture of the North. The satellite invasion of the 1990s, then the development, as much technological as economic and cultural, since the beginning of the new century, have completely changed our understanding and endorsed a real "communications revolution".

If, in the Southern States, the current situation of media education is very inconsistent – integrated or not in the school curricula and practiced by active groups, notably feminine, or members of SIGNS[2] – it is probable that such actions are carried out in the Northern States and the universities and private institutes in that part of the country train media professionals without any critical frame of reference. Confirmation – as given by the Chairman of the Research Division on Media education at IAMCR[3] – of the decline, on an international scale, of the movement for media education, Keval J. Kumar ended by insisting, as he did in 1990 at the Toulouse Symposium[4], on the necessity for developing countries to adopt a specific approach to media education, taking into account the local needs and resources, keeping in mind the mass medias which remain predominant and their economic dimensions, not only linguistic but also the inter-relations between the national and multi-national perspectives of former and new medias. In a word, media education requires a radical change and new research, theories not copied from developed countries, which take into account education for citizenship and tie up media education and development: the main challenge for future educators for the medias seems to be to maintain the balance between saving democratic liberties and resisting pressure groups and other lobbies; *otherwise said, to think of media education as a political action in the service of "critical autonomy" and not as an academic or professional matter.*

It is a new cultural context affirmed the following speaker, Samy Tayie, Professor at the University of Cairo and Chairman of the Association *"Mentor"*: that of the Arab countries which are currently becoming aware of this type of preoccupation as was highlighted in the *"First International Congress on Media education" held in Riyadh, Saudi Arabia, in March 2007.*

The technological evolutions have affected the Arab countries just as others via satellite television watched by 90% of the population and Internet now accessible to 75% of the children. If research on relations between the younger generation and the medias started in the early 1980s, it was not really developed until the last 5 years and bears witness, as all over the world, to social and geographic differences; media practices only rarely concern destitute children and do not take into consideration the role of parents. There is no tradition of surveillance or parental control and the television, like the cinema, remain the medias most appreciated, given the level of illiteracy in most of these countries. Suffice it to say that there is a necessity for media education as much for the children as for the parents and teachers: and if at the beginning of the 1990s most governments insisted on the creation of "multi-media laboratories" for the schools, no specific action in favour of media education came about before the Workshop organised in 2002 by UNESCO in Egypt, after that organised in Tunisia. It is in this context that the *Association Mentor* organised, with the support of UNESCO and the European Commission, and in the presence of Ministers of Education from the Arab countries and members of the Saudi Royal Family a *First International Congress on Media Education*[5], followed by 1500 participants who came from different continents: teachers, students, university professors and media professionals, which enabled us to open up an intercultural dialogue. Other events are envisaged: the next Congress will be held in the United Arab

Emirates in March 2008, as well as a comprehensive training programme lasting 6 months for 3,000 Saudi teachers which will take place partly in Saudi Arabia and partly in Europe. This should contribute to clarifying *the great confusion which reigns in these countries as to what should be the concepts and objectives of media education.*

If, on the other hand, there exists in Europe a long tradition of critical analysis of the medias and support for juvenile media productions, this does not mean to say that the definition of media education is clear for everyone and that there are not steps to be taken to achieve a European approach. It is this objective which the European Commission has set itself, as explained by Aviva Silver, Head of a Unit for the General Directorate of the Information Society, responsible for the programme called MEDIA.

Based on three essential elements – access to the medias and their contents, critical approach, aptitude to decode media messages and expertise as to their working methods, capacities for creation and media productions – "media literacy" should concern all the medias, be a pre-requisite for juveniles and the not-so-young in order for them to take an active part in citizenship by being vectors of European cultural identity and to foster both protection against harmful media effects and involvement as producers and not only as information consumers.

Specific actions in favour of "media literacy" projects were then mentioned and concerned those carried out between 2002 and 2005, then as from 2007, and included article 26 of the Audiovisual Media Services Directive (AVMS) which requested the Commission to produce "a report on the level of media education in all Member States", the constitution of a Group of European Experts to promote "good practices", a major public consultation launched at the end of 2006, a study entrusted to the Autonomous University of Barcelona on "Tendencies and trends of media education in Europe" (http://ec.europa.eu/avpolicy/media_literacy/index_en.htm); finally to complete this roundup, end of 2007, a Communication on "media literacy" which will be adopted by the Commission.

In summing up, Aviva Silver recalled that it was up to the competent authorities of the Member States to decide to include "media literacy" in their school curricula and up to local authorities, closer to the citizens themselves, to support initiatives in the area of non-formal education, the role of the European Commission being to strengthen European identity: this should enable us to attain the objectives fixed at the European Council in Lisbonne in 2000, in particular as concerns competitiveness in the economy of knowledge in the service of the Society of Knowledge.

After recalling the major principles on which media education was based and the current reasons for reinforcing their development in the different contexts mentioned by noteworthy speakers, the three roundtables which followed had for objective to give precise information as to progress, obstacles and trends since the Grünwald Declarion, at the same time taking into consideration practices and strategies in formal and non-formal education systems.

What Pedagogical Methods Have Been Developed Throughout the World?

The participants agreed to make a relatively positive intermediary inventory underlining new introductions and acquisitions, as well as the positions consolidated in media education, despite the relative "newness" of the field. Practices are many, with notable successes, but on a small scale, that of a class or a region. Changing to a higher national scale is rare and, when it takes place, is proposed mainly on an optional basis. There is a strong feeling of limited duration and of the window of opportunity which will open for a second phase concerning media education, of pedagogical experimentation for the general diffusion of practices because the social need for this expansion is made felt, aggravated by technological advances in the media world and by globalisation and new challenges from the information society, which UNESCO prefers to call "the knowledge societies". Frequent obstacles were nevertheless underlined, despite certain progress which has given rise to partial implementation of media education in many countries. Some are structural, others intellectual and cultural.

The weaknesses in the system come from the insufficiency of media education in the initial training of teachers, despite lobbying by certain sectors of civil society. In contrast, lifelong education for teachers is more developed and more efficient. The reality shows that "teachers are recycled rather than specialised" according to Thierry de Smedt (Belgium). An absence of the subject matter in universities contributes to this stagnating structural situation because the field has difficulty in asserting itself. The result is a lack of general conceptual framework which is needed to consolidate practices as well as a lack of theoretical models transformed into methods.

Other weaknesses vary according to the educational contexts and the understanding of the role of the school in a given society. They arise from a lack of availability of media education on the part of the teachers, seen as the weak link in the chain of scholastic transmissions. The majority of teachers expect formulas and a "ready to teach" model according to Jacques Piette (Canada). They suffer also from a lack of coordination and priorities from their governing and evaluating bodies (ministries, rectorates, inspectorates). A lack of diffusion of research can lead to confusion between education *with* medias and education *about* medias, between effects and treatment, without speaking of a kind of "ingenuity" of technology about which judgement remains strong in certain mentalities, according to Roxana Morduchowicz (Argentina).

Major advances have nevertheless been made if we take into consideration the fact that media education is relatively recent. The most promising avenue is that of pedagogical innovation which has the potential to modernise schools, even to "modify the medias" according to Toshiko Miyazaki (Japan), because it changes apprentices into active, critical and demanding users. Media education is seen as a transversal skill which has for objective to develop critical and analytical thinking and, as such, should become part of the foundation of basic skills, common to all school curricula.

Another promising advance comes from media teaching aids themselves. Initiatives can be taken by hybrid bodies outside school, such as the National Audiovisual Institute (Institut national de l'audiovisuel (INA)), which develops media tools "conceived according to pedagogical demands" according to Xavier Lemarchand (France). The digital materials are calculable and dynamic and allow for the segmentation of data, on the one hand, and "intelligent" research on the other. It is thus now possible to put at the disposal of teachers and apprentices tools for annotating, segmenting and recomposing audiovisual and multi-media materials. The advantage is that they can be put back into their context, we can reintroduce elements of production in their original form, and modify them afterwards. However, it has to be noted that sometimes the offer proposed by these efficient tools is too sophisticated and disproportionate in comparison with what a school can undertake in its everyday existence, which opens the possibilities for self-training, as much for the teacher as for the apprentice.

The challenges for the future stem from the initial diagnosis. They consist especially in finding more room for media education in initial teacher-training (where it competes with other subjects, such as education and sexuality, citizenship, etc.). It would seem urgent to work in close harmony with teachers, taking into account contributions from apprentices as soon as teaching materials and methods have been worked out. The articulation between critical analysis and production of media contents is vital here. It is most important to avoid formulas but to propose, for the foundation of basic skills, a real legibility and visibility of media education. The implementation of a curriculum which openly declares its priorities, the teaching methods and their evaluation would seem to be the cornerstone of this process. A modular approach, used in the kit on media education and published by UNESCO (2007) is adhered to by most of the participants, the case of Russia, presented by Alexander Fedorov, being exemplary for its feasibility approach and its capacity for localisation.

Taking up such a challenge would imply an investigation into the nature and role of media education for the standard school, with a need to debate interests at stake and the resources. In the face of challenges from the information society, universities and other standard training places are not the only ones to have curricula with a media and technological component, and to counteract the onslaught from the private sector, the incursions of which are evermore numerous in media education, it would be necessary to adopt "an integrating policy" to use the expression of Javier Arevalo Zamudio (Mexico). International exchanges and the comparison of practices would seem to be worthwhile ways to share expertise and an opportunity to take stock of cultural diversity, as much for the school as for the medias.

What Actions Have Been Taken to Integrate Media Education in Educational Policies Throughout the World?

If we are all in agreement in considering that Grünwald has made decisive steps forward for the study on media education, this roundtable feels it necessary to ask two questions. What was the actual follow-up for education systems? In the future, what will be the principal guidelines for media education and their impact on educational policies?

After expression, creativity, participation, training, research ....what will be the new key words for this education?

Such were the questions of Susane Krucsay (Austria) to the participants in this roundtable.

With regard to the history of schools and their branches of study, the history of media education is very short. Between the current situation and future prospects, the question of a change in status for school practices will henceforth have to be made. This question should, of course, be relativised and viewed differently according to historical, cultural and economic contexts. As the participants emphasized, it should be considered with certain precautions but without forgetting that the rapid changes in the society of information necessitate everywhere an urgent response.

Catherine Bizot, General Inspector for Language and Literature, asks herself how, bearing in mind a survey of French education concerning obstacles which have blocked progress, and despite a work of quality during 25 years on all the aspects envisaged by the Grünwald Declaration, it is possible that this field of interest has not gained in importance and visibility. These obstacles are structural, cultural, psychological or administrative in nature and remain numerous and only a strong political directive on this question would be able to bring about change. Media education also lacks, without doubt, sufficiently clear definitions as to the areas to be covered and ambiguity on their precise content remains very evident.

Mustafa Ennaïfar also spoke about obstacles which exist in Tunisia. They are probably of another dimension because media education has not been on the agenda for a long time as such and mostly in two specific fields: images and information and communications technologies. All measures talked about for other education systems (teacher-training, equipment, production tools) will probably have positive effects but he remained convinced that the compulsory character of this teaching remains the decisive factor to prompt a real evolution.

In Turkey, media education, is also in its teething stages, but it is a necessity which is clearly felt and in a revolutionary context of the medias themselves. Yasemin Inccoglu talked about the media education courses recently implemented in the upper grades of the lower secondary schools at the joint initiatives of the Ministry of Education and the regulating authorities. Of course, we are still far behind a 'media educated' country but we have not to be pessimistic because this topic demands particular attention at a moment when Turkey, wishing to enter the European Union, gives thought to this perspective in the light of respect for human rights and the development of a democratic society.

A perspective which systematically privileges the Council of Europe for which media education is part of the logic concerning the right for freedom of expression, for information, and for professional training for journalists. Apart from this, Bernard Dumond recalled that the education systems had a fundamental responsibility for their programmes, their equipment, but also for evaluating experiential learning and competencies. Moreover, they are not the only ones concerned and today the question of media education should be, like many others, accepted as part of the logic of lifelong education and training.

Roxana Morduchowicz was convinced that the groundwork undertaken with parents had given fruit because Argentina had developed a series of actions and dynamic initiatives to involve families in the work of media education. Its fundamental objective is to reinforce, in the long-term, actions undertaken to fully legitimise media education in schools. For her also, obstacles have been created, especially by the teachers, who appear to have rather negative sentiments vis-à-vis the medias and the youth culture they promote. Media education was recently mentioned in a new law concerning education but the challenges to be taken up are still numerous.

The participants expressed the desire and the necessity to see media education ratified as part of the curricula in their education systems. But if a change of scale becomes indispensable, it should be accompanied by a change in culture which teacher-training cannot ensure alone. A strong political directive matching the social demand is necessary everywhere so that media education becomes part and parcel of teaching priorities for schools.

The richness and great diversity of operations so far conducted indicates the profusion of media education. Perhaps today we should, in order to better organise the future, determine more clearly the guidelines, give a clearer structure to this diversity, study and define this education in such a way that it can be shared more broadly.

Which Actors Have Been Mobilised Outside the Educational Framework?

Because media education is not considered as an instruction exclusively scholastic, because it concerns and involves numerous actors outside the teaching profession and because it is designed not only for children but equally for adults, it is fundamental to show interest in activities related to media education which can be developed outside the school, to question their links with the educative system and on ways to better encourage and mobilise all actors involved outside schooling in order that they become a driving force in favour of universalising media education as a component for lifelong education.

By its very objective, media education should associate the medias, that is to say the journalists, the editors in chief, programme makers, producers, mediators, schools of journalism, etc. Now, in the same way that the school has difficulties to open up to the outside world, the medias tend to constitute a relatively closed circuit and paradoxically they are little inclined to debates and external criticism. The mediators, such as Jean-Claude Allanic, former mediator for France 2, have precisely the mission to encourage the opening up of the medias and exchanges with the public. The medias should be more alert to the expectations of the public, to their social responsibilities with regard to citizens as makers of opinion and the fourth power in democratic societies. In this regard, the training of journalists should include more in-depth instruction in legal and ethical matters.

The medias have, anyway, a commercial interest in drawing closer to their audiences in order to better appreciate their desires and to match their offers to demands, and finally to make known and stimulate the interest of a public or potential readers. This way of sharing interests has been well understood by the World Association of Newspapers (Association mondiale des journaux) which has, for a number of years now, developed an introductory programme to journals for schools. This has been used as a pedagogical tool and support for different projects. It encourages the learning of democratic values and takes part in active education for citizenship, stimulates children's performances and inspires children to become future readers, as underlined by Aralynn McMane.

Local or community medias, such as Bush Radio in South Africa (known as the "mother of community radios in Africa"), which maintains closer links with their essentially participative audience, have a strong sense of their responsibility with regard to society and set up projects which enable the population to take part in their activities and, above all, interact. The very objective of Radio Bush is to allow the communities to affirm their dignity, their identity and promote their social responsibility and critical analyses. Thus Bush Radio launched a project in 1996 destined for youngsters with a twofold objective: put at their disposal tools to understand the medias and give them a voice. This project, which has a training and evaluating component, has met with an unqualified success. For Adrian Law, freedom of expression and media education go hand in hand.

OFCOM (The Office of Communications, which is the regulator of all British commercial broadcast media) agrees with this approach and considers that media education helps to encourage self-regulation by users. When the media world is experiencing major changes and the regulating system tends to evolve towards co-regulation, the users should exercise a part of the responsibility in parallel with the traditional regulation ensured by independent authorities. With the development of high speed Internet, cell phones, etc. media offers are experiencing a phenomenal increase and adolescents have a high consumer capacity and take part actively in the development of new practices on Internet. The medias thus occupy an ever increasing place in our everyday lives. In such a context, knowledge of the medias and what they are used for becomes a useful and necessary condition for real and effective participation in society. Such knowledge constitutes an instrument to combat social exclusion and becomes indispensable in the same way as learning to read and write. With the development of Internet, we must avoid the dangers of a training which concentrates on the use of tools and which neglects critical analysis of contents, and we should also help the adult population which has not benefited from training within the school framework. Media education is a statutory objective of The Office of Communications (OFCOM), as recalled Fiona Lennox.

In 2006 OFCOM published a survey in the United Kingdom on knowledge and skills as regards media education which it uses to make the different actors aware of the hazards of media education and to help with the coordination and coherence of messages addressed to consumers and citizens. At its suggestion, the BBC and Channel 4 initiated innovative and strategic projects to alert the public to what is at stake in media education. These projects give adolescents the skills needed to enable them to produce their own programmes and present their analyses of a subject. OFCOM has also encouraged the development of actions intended for elderly people over the age of 65 who have little use for Internet because they do not understand the range of possibilities and consider that they have no utility, either through lack of confidence or lack of technical know-how to use the services on offer. OFCOM, for example, supported "the week for adult learners" covering events organised in different places (cafés, hospitals, museums, prisons, etc.). The last three programmes concentrated on media education and have mobilised more and more participants each year.

Outside the medias and regulating bodies, associations are among the key actors of media education and have often been, in many countries, the first to make people aware of the important interests at stake in media education and to campaign in favour of its development. Kathryn Montgomery from the American University contributed her experiences as co-founder and former director of an NGO, the Centre for Media education (le Centre pour l'éducation aux medias). Outside associations devoted to media education, many others work on topics closely related to this field whether they be parent-teacher associations, associations for professionals of medias, or associations defending fundamental liberties. Thus broadcasting associations or operators have seen in the promotion of media education an instrument to encourage auto-regulation and a strategic argument to combat attempts to control contents by the American government. The development of electronic medias by giving users the possibility of increased participation, creativity and inter-activity (through blogs, exchange platforms and social networks) should enable a reinforced awareness as to the link between media education and education for citizenship. In the United States this evolution in the media world has brought about a renewed vision concerning media education, its role and functions when it was mainly centred on child protection and a guarantee as to quality of the media environment for children.

Take the example of the Inter-Associative Group for Children and Medias (collectif inter-associatif enfance et medias – CIEM) which in France groups together associations dealing with education, youth, children's parents, family matters, and research, and participates in mobilising civil society in order to bring more weight to public debates and influence political decisions. For this group of very diverse NGOs, media education is not limited to the field of education but covers the interests of democracy, society, participation, freedom of expression, citizens' rights, etc. It is the reason why it has adopted a strategic multi-actor approach and intends to bring the citizen's power to the fore next to public powers and the media enterprises in debates concerning medias which enjoy increasing commercial success. It defends the principle according to which media education should be the object of shared responsibility for all actors involved, not exclusively that of teachers, and should be considered as "education for all", that is finding a place in informal education and also for adults, in particular "resource" people. The medias should consent to make efforts to implement a policy of promotion and creation of programmes of quality for children containing a citizenship dimension, taking into account cultural diversity and receiving support from public powers. Research on relations between the medias and children should be equally developed. To each level of action and concerning each of the key actors, the public powers should play a role in which they openly declare a policy of engagement which supports the mobilisation of all partners and permits a real change in the system.

The motives which are primordial and fundamental to the generalisation of media education and which will give it another status, as pointed out by Regina de Assis, in the name of the Brazilian Association, Multirio, remain political engagement which will determine the choice of priorities and mobilisation of sufficient resources at all levels.

Notes

1. International Catholic Association for Radio, Television and Audiovisual
2. World Catholic Association for communications
3. International Association for Research Studies on Information and Communications
4. Media education throughout the world : new orientations, Bazalgette, C., Bevort, E., Savino, J., (coord) UNESCO/CLEMI/BFI, 1992, pp 181-184
5. See the text published by the International Clearinghouse on children, youth and media: http//www.nordicom.gu.se/clearinghouse.php

Reference

Media Education. Advances, Obstacles, and New Trends Since Grünwald: Towards a Scale Change? Proceedings, Synthesis and Recommendations, International meeting organized by the French National Commission for UNESCO, 21-22 juni, 2007, Paris, http://www.unesco.fr

The Paris Agenda
12 Recommendations for Media Education

25 years after the adoption of the Grünwald Declaration that paved the way for media education at the international level, experts, education policy-makers, teachers and researchers, NGO representatives and media professionals from all the regions of the world met in Paris, on 21-22 June 2007. In a cooperative framework gathering all the stakeholders, this joint initiative of the French Commission for UNESCO and UNESCO, supported by the Council of Europe and the French Education Ministry, aimed at taking stock of the progress made and the obstacles met in developing media education through the implementation of education policies or practical experiences; it also intended to formulate recommendations meant to scale up media education and to mobilize all the stakeholders.

The participants reaffirmed the relevance of the Grünwald Declaration. The statements made in 1982 have an increased acuteness with the advent of the information society and knowledge sharing in a globalized context. The place and role of media have strengthened in our societies. More than ever citizens need to have a critical analysis of information whatever the symbolic system used (image, sound, text), to produce content by themselves and to adapt themselves to professional and social change. All the stakeholders must be involved in media education.

The continuing appropriateness of the Grünwald Declaration is both symptomatic of the accuracy of the analysis made and of the lack of recognition of media education. For the last 25 years numerous and rich experiences in media education have been developed both in schools and out of schools. Empirical and theoretical works have elaborated a well-defined field of research in all the regions of the world. These experiences and this body of research remain insufficiently known and shared with the result that media education has not yet moved from the phase of experimentation to the phase of widespread use.

The participants underlined the fact that international mobilization for scaling up media education was a matter of urgency and that their was a need for regular evaluations to assess and update the implementation of the proposed recommendations. They also mentioned that these actions were coherent with the international commitments and that they came within the framework of the agenda of the international community regarding the Millennium Development Goals and the World Summit on Information Society.

The stock-taking of this two day-meeting resulted in the elaboration of twelve recommendations for priority actions intended to foster the operational implementation of the four Grünwald guidelines that remain valid:

I.   development of comprehensive media education programs at all education levels;

II. teacher training and awareness raising of the other stakeholders in the social sphere;

III. research and its dissemination networks;

IV. international cooperation in actions.

These recommendations which make up the Paris Agenda apply to all stakeholders at all levels of intervention and coordination, whether local, national, regional and international.

I. Development of comprehensive media education programs at all education levels

Recommendation 1: To adopt an inclusive definition of media education

The integration of media education in school programs requires a clear definition of the scope of media education. Today the question is no longer how to distinguish between education "with" media as pedagogical tools and education "about" media as a subject for study but to place media education within an economic and social environment undergoing massive changes due to the development of information and communication technologies (ICTs). Media education applies to all media whatever their nature and the technologies used. Far from challenging media education practices these changes enrich them with new skills regarding information knowledge and interactive communication including the social, legal and ethical dimensions involved.

An inclusive concept of media education has three main objectives:

- to give access to all kinds of media that are potential tools to understand society and to participate in democratic life;

- to develop skills for the critical analysis of messages, whether in news or entertainment, in order to strengthen the capacities of autonomous individuals and active users;

- to encourage production, creativity and interactivity in the different fields of media communication.

Recommendation 2: To strengthen the links between media education, cultural diversity and respect for human rights

Built on these common bases, curricula will be adapted to the diversity of the cultural, educational, social and economic contexts in order to avoid the adoption of models that would not suit local realities.

Given the development of international exchanges and the globalisation phenomenon, media education should foster intercultural understanding and promote local cultures everywhere.

Media education contributes to people's empowerment and a shared sense of responsibility in society and as such is part of citizenship and human rights education.

Recommendation 3: To define basic skills and evaluation systems

According to these principles, the basic skills and knowledge to be acquired are both transversal and interdisciplinary and should be specified for each level of the school system. Their evaluation should take into account students as well as teachers in training. These programmes could be compiled and analysed in a comparative study that would highlight their common features and differences; they would help to structure media education and improve the relevance and effectiveness of its curricula.

II. Teacher training and awareness raising of the other stakeholders in the social sphere

Recommendation 4: To integrate media education in the initial training of teachers

Initial training of teachers is a key element of the system and must include theoretical dimensions and practical skills; it needs to be based on a good knowledge of young people's media uses. In times of rapid change, this training must rely on institutional actions and self-training, using teaching aids that have been tested and validated by teachers and students.

Recommendation 5: To develop appropriate and evolving pedagogical methods

The main purpose is to set up new "active" methods that are incompatible with ready-to-teach recipes and require an evolution of the teacher's role, a greater participation by students and also closer relations between school and the outside world. Teaching materials and tools, either free of intellectual property rights or with fair and negotiated copyrights, have to be developed to be fitting with such new methods. They need to be produced in close collaboration between teachers and students, whatever their formats, covering the whole range from printed manuals to digital spaces of collaborative work.

Recommendation 6: To mobilize all the stakeholders within the education system

The integration of media education in the education system has to mobilize all stakeholders. The awareness of curricula managers, school directors, chief education officers, etc., must be increased in order for them to assume the responsibilities that legitimize these actions. In the framework of regional and national missions, experts could be at the disposal of official education authorities to launch awareness raising initiatives.

Recommendation 7: To mobilize the other stakeholders of the social sphere

Media education cannot be limited to the school environment; it is also the concern of families, associations and media professionals.

Parents and families along with civil society associations must contribute to it in the schools and outside the schools, in non formal locations, if media education is to move from the experimentation phase to widespread innovative implementation.

Media education should be integrated in the professional training of journalists and include legal and ethical knowledge. It also applies to all media professionals, content producers, editors, broadcasters, etc. Efforts have to be made in order to encourage the production and broadcasting of good quality programmes devoid of stereotypes, especially about young people. They should promote dialogue and bring together media professionals, educators and citizens. The regulation authorities have also a vested interest in participating in media education initiatives as self-regulation and co-regulation play an increasing role in parallel to regulation.

Summer schools organized at regional and national levels can encourage exchanges and the dissemination of best practices. They can contribute to the continuous training of teachers and to the spread of media education. Festivals and workshops can give more visibility to the productions of young people and increase the value of media education initiatives.

Recommendation 8: To place media education within the framework of lifelong learning

Media education is not only for young people but also for adults whose main information and knowledge sources are media. In this context, media education is a process of quality lifelong learning. It is important to provide adults who did not have this opportunity with continuous training modules that will help them to become freer and more active citizens in society. Tools of various kinds have to be put at their disposal to raise their awareness and train them. The continuous training and self-training of adults have to be implemented at the local level with the support of civil society associations, NGOs and experts.

III.   Research and its dissemination networks

Recommendation 9: To develop media education and research in higher education

Higher education is the link between training and research as there is a need to guide and monitor empirical practices. It is necessary to develop different directions for research:

- theoretical research so that media education initiatives can follow ongoing evolutions whether technological or social; such research should include the various conditions of production, broadcasting and use of media;

- evaluation research as close as possible to teacher and student practices in order to assess their possible impact better;

- research-action in order to mobilize stakeholders, give support to the current actions and contribute to the continuous training of teachers and educators;

- investigations on the behaviour and the role of parents and other stakeholders in media education.

Media education has to be dealt with in the framework of interdisciplinary research (education, information and communication sciences, sociology, etc.). It must be developed in close connection with studies on pedagogical innovation, on the role and impact of technologies in education and training and especially on e-learning, as well as with those focused on citizenship, human rights and sustainable development.

Recommendation 10: To create exchange networks

It is essential to build up and to share research questions as well their results in order to contribute to the much-needed change of scale in media education. Networks of researchers organized in thematic groups at regional, national or international levels will allow such sharing of knowledge. Their works should lead to the elaboration of ethical recommendations likely to result in an international charter. Calls to tender launched by national or international research bodies will also stimulate research.

IV. International cooperation in actions

Recommendation 11: To organize and to make visible international exchanges

International exchanges need to be stimulated and well organized in order to spread good practices and existing works, to grasp the diversity of the concrete situations and to encourage cooperation of all types. In that respect international organizations, like UNESCO, as well as regional organizations such as, for Europe, the Council of Europe and the European Union, have an important role to play in order to support both local and global initiatives and coordinated actions.

The creation of an international clearinghouse on media education would allow to collect, translate and put at the disposal of all a body of relevant data on media education: quality works whether in the research field or on education policies and strategies of integration of media education in curricula within the education systems. This clearinghouse would contribute to the creation of a network of key-stakeholders helping to monitor scientific and pedagogical development in this field.

The organization of regularly scheduled international events with a precise agenda is also necessary:

- international symposia with high level experts in order to assess current practices and to update recommendations. National education ministers and other relevant bodies should be kept informed of such activities and their conclusions;

- annual meetings of national specialists designed to share, transfer and increase their expertise particularly in countries newly engaged in media education;

- international festivals of media productions by young people, possibly in relation with national events, with specific awards and the opportunity of broadcasting in national media.

Recommendation 12: To raise awareness and to mobilize political decision-makers

Media education cannot come into general use without an effort to raise people's awareness and to mobilize all stakeholders and particularly high-level political decision-makers in all countries. Beyond actions taken at the national level to mobilize public opinion, UNESCO in cooperation with other international or regional organizations, such as the Council of Europe and the European Union for Europe, could launch a variety of initiatives among which:

- an international campaign to raise awareness on the importance of media education for the training of the citizen of the XXIst century;

- an international meeting of education ministers that will aim at creating a strong mobilization in favour of the integration of media education in education policies;

- the involvement of the UNESCO Schools Networks and Clubs in media education events and more precisely in the creation of a festival for young people's productions;

- the creation of "media education" UNESCO chairs that will keep researchers from losing sight of local realities and will enrich theoretical frameworks as well as practices in media education throughout the world.

Paris, 22 June 2007

Grünwald Declaration on Media Education

This declaration was issued unanimously by the representatives of 19 nations at UNESCO's 1982International Symposium on Media Education at Grünwald, Federal Republic of Germany. It is reproducedhere since media teachers may well find it useful to quote or cite in preparing rationales, justifications orexplanatory documents relating to media education.

'*We live in a world where media are omnipresent:* an increasing number of people spend a greatdeal of time watching television, reading newspapers and magazines, playing records and listening to theradio. In some countries, for example, children already spend more time watching television than they doattending school.

'Rather than condemn or endorse the undoubted power of the media, we need to accept theirsignificant impact and penetration throughout the world as an established fact, and also appreciate theirimportance as an element of culture in today's world. The role of communication and media in the process ofdevelopment should not be underestimated, nor the function of media as instruments for the citizen's activeparticipation in society. Political and educational systems need to recognize their obligations to promote intheir citizens a critical understanding of the phenomena of communication.

'Regrettably most informal and non-formal educational systems do little to promote media educationor education for communication. Too often the gap between the educational experience they offer and thereal world in which people live is disturbingly wide. But if the arguments for media education as a preparationfor responsible citizenship are formidable now, in the very near future with the development of communicationtechnology such as satellite broadcasting, two-way cable systems, television data systems, video cassetteand disc materials, they ought to be irresistible, given the increasing degree of choice in media consumptionresulting from these developments.

'Responsible educators will not ignore these developments, but will work alongside their students inunderstanding them and making sense of such consequences as the rapid development of two-waycommunication and the ensuing individualization and access to information.

'This is not to underestimate the impact on cultural identity of the flow of information and ideasbetween cultures by the mass media.

'The school and the family share the responsibility of preparing the young person for living in a world ofpowerful images, words and sounds. Children and adults need to be literate in all three of these symbolicsystems, and this will require some reassessment of educational priorities. Such a reassessment might wellresult in an integrated approach to the teaching of language and communication.

'Media education will be most effective when parents, teachers, media personnel and decision-makersall acknowledge they have a role to play in developing greater critical awareness among listeners, viewersand readers. The greater integration of educational and communications systems would undoubtedly be animportant step towards more effective education.

'We therefore call upon the competent authorities to:

1. initiate and support comprehensive media education programs - from pre-school to university level, and inadult education - the purpose of which is to develop the knowledge, skills and attitudes which willencourage the growth of critical awareness and, consequently, of greater competence among the usersof electronic and print media. Ideally, such programs should include the analysis of media products, theuse of media as means of creative expression, and effective use of and participation in available mediachannels;

2. develop training courses for teachers and intermediaries both to increase their knowledge andunderstanding of the media and train them in appropriate teaching methods, which would take intoaccount the already considerable but fragmented acquaintance with media already possessed by manystudents;

3. stimulate research and development activities for the benefit of media education, from such domains aspsychology, sociology, and communication science;

4. support and strengthen the actions undertaken or envisaged by UNESCO and which aim at encouraginginternational co-operation in media education.'

Grünwald, Federal Republic of Germany, 22 January 1982

Media Education: quand il n'est plus temps d'attendre...
Media Education: When the Waiting is Over

Geneviève Jacquinot-Delaunay

Education in the different media is practically as old as the media themselves[1] – whether this involved concerns over their negative influence, placing high hopes of democracy in them, or using them as a channel for constructive teaching practices. How many know that the first French school newspaper documented in the French National Library dates from 1830? The foreword written by young pupils from Marseilles as we can see displays both their critical-mindedness and the ability of their teacher to foster their right of expression:

> The recent educational reform makes it incumbent on pupils to think for themselves as much as through the authors they are reading; no longer is the teacher that stern master who from his rostrum solemnly imposes on his disciples his opinions and utterances. The pupil is called upon to give his own views and challenge those of the teacher, if he feels they are not the best. The result of this contest is that the pupil learns to form judgments early. His thinking becomes clearer and he can then offer his ideas at an age at which the youth of former times had to remain silent...[2]

However, it is also worthwhile remembering, taking only the French print press as an example, that before 1976 (and a letter from the then education minister René Haby to the head of the national inspectorate) the use of the print press in class could incur penalties. This is tantamount to saying that *media education – and this is it foremost attribute – has always been a militant activity.*

In effect, beyond differences in time and place, whichever the media considered, these pioneering activities were always initiated by individuals or groups who on the one hand shared a certain "liberating" view of education (were it Freinet's modern – or "active" – school movement in Europe or Paolo Freire's "conscientisation" in Latin America, to take just two examples) and on the other hand considered that the media of their time were too important to be left in the sole hands of media professionals. This is still how we present our review

MédiaMorphoses[3] which aims to publicise the most recent research findings on changes in the media and information and communication technologies with a view to making professionals aware of their new responsibilities and helping trainers at all levels to design specific educational activities.

However, it was primarily from the 60s that work developed taking the successive media channels – print press, cinema, television, video, the Internet, mobile phones, and all their derivatives – as specific focuses of study and that teaching practices were established to analyse them and have learners produce them. Such work has prompted much controversy that, when overcome, has proved productive: should analysis or production be promoted? Should media education be a separate (and additional) subject or cut across several subject areas? Specially trained media teachers or media education included in all teacher training? Work medium by medium or take the media environment as a whole? Or, more fundamentally, use media education as a complement to teacher training or an opportunity to rethink education in the new media context?

It must also be recognised that as they became institutionalised, some of these activities tended to reify and their original scope was forgotten: between initial vocational training and an academic exercise, media education sometimes lost sight of its "political involvement for the purpose of critical autonomy".

Nonetheless, whether it is public or private, secular or denominational, institutional or alternative, proposed by professionals or volunters such training of the critical-minded citizen has not had, and will not have, the same meaning:

– in a country "with a tradition of democracy", and on a continent or in a region still struggling to attain "freedom of thought and expression" for all citizens;

– depending on the local media situation, in a region where the media are free or where they are tightly monitored or in the hands of "fundamentalist" groups (as the "globalisation" phenomena characteristic of current media development do not abolish such differences but even revive them);

– also depending on the cultural and educational traditions of each country: in 1990, in Toulouse at another international meeting under the auspices of UNESCO, voices were raised to recall that *international* does not mean *universal*. On behalf of participants from Asia, Africa, and Latin America, they called for a less "UNESCO-type" definition of media education than the one used at the time[4]. They wanted a definition that laid greater stress on "communities" for "development" and/or "liberation" than on "the training of autonomous individuals endowed with a critical sense and clear-sighted adults". Educational models also play their role and can create paradoxical situations such as in Japan where the absence of a tradition of criticism in the public education system – despite the advent of democracy – is in conflict with the crux of media education, "even when the mistake is not made of equating critical-mindedness with opposition to the established order or government[5]"

In other words – and *this is its second characteristic – media education is a highly contextualised activity,* and one must be careful about transferring models, theories, and practices from the North to the South as pointed out again at the meeting in Paris.

Finally, and *this is the third characteristic, media education activities are – allowing for exceptions – very fragmentary, unstable, and mostly unsupported by specific theories and research.* "Media education" is often confused with "education *by* the media". In fact, the two approaches are complementary to communication. One is "instrumental" (a means used to impart content) whereas the other is "thematic" (a subject for study). They have different aims but require skills that must be mastered equally by teachers and pupils, for to learn with the media and technologies it is better to know how they operate. There is also confusion between media education and research into the relationships between young people and the media that are a pre-requisite. Moreover, too often has the research been reduced to an inventory of young people's preferences or an illusory measurement of the time they devote to this or that medium whereas much research has shown the complexity and variability of relationships children maintain with "their" media. From this point of view, the International forum of researchers held in Paris in 1997 and in Sydney in 2000 on the initiative of UNESCO[6] marked an important step in the necessary evolution of research hypotheses and consequently of media-education practices: a shift towards research and practices that take more account of developments in society, the social and media experience of young people[7] – family life, the conceptions of childhood and adolescence, communication practices, and references to gender, identity, and ethnicity... not to forget media specificity in this digital age.

Many other initiatives – local, national, and international – especially by UNESCO through assignments such as the one entrusted in 1997 to the *Nordicom Centre* of Göteborg[8] University as a direct follow-on from the International Convention on the Rights of the Child or more recently through the *Mentor* Association, which focuses more on Mediterranean countries and the Middle East, have sought and are seeking to continue this work. For despite the current relevance of the basic Grünwald proposals, there have been many changes in media communication and in society, culture, and education. This was recalled in Riyadh as well as in Paris. However, with few exceptions, media education has not kept pace with these changes. The media education provided in some European countries since the 60s – both in and out of school – (sometimes as an integral part of schooling) needs a total overhaul that begins with a more comprehensive understanding of the present situation. This does not mean seizing on the latest technological invention, e-TV, or the blog to replace the television newscast or the use of video. Rather, as with any education it requires a tight definition of the types of knowledge and skills needed to train a citizen of the world and the ability to evaluate them[9].

All the media are part of media education and, as was said by the representative of the European commission at the Paris Meeting, an individual is "media literate" if he/she can make choices and assess the reasons for those choices, if he/she can protect him/herself and his/her family from objectionable content, if he/she has acquired knowledge and know-how enabling him/her to use the media as a responsible citizen and play a full part in the life of society... then media education involves everyone, and constitutes a "fundamental right of humankind".

To achieve this, we must draw on past experience and achievements but also envisage entirely new outlooks: the three characteristics of media-education processes already identified have to evolve. Fragmentary, unstable practices not backed by an explicit theoretical framework and seldom evaluated must now give way to a conceptual and operational framework translating into a precise delineation of what media education is and how it – with other activities – can help make the pupil and citizen "literate". While taking into account contexts that are at once political, cultural, and local-media based, such work must transcend this diversity to get at the transnational dimension of the current challenges facing society. Lastly, such practices should shed their marginal and activist status so that they are incorporated – by way of forceful political commitments – into the various education and media.

And these are the challenges we now face: how can we avoid reinventing the wheel; how can we scale up initiatives that have remained all too often experimental; how can we enable those who only now are embarking on the task avoid going through all the stages we underwent and getting the living and learning conditions of the 21st-century citizen wrong? We need testimonies on the diversity, wealth, and creativity of initiatives taken throughout the world; by identifying the recurrent hindrances and obstacles to their extension; and finally by reformulating and updating recommendations designed to go further than pious hope and to support operational work that can adapt to each local context.

Notes

1. A few dates: print press mid-19th century; cinema 1895; radio 1920; television 1950; computers 1980; the Internet 1995; and so on...
2. In *La presse des lycéens et des étudiants au 19ème siècle*, Corroy, L., INRP, Education, Histoire, 2004, p 77-78.
3. Published by the Institut National de l'Audiovisuel in partnership with Armand Colin, publishers http://www.armand-colin.com/revues_info.php?idr=24&par=1
4. *All manner of learning and teaching at all levels and under all circumstances... of the history, creation, use, and evaluation of the media as practical and technical crafts, as well as the place the media occupy in society, their social impact, the implications of media communication, participation, the modification of the mode of perception they generate, the role of creative work, and access to the media, UNESCO, 1979.*

5. M Suzuki,M F., "Osez exercer votre esprit critique" in *L'éducation aux médias dans le monde,* (media education throughout the world : new orientations) Bazalguette, C., Bevort, E., Savino, J., (coord) Unesco/CLEMI/BFI op cit, p 181-184

6. Organised by the GRREM Association. The main proceedings are published in *Les jeunes et les médias, Perspectives de la recherche dans le monde,* Jacquinot G., (ss dir), L'Harmattan, coll. Débats JeunesseS,2002.

7. Buckingham,D., *Media education, literacy, learning and contemporary culture,* UK, USA, Polity Press, 2003.

8. Every year, *the Clearinghouse on Children, Youth, and Media* publishes a book of reflections and research findings on the media and media education (Editors, Ulla Carlson and Cecilia von Feilitzen). www.nordicom.gu.se

9. In France, work is underway at CLEMI, the *Centre de liaison de l'enseignement et des moyens d'information* (liaison centre for education and the media) into the "common core of knowledge and skills in media education"

III. Young People's Media Culture in the Digital Age

Children and Mass Media in the Arab World
A Second Level Analysis

Samy Tayie

In the old days, childhood was not well nurtured. Children were seen as savage creatures that must be avoided. No one cared for children, and they were far down the list of priorities in the family and human interest. This was the case in ancient times and even during the middle ages. The child was savage with respect to its behaviour, and education was crucial in changing this behaviour.

Jean Jack Rousseau was a pioneer who brought about some changes in this view. Ever since, the interest and care devoted to children moved to different sectors. The child who was nothing now became everything.

This new view of children prevailed around the world. Attention and care given to children accompanied the introduction of the cinema at the turn of the nineteenth century. It was natural that the cinema paid a great deal of attention to children as this was in fashion during that era. This interest in children and production of children's movies continued through World War I, and were followed by the introduction of children's programmes on television during the 1950s.

Care for children became very obvious in all countries of the world around the turn of the twentieth century. In 1989, a world summit for childhood was held. Starting from that date, most countries began offering special care for children. The needs of children were to be given the greatest priority, and attention to children was also obvious in the universities and academies, where a great deal of study and research was focused on children, their general and cultural needs and education.

When we talk about children and media, the most common media are the cinema and television. In fact, they have more effect on children than do other media such as print or theatre. Although these two media contradict each other, and actually compete (television has been accused of stealing audiences from the cinema, especially in the Arab world [Dehny, 1993, pp. 38-42]), they complement each other.

This paper contains two main parts: the first concerns a review of children and massmedia research literature in the Arab world and presents findings from different research projects and studies conducted in the Arab world. The number of these studies is great; we manage to cover most of this volume. It was found that most of the reviewed studies were conducted during the 1990s and were mainly Egyptian, but also came from Saudi Arabia, the United Arab Emirates and Jordan. The second part presents a second level and an overall analysis of the findings of these studies, i.e. a conclusion and recommendations.

Reviewed studies were classified into four categories:

- Children and mass media in general

- Children and television/cinema

- Children and print media

- Children and radio

Children and Mass Media in the Arab World

This section discusses the findings of studies related to children and mass media in general.

Findings of a study conducted on Egyptian children's use of media, on a sample of 1800 children aged 8 to 15 years and 600 parents (mothers and fathers), have shown that the most important time for watching television was the peak time from 6 to 9 p.m. (El Hadeedy et al., 1991). Most children (99%) mentioned that they watch children's programmes, which came in first place as the most mentioned programmes ahead of Arab movies, cartoon films and commercials. Children's preferred programmes were cartoons, magic games, stories and tales, children's series and puppet shows. Topics preferred were police adventure, religion and social issues.

Children also mentioned that they listen to radio (45%). The peak listening time was 6 to 10 a.m., and then 3 to 6 p.m. Preferred radio programmes included music, songs and religious programmes. Children's programmes and news bulletins were also preferred. Preferred radio subjects included stories and tales. Musical programmes, songs and contests followed suit.

With respect to parents, it was found that more than two-thirds of parents watch children's television programmes, whereas only 8% listen to children's radio programmes. Parents encourage their children to watch certain kinds of programmes, such as religious programmes and children's programmes rather than adult programmes. Parents mentioned that they prohibit their children from watching violent programmes. They also mentioned that they feel that some television commercials cause problems for children as they feel they cannot afford to buy the advertised products, and that some of these commercials do not match the ethics and values in society.

A study on Egyptian children's use of the book, cinema and theatre was conducted on a sample of 440 children from Cairo aged 6 to 15 years (Kandeel, 1997). Variables of age, gender, geographical area, social background and level of education were taken into consideration. Findings have shown that 49% of the children do not read books and that children who read books regularly represent only 22%, with the books they read being mainly stories, adventures and police books. It was found that the social background factor has an influence on children's reading of books, as middle and upper-class children were more frequent readers than working class children were.

With respect to the cinema, findings have shown that nearly a quarter of the children interviewed (26%) go to cinema. Action and violent films were the most preferred (95%) by children. More than half the interviewees (56%) preferred Arab films. Children from working class families are heavier users of the cinema than are middle and upper-class children.

Children almost never go to the theatre, but do mention a preference for comedies and puppet shows. Circus and children's choral performances were not mentioned at all.

Egyptian children's use of mass media was the topic of another study (Kandeel, 1993) conducted on a sample of 260 children aged 8 to 12 years, boys and girls, from urban areas. The findings show that more than half the interviewed children read newspapers (57%) and magazines (62%). There was no significant difference between boys and girls in this respect. Listeners of radio represented 67% of the sampled children and television viewers represented 97%, showing that television was the most used medium.

Findings have also shown that children's reading of newspapers depends to a great extent on their socioeconomic status and ability to read and write. Therefore, older children read the newspaper more than younger children do. Children's motives for reading the newspaper included searching for news and current affairs as much as for entertainment.

Children's preference among newspapers depended on their availability newspapers and easy access. The use of coloured pictures and drawings and easy readability, as well as coverage of crime and show business, were the most mentioned reasons for reading a given newspaper.

Due to the higher prices of magazines compared to newspapers, it was found that children's use of magazines depended largely on the economic situation of their family and their parents' opinion on the importance of magazines. Fun and entertainment were the main motives for reading magazines, and those with pictures and colours are more attractive to read. Stories and tales also determine children's preferred magazines.

The peak time for listening to radio was early morning before school (before 7:00 a.m.). It was also found that listening to radio was mainly for fun and entertainment. Therefore, music and songs were the most preferred radio programmes. Listening to news and seeking information were less important.

Regarding television, entertainment and passing of leisure time (35%) were the most mentioned motives for viewing television. Taking a rest from studies (29%) and seeking information (24%) were also among the motives.

In a Jordanian study on the influence of mass media on the child, conducted on a sample of Jordanian children (Hindy, 1998), the aim was to examine the influences of television, radio, the press, cinema and video on the child. The findings show that the influence of mass media on the child is accumulative and varies from one medium to another. Television was found to be the most influential medium on the child, followed by video. Other media were less effective. The study also found that media have both positive and negative effects on the child. The family and the school also play certain roles in determining the child's use of mass media. Generally speaking, all children's materials were not of high quality compared to those directed at children in Western countries.

Findings have also shown that people working in the field of production and presentation of materials for children were not qualified enough and need serious training. Finally, the study found that there is a great difference between findings of Arab studies and those from other countries, due to different cultures and environments.

Labib (1994) conducted a study on the child's right to adequate media materials. He found that although the amount of books for children has increased recently, economic circumstances and the high price of books have made it difficult to buy them. Children's magazines were also not very successful. They were merely translations of foreign material and did not sufficiently inform children about current events, nationally or internationally.

Spaces devoted to children's material in the Egyptian newspapers were very limited, irregular and mainly addressed children over ten years of age. Material for children under ten years was hard to find.

Egyptian television was an important medium for children. Television has managed to take listeners away from radio, and also attracts children to watch their own programmes as well as those of adults. It was also found that the Egyptian child has free access to television except during exam time. Egyptian children are exposed to a great deal of imported foreign materials and commercials in addition to programmes on satellite channels. This material was found to comprise useful sources of information for children in different domains of life.

The role of mass media in increasing Egyptian children's cultural awareness was the topic of another study (Sabry, 1995). It aimed at examining the role of mass media in satisfying the child's cultural needs. Its findings show that television was the most important medium for children. Eight percent of its programmes was devoted to children, of which 90% were foreign programmes, mainly American. It was also found that violence was very common in children programmes. According to the study, this type of programmes increases children's tendencies toward actual violence.

In his study on the role of local Egyptian media in providing the child with information, Hassan (1989) conducted a content analysis on a sample from television children programmes, newspaper materials and radio programmes. The study also included interviewing samples of individuals who work in media, who are in charge of children's programmes and materials, as well as 400 children aged 9-12 years.

Findings from the study show that all three media present something for children, weekly or on Sundays. Children participated in their television programmes (72.2%), print materials (52.2%) and radio (25%). Religious information was the most common in all three media.

Interviewed children mentioned that they need more information on topics such as Egyptian history and public figures, as well as animals and new discoveries. With regard to children's admiration of their own programmes and materials, TV programmes came in first place (91.6%), print materials in newspapers second (89.6%), and finally radio programmes (44.2%).

Findings from interviews with those in charge of children's programmes and material have shown that they were all qualified and university graduates. They all agreed that most of their programmes and material were directed to children aged 6 to 12 years.

Children and Television/Cinema

Studies related to children and television/cinema will be reviewed on the following pages.

El Semary (1995) conducted a study on the influence of exposure to television on the reading habits of the Egyptian child. The study was performed on a sample of 300 children, males and females, aged 9-12 years from Cairo (urban area). Its findings show that television affects children's reading habits, especially in the case of older children who can read and write. For example, they may read while watching television or while talking to other members of the family. Television also influences children's preferred reading materials. It was also found that there were other reasons, besides television, that discourage children from reading, e.g. heavy homework load, lack of parental encouragement to read and a failure of the school to support their reading.

In a study on children's perception of the personality characteristics portrayed in children's programmes, Kamel (1995) found that television was an attractive medium in influencing children. Kamel's findings show that there were differences between boys and girls with respect to the influence of television. Girls were more influenced by characteristics such as friendship sincerity, whereas boys were more influenced by characteristics of honesty and trust. Boys were also more influenced by violence and aggressiveness than girls were.

The findings also show that boys were more influenced by characteristics of cooperation and girls were more influenced by belongingness. It was also found that boys were influenced with characteristics of egoism and individualism. Girls

71

were more influenced by characteristics of "not liking to work" and "staying at home". It was also found that girls were more likely to appreciate beauty than were boys, who were more influenced by comedian characteristics.

Finally, the study concluded that television's influence on children depends on their interests and attitudes as well as their socialization.

A study on children's perception of the difference between screen personalities and those in real life (El Sayed, 1996) examined the influences of factors of age, gender and social circumstances. The study was conducted on a sample of 114 children, boys and girls. The sample was divided into two groups: pre-school (3-5 years) and primary school (6-8 years) children. An experimental approach was used, by which data were collected from children after exposing them to specific children's programmes. The study's findings show that there was a negative relationship between the age variable and perception of the televised reality. The relationship was also negative between watching television with others and the perception of televised reality. The gender variable did not show any influence on the children's understanding of televised reality.

Hassan (1995) conducted a study on a cluster sample of 540 Egyptian children aged 12-15 years from urban and rural areas. The study aimed at examining children's attitudes toward their programmes. Its findings show that children were more interested in adventures and action programmes (fun and entertainment) than other programmes, and were less interested in educational, scientific and economic programmes. The study recommended that special programmes for teenagers be introduced.

El Hadeedy (1990) conducted a study on children's cinema in the Arab world. The study's sample was taken from children aged 8-12 years, boys and girls from 12 Arab countries. It was found that children's cinema was available in all the studied countries except two, Mauritania and Djibouti. Children's films are available in many places, and are watched in cinemas, schools and public places. It was also found that production of children's films was available in only four countries, i.e. Egypt, Sudan, Iraq and Qatar. Besides local production in these four countries, all Arab countries rely mainly on importing children's films and programmes (i.e. animated films, puppet shows, documentary films, experimental films, variety shows and educational films) from Western countries, especially the United States and England.

With respect to children's preferences, it was found that they like Arab films as well as foreign ones. Adventures and action movies were preferred by boys, while girls preferred social and love stories.

Another study on children's cinema in the Arab world (El Abd, 1988) examined the availability of children's films in 12 Arab countries, i.e., Egypt, the United Arab Emirates, Iraq, Syria, Jordan, Qatar, Djibouti, Sudan, Southern Yemen, Mauritania, Somalia and Bahrain. The study's findings show that children's programmes are shown in all studied countries except Mauritania and Djibouti. With respect to production, children's programmes are produced in only four of these countries

(Egypt, Iraq, Qatar and Sudan). All Arab countries present foreign children films imported from abroad due to the lack of local production and low cost.

Topics of children's films were mainly motion pictures (100%), variety (70%), drama (70%), documentary (70%), experimental (40%), and educational (30%). Only Egypt and Iraq have participated in international festivals and contests related to children's films.

Reda (1994) conducted a study on the impact of televised violence on children's behaviour on a sample of 200 parents from Cairo and its surrounding areas. The study's results show that 64% see television as a major responsible element in children's violent behaviour and believe that television is to blame for the bad language that children use. Parents also mentioned that they are obliged to interfere in most cases to determine what their children should and should not see, especially as children watch adult programming in most cases.

The majority of parents (83.5%) also mentioned that foreign programmes and films were mainly to blame for their children's violent behaviour. This situation was even worsened with the introduction of satellite television. A strong relation was also found between the educational level and socioeconomic status of parents and their awareness of the danger of television in increasing their children's violent behaviour. The same factors influence parents' control of what their children watch on television. Parents from higher classes and with higher educational levels were more likely to control their children's use of media in general, and of television in particular.

The role of animated films in the cognitive development of children was examined in a study conducted on a sample of Egyptian children, boys and girls in primary schools aged 7-8 years. The study included a content analysis of a sample of 19 television series and 14 animated films (Hassan, 1998). The findings show that screening of children's programmes occurred at the wrong time, when children were not at home; programmes were screened more on schooldays than during weekends and holidays. Therefore, children's exposure to these programmes was very limited.

The study recommended that the timing of children's programmes must change to allow children to see more of them during their leisure time and days off from school. Most of the screened programmes were translated foreign programmes; there is a real need for the production of pure Arab programmes that take into consideration the interests of the Arab child.

A content analysis study was conducted to examine the portrayal of homeless children (Ibrahim, 1994) in a sample of Egyptian televised programmes from the main three channels, as well as in the press. The sample period was three months (July-September 1992).

The results show that the portrayal of homeless children in most television programmes as well as in the press was very weak and superficial. There was more concentration on models of example children, children's festivals and feasts. In the press, homeless children received more coverage in human-interest stories and accidents. The press coverage of stories on these children tends to consider lack of education, large number of children and domestic problems the main reasons.

In a content analysis on a sample of 608 TV commercials, the role of television advertising in forming children's values was examined (Rezk, 1995). It was found that only 8.2% of commercials were directed at children. These were commercials for products for children (e.g. diapers, ice-cream, sweets, etc.). This may ultimately teach children consuming habits that sometimes do not match the standard of living of their family, and this causes the child to ask for things their parents cannot afford to buy.

It was also obvious that a great deal of the commercials (65.5%) speak to the upper middle class in society, concentrating mainly on consumer goods and cosmetics or welfare goods such as expensive cars and trips. This, according to study findings, may lead to depressing children who cannot afford these kinds of products. There was also a tendency to impose on the child a cultural alienation, especially Western style, rather than belonging. This leads to a conflict between culture of society and other imported cultural patterns.

A study was conducted on the role of television in increasing Egyptian children's environmental awareness (El Keleeny, 1993), on a sample of 300 children (aged 10 years) in primary schools in Cairo. The study's findings show that television plays an important role in spreading awareness among children with respect to the environment and its problems. However, it was found that the role of television in creating pro-environment behaviour of children was absent.

The findings also show that interpersonal communication plays an important role in increasing children's environmental awareness. This may lead to the conclusion that the socialization process has a role to play in this respect.

A content analysis was performed on a sample of children's programmes screened on both the first and second channels of Egyptian television for five months (August-December 1982) (El Abd, 1988). The content analysis was followed by a field study on a sample of children from primary schools in urban and rural areas.

The findings show that the most common subjects in these programmes were science (18.4%), art (13.4%) and translated foreign subjects (10.9%). Social, economic, military and psychological subjects were less frequent. Personalities in children's programmes were mainly males, and information on females was rare. These personalities were mainly artists (21.9%), religious figures (17.2%), scientists (15.2%) and politicians (12.4%). Students and sportsmen were less frequent personalities in children's programmes. Information on farmers and workers was not available at all.

With respect to subjects on which information was presented, these were mainly the men (15.5%), places (13.2%), animals (12%) and tools/equipment (10.2%). Information was general in 42% of programmes, on Egypt in 26.2%, on foreign countries in 25.3% and on other Arab countries in 6.5%.

Sources of information for children's programmes were mainly producers (72.1%), children themselves (17.4%) and finally interviewed guests on the programmes (10.5%). These guests were from various domains, excluding politics.

With respect to illustrations in children's programmes, these included photographs (20.4%), documentaries (16%), models (8.6%), puppets (8.3%), animated films (4.8%) and hand drawings (4.4%). Illustrations such as written boards and maps were less frequent.

A study on the role of television drama in providing children with social values was conducted on a sample of children who had left education (340 children) (Asran, 1998). The study's findings show that all the respondents watch television (81.6% often, 30.9% sometimes and only 7.3% rarely). With respect to children's preferred programmes, drama came in first (30.3%), followed by cartoons (15.4%), advertisements (13.8%) and sports programmes (13%).

It was also found that entertainment and fun were the most mentioned motives for watching television drama. With respect to positive values that children learn from television drama, helping the needy (70.2%), being faithful to one's parents (20.2%) and sticking to religion (19%) were the most mentioned. The most mentioned negative values included underestimation of the importance of education (13.9%), violence (12.4%) and favouritism (12.1%).

El Abd (1993) conducted a study on children's programmes on Omani television, which also included a sample of 500 children (males and females). All the interviewed children mentioned that they watch television. More than half (58%) mentioned that they watch television after completing their homework, 20% before starting their homework and only 6% while doing their homework.

With respect to the preferred programmes, all children mentioned animated films and children's programmes, of which Arab series (99.4%), songs (98.6%) and Arab films (94.6%) were among the most preferred. Advertisements (92%), sports (79.8%), variety shows (79.6%) and religious programmes (75%) were also mentioned.

With regard to parents' interference in their children's exposure to television programmes, it was found that parents interfered in 32% of the cases. They prohibited their children mainly from watching some Arab films (81.3%), foreign programmes (68%) and some Arab series and some sports programmes (31.3%). Parents also prohibited their children from watching news (25%), sports programmes (12.5%) and advertisements (6.3%).

Regarding children's evaluation of their programmes, most respondents (84%) mentioned being satisfied with their programmes and 16% saw them as acceptable. The majority (98%) mentioned that they learn a great deal from local children's programmes. In addition to Omani television, the respondents watch other television channels such as Dubai, Abu Dhabi, the Egyptian Satellite Channel (ESC), MBC, Saudi and Jordanian television; again, their most preferred programmes are children's programmes (90.3%).

El Keleeny (1995) conducted a study on the negative aspects of new children's video games and the kind of children who visit video clubs, on 40 Egyptian children aged 12-15. The findings show that there were certain kinds of traditional games that children play most of the time. It was also found that playing video games in video clubs might help to strengthen relationships among players. However, the video games may cause many negative effects such as keeping the child away from social life, exposure to cultural content that varies from that of the society, and associating with people from different social classes, which may lead to bad habits such as smoking and drug use. The negative effects also included the fact that most children who go to the video clubs belong to higher social classes, where parents are busy most of the time. This may lead to a situation in which these children are more influenced by these games with the absence of family control. It was also found that there is a correlation between visiting these clubs and poor performance in school, due to the waste of study time. Also, video games train children in violence and aggression and take them to a different world than their own real one.

The findings of a study on children's television programmes (El Abd, 1988) from 13 Arab countries (i.e., Egypt, Iraq, Jordan, Djibouti, the United Arab Emirates, South Yemen, Sudan, Mauritania, Bahrain, Syria, Somalia, Qatar and Saudi Arabia) show that there were television programmes for children in all the above countries. Each country feels that its children's programmes were sufficient. Children take part in their own programmes in all countries except Djibouti. Children's programmes are screened as recorded programmes in all countries except Egypt, the United Arab Emirates and Sudan, which offer live programmes for children. Only five countries (Egypt, Syria, Iraq, Sudan and Qatar) conduct research on children's programmes.

It was also found that the sources of children's programme production were local (28.7%), foreign (23.8%), Gulf (21.4%) and Arab (19%). Programmes imported from other countries were animated films (22.8%), children's series (19.4%), children's films (14%), puppet shows (14%), children's songs (12.3%), circus programmes and acrobat shows (10.5%) and full packages of children's programmes (7%). Most countries participate in international festivals and contests for children's programmes, with the exception of South Yemen, Mauritania, Djibouti and Somalia. The study also found that children's programmes have certain problems in all countries except Iraq. These problems may be due to the lack of financial support and qualified people, as well as the overuse of foreign programmes. Some countries (Egypt, Iraq, Jordan, the United Arab Emirates, Bahrain and Qatar) have local production, which is run by the respective countries' governments. Only two countries (Egypt and Jordan) allow private production.

In a study on the planning and production of children's programmes on the United Arab Emirates television (El Aly, 1992), it was found that 70% of the interviewees mentioned that the appearance of children was important in their own programmes. The findings also show that presenters of these programmes must be local, male and female, and that the programmes must also be presented through four artistic types: songs (100%), animated pictures (70%), stories (30%) and direct talk (30%).

A Saudi study was conducted on Saudi children's use of video, on a sample of 163 mothers (Zeenada & Beet El Mal, 1991). The findings show that 31% of children use video heavily (5-7 times a week), mainly late in the evening and during the afternoon. Children preferred cartoons (54.6%), commercials (28.8%), translated films (28.2%) and adventure (16%).

More than one-third of the interviewed mothers (38%) mentioned using video as a tool in punishing their children; if children misbehaved, they were not allowed to use the video. Children were also not allowed to use video in their own rooms. A percentage of 63.8% of the mothers mentioned buying videotapes for their children upon their request. The study concluded that the use of video has three main effects on children: social, cognitive and behavioural.

Another study on children's programmes (El Mishmishy, 1993) on Saudi television included a content analysis of children's programmes on the first Saudi TV channel and interviews with the planners and producers of these programmes. The findings show that television did not distinguish among different age groups, and that programmes were screened to children in general and were not very attractive to them.

Programmes were mainly local (73.2%). They were promotional (31.6%), educational (16.1%), social (9.3%) and religious (2.7%). Surprisingly, religious programmes were the least screened programmes.

A percentage of 64.3% of the interviewed planners and producers mentioned that they worked on a part-time basis, with 42.9% not having any type of training and 28.6% not being university graduates. They also mentioned experiencing a great deal of difficulty in conducting their work, due to a lack of technicians and supporting qualified staff.

A study was conducted on the role of television in increasing Egyptian children's health awareness (Jaffar, 1998). The study's sample was 240 children, and relied on the experimental approach. It was found that there was a great difference between those who watch television and those who do not, with respect to their information on health affairs. Television was ahead of other print media with respect to its capacity to increase children's knowledge about health matters. It was also found that children from the middle class had more information on health matters than did those from the working class.

Females had more information on health than males did.

Lotfy (1992) found, in a study on the influence of television advertising and Arab serials on the Egyptian child, that children are greatly negatively affected by television. The study was carried out on sample of 627 commercials, 400 children (10 to 12 years), and a sample of parents.

The study found that television was to be blamed for spreading certain bad behaviour among children. Parents said that their children exaggerated about the amount of time they spent watching television. Children from the middle class were more under parental control than were those from the working class. Children, by contrast, mentioned that their parents controlled their exposure to television.

77

It was also found that children were encouraged by television commercials to buy things they did not need.

The child's appearance in television commercials was the topic of a study conducted on a sample of 1284 commercials, 33 programmes, planners and directors, a sample of 100 children and a sample of experts and psychologists (Jaffar, 1991).

It was found that programme directors use both males and females in their programmes (62%), as the target audiences for their products and services are both boys and girls. Programme planners and directors also mentioned that they prefer using older children (6-12 years), and 56% of commercials use children in this age category. Ninety-two percent of commercials relied on children from urban areas, and 86.7% of programme directors use this type of child.

Children and Print Media

This section reviews the findings of studies related to children and print media.

El Abd (1988) conducted a study on children's print material in 13 Arab countries, i.e., Egypt, the United Arab Emirates, Saudi Arabia, Iraq, Djibouti, Jordan, Bahrain, Syria, South Yemen, Sudan, Mauritania, Somalia and Palestine. The data were collected through a questionnaire sent to those in charge of children's print media during the months of July, August and September 1988. The study's findings show that special materials for children exist in only nine of the countries, i.e. Egypt, the United Arab Emirates, Iraq, Jordan, Bahrain, Syria, Sudan, Somalia, Djibouti, Southern Yemen, Mauritania and Palestine.

Two of the above countries (Egypt and the United Arab Emirates) offer regular daily material for children in the print media. Eight countries (Egypt, the United Arab Emirates, Saudi Arabia, Iraq, Jordan, Bahrain, Sudan and Somalia) offer regular weekly material for children. One country (Syria) offers material for children once a fortnight, while another (Iraq) offers monthly material for children.

With respect to the kind of children's material, it was found that general information (100%) stories (100%), hobbies (88.9%), entertainment (88.9%) and news (44.4%) were the most mentioned. It was found that the children's participation took on two forms: as correspondents in their schools or as taking part in editing their own material by submitting information for publishing.

Regarding children's newspapers and magazines, it was found that they exist in ten countries: Egypt, the United Arab Emirates, Saudi Arabia, Iraq, Jordan, Bahrain, Syria, Southern Yemen, Sudan and Palestine. They are issued by either ordinary news organizations or special organizations for children. It was also found that publishing houses rely on specialists from outside the organization (freelancers) to edit and prepare children's magazines. A percentage of 42.9 of the magazines are printed in colour, 42.9% combine colour and black and white, and 14.2% are printed only in black and white.

El Laban (1995) conducted a content analysis study on an Egyptian weekly magazine for children (*Aladdin Magazine*) for two years (1993-94). The study aimed at examining the physical and psychological dangers of the use of colour in children's magazines. It was shown that the studied magazine was very successful with respect to the quality of glossy paper and colour used. The use of glossy paper may lead to the reflection of a great deal of light while reading, which may cause fatigue to the child's eyes and increase the number of children who are not used to reading for long periods of time. The magazine used high quality printing ink that does not rub off on children's fingers while reading. The study's findings also show that the magazine was successful in the use of illustration, especially simple drawings appearing on white backgrounds, which enhances visibility. The magazine used psychological and religious appeals to attract the children.

Children's magazines were the topic of another study (Amer, 1993), conducted on *Samir Magazine* (Amer, 1993). Material from the magazine were analyzed from June 1989 until December 1991. The sample included 394 scientific topics that were published in 135 issues.

It was found that a great deal of the magazine's content is devoted to scientific topics. The main translated topics were related to industrial technology, space and planets, science, astronomy and international scientific news stories. Science-fiction stories formed a large share of the scientific content of the magazine. Material related to contests on scientific topics was also published frequently. Stories related to computers and robots were also widely covered.

With respect to the format and presentation of scientific materials, *Samir Magazine* uses simple scientific terms to transfer meaning quickly and relies on coloured pictures and drawings to simplify things. The findings also show that the magazine does not provide children with any information on Arab scientific life, ancient or modern. Finally, it was concluded that the magazine lacks a qualified professional scientific editor who can blend news and science.

In line with the above study, Mabad (1995) conducted a study on trends in the fictional stories directed at the Egyptian child on a sample of three monthly children's magazines specializing in science fiction, i.e. *Nova*, *The Future File* and *Seef El Adalah*. These are the most important magazines specializing in this area. A content analysis was performed on the material published in the magazines in 1994. It was found that the above magazines imitate Western magazines to a great extent, and that their format is identical to that of American magazines with respect to the handbook size, cheap paper and low price. They always start with a short introductory editorial and contain short stories accompanied by pictures and drawings, often taken from foreign magazines.

The trend to remove the human race and replace it with another was the most mentioned trend (79.5%) in the studied magazines. The control of machines and computers on human beings (19.6%) and the trend to occupy other planets (10.6%) were also among the trends. Using space for spying and travelling to other plantets were less mentioned trends.

Findings from a study (Kamel, 1995) on translated magazines (*Mickey*) show that a great deal of material comes in the form of drawings. Critics express a great deal of reservation regarding this kind of drawing, as it may kill children's ability to create and imagine. Findings also show that children were less interested in reading short stories in magazines, and this shows that the magazines did not present a good press service to the children. Pictures and drawings do not present everything a child needs. The magazine's content is very weak and superficial, and is far from the Egyptian cultural, social, economic and political realities. It also lacks religious, historical, sports and artistic content. It does not pay any attention to the child, as it does not offer any sign of help for solving his/her problems. It also does not motivate the child or provide any help in developing the child's ability to create or invent. In all, the magazine does not satisfy the needs of the Egyptian child.

Kaheel (1995) conducted a study on the influence of magazine advertisements on children in *Aladdin Magazine*, i.e. the most popular children's magazine in Egypt. All advertisements published in the magazine during the sample period (August-December 1993) were analyzed. The study's findings show that most advertisements were for children's toys, clothes and other articles, which are not essential to children. It was also found that there was a contradiction between the drawings and pictures in the studied advertisements and the values of Egyptian society. The same contradiction was found between the values portrayed in the advertisements and values spread among children in society. This may lead to unwanted consuming habits and the spread of negative values among children.

Another study was conducted to examine children attitudes and interests regarding content in children's magazines, on a sample of 600 children aged 8-12 years; 450 from Cairo (urban areas) and 150 from rural areas (El Hadeedy et al., 1989). The study's findings show that more than half the interviewed children (58.3%) read magazines. The reading of magazines was more frequent among children from urban areas (70.1%) than it was among those from rural areas (20%). With respect to reasons for not reading magazines, it was found that lack of access to magazines, lack of time and not liking the content of children's magazines were the main reasons. Children also feel that there is a real need to increase the space devoted to stories in children's magazines, as this is their most preferred material.

It was also found that children feel there is a need for a new magazine to meet their needs, and that it should be a weekend (Thursday) magazine. This shows the importance of timing in children's magazines.

What children expect from a new children's magazine is fun and entertainment. This shows that children's magazines should not be seen as educational or scientific media, but should entertain rather than teach. It was also found that the price of any new magazine should be reasonable.

Children's use of their magazines was the topic of another study (El Hadeedy, 1997), which aims at examining children's motivation for using children's magazines. The study was carried out on a purposive sample of 405 Egyptian children aged 9 to 12 years. It found that children read 14 magazines, the most mentioned being *Alaa El Din* in first place (22%), followed by *Mickey* (17.1%) and *Majed* (11.1%). With respect to access to children's magazines, they are bought by a family member (29.2%) or by the children themselves with pocket money (26.1%). The children's magazines were also borrowed from friends.

Nearly half the interviewed children (44%) read alone, 22.2% with friends, 21.9% with family members, and 11.6% with a teacher. Preferred material included comedy, games, competitions, entertainment and general information. Factorial analysis shows that children read magazines for five factors: information, entertainment, interaction, social communication and tales.

Children and Radio

On the following pages, findings from studies on children and radio will be discussed. The number of these studies was very limited.

Reda (1990) conducted a study on a sample of 200 children aged 10-12 years, selected from schools in rural and urban areas. The main objective of the study was to examine children's programmes on local radio stations and their influence on the formation of children's concepts and values. The sampled local station was the Wasat el Delta radio station. Concepts of the religion, nature and belonging were three important concepts introduced in 72% of children's programmes on the station. "The religion concept" came in first place (24%), followed by "the nature concept" (22%). The "belonging concept" came in third (18%).

Children mentioned liking the children's programmes aired on the station because they present useful information (68%), music and songs (55%), and stories and tales (53%). The study recommended that the time devoted to children's programmes be increased and more attention be given to the needs of children in rural areas.

El Abd (1988) conducted a study on children's programmes on radio in 13 Arab countries (Egypt, Syria, the United Arab Emirates, Sudan, Northern Yemen, Southern Yemen, Djibouti, Bahrain, Jordan, Somalia, Iraq and Qatar). The study found that there were special radio programmes for children in all countries except Djibouti. With respect to the number of daily children's programmes, the findings show that five Arab countries (Northern Yemen, Southern Yemen, Mauritania, Bahrain and Jordan) broadcast only one programme, Syria two programmes and Somalia three. Egypt and Iraq have more than 12 daily programmes for children, while other countries have a range of five to six daily.

Aims of the children's programmes included developing children's skills of thinking and information seeking, increasing their national spirit, entertaining and creating the child's own world and linking them to the real world.

According to producers of children's programmes, the number of children's programmes was sufficient only in Egypt and Iraq. Children participated in some programmes in most countries (83.3%), with the exception of Qatar and Syria. The findings also show that planning was done for children's programmes in six countries, i.e. Egypt, Sudan, Bahrain, the United Arab Emirates, Iraq and Qatar. The planning of children's programmes relies on some principles such as the state's general plans, providing the child with the right values and information, satisfying the child's needs, connecting the Arab child with children in other parts of the world and suitability of programmes for different age groups. The programmes must also match current events, the child's cultural environment and the different seasons of the year.

In most countries, regular evaluation was performed on children's programmes. It was also found that children were corresponding with their programmes with the main motives of broadcasting their names and participating in the programmes. Budgets for children's programmes were not sufficient in Egypt, Sudan, Northern Yemen, Southern Yemen, Jordan, Somalia and Mauritania, but were adequate in Iraq, Qatar and the United Arab Emirates.

Sources of materials for children's programmes were national production (54.5%) and joint Arab production (45.5%). Control over children's programmes was found in all countries except Bahrain. The main problems which face the production of children's programmes included lack of financial resources, lack of qualified staff and low participation of children in their programmes.

Conclusion and Recommendations

If the rise of mass media goes back to the beginning of the 20th century, the study of children and media is more recent. Works in the field of children and mass media rely on the contribution of scholars from different approaches, i.e. mass communication, psychology, social psychology and sociology. Due to the importance of mass media and its strong relationship with human beings, scholars in the fields of education and mass media are more interested than others in studying the influence of mass media on the child.

The child's very limited experience in life leads to his quick response to stimuli without critical thinking. Critics were divided among themselves with respect to the influence of mass media on the child. While some see that mass media have positive effects on the child, others see negative effects.

The above review shows that the number of studies conducted during the 1990s, especially the mid-1990s, was great compared to during the 1980s or 1970s. This may be due to the great amount of attention the governments in Arab countries have started to give children. A great number of children's organizations have been established under the supervision of governmental and non-governmental organizations. Academic and scientific centres for the study of children have also been established across the Arab world. There has also been a pan-Arab interest in the child, reflected in the establishment of the Arab Institute for Childhood Studies in Cairo within the Arab League. In Egypt, for example, there was a presidential decree to consider the decade 1989-1999 the childhood decade, and during that time a great deal was done at official and private levels to improve the quality of the services provided to the Egyptian child. This may also explain the great care taken to study children during this decade.

Most of the reviewed studies were related to children and television, i.e. types of children's programmes on television and children's exposure to these programmes. While some of these studies mainly analyzed the programmes, others were concerned with children's exposure to them, their preferences and the influence of the programmes on the children. Some of the studies were also related to communicators (programme planners, producers and directors). Finally, a few examined parents and the extent to which they influence their children's use of television. Studies on children and media in general, print media, radio and other media such as video were less frequent.

It was also found that social status and geographic area factors have a great influence on children's use of mass media. Those from the upper and middle classes have access to most media, whereas television was the most used medium for children from a working-class background. The difference was also clarified in preferences: Middle-class children prefer variety shows and musical programmes, whereas working-class children prefer traditional and religious programmes and material. Middle class children also used magazines and other print media more than working-class children did. It was also found that children in urban areas have access to more media than do children in rural areas, who stick mainly to television as their main medium.

No attention was given to the problem of poorly educated and homeless children. Official organizations continue to address children's problems, but nothing is ever mentioned about the role media may play in this issue. This problem is very common in all Arab countries, but unfortunately very little is done about it.

Arab children are different from those in other countries, especially Western societies, with respect to their dealing with media, especially television. In most families from different social milieus, children are left to watch television without any control or interference from the family. The danger in this situation increases with the introduction and spread of satellite television. In most Arab countries, children know more about satellite programmes than do other family members, and they use these channels more often than do other family members.

According to the studies discussed above, television is the most dominant medium and most children watch television for different forms of gratification, especially entertainment and fun. Cinema is also one of the most important media for children. The importance of films is special in the Arab world because of the spread of illiteracy, which makes children more prepared to respond to films and motion pictures.

Writers and specialists agree on what is meant by films for children, distinguishing between different kinds of films as follows (Shokry, 1995, pp. 9-15):

- Films in which children are the principal personalities, or whose main theme is the child

- Films that parents feel suit the requirements of their children

- Sports films

- Animated films that give life and action to inanimate objects such as drawings, puppets and cartoons, which rely on the persistence of vision (Davies et al., 1975). This kind of film creates a magic world for children who live in the world of Tom and Jerry, Mickey Mouse, Donald Duck and Pluto.

- Documentary films, which children may see in the classroom

- Educational and cultural films

- Special films for children

The use of newspapers was affected by the age factor: Older children (10 years and above) use newspapers more than younger children do. The same applies to magazines. Children's use of print media was also affected by the socio-economic status of the family. Children in middle-classes families were more likely to use print media than were working-class children, who lack sufficient financial resources.

Timing of children's magazines and prices are also crucial issues. Publication should be near the weekend. Most children see magazines as entertaining rather than educational. Therefore, they prefer to read magazines during their days off from school. This point should also be reflected in content, which must be light to satisfy children's needs and expectations.

It was obvious in the literature that there is a problem with respect to specialized writers for children in the print media. Specialized writers were very few, and most were not up to standard. This applies to those whose material covers the very limited space devoted to children in newspapers, and may also apply to magazines or even children's magazines.

The situation was different in radio and television, where children's programmes presenters were relatively more experienced. This matter could be seen clearly on Egyptian radio and television. Egyptian television screens a wide variety of programmes for children and for different age groups, and the rate of viewing by the target young audience is high. The rate of listening to children's programmes on the radio is also high among the target audiences.

Lack of financial resources was a major problem for children's media in most Arab countries, with the exception of the Gulf countries. Budgets allocated to children's programmes for radio or television were far lower than those allocated to other kinds of programmes. The same applies to the situation of children's films, which suffer from a lack of financial and other resources. It is also difficult in most cases to produce children's films in which children play principal roles.

Another problem includes the lack of specialists and staff in the field of production and presentation. At the same time, those who work in the field of children's programmes were paid less than others were. This leads to a situation in which people who produce children's material and programmes are viewed as less qualified than those who produce other programmes. This was common in most Arab countries.

Although a great deal of research on children and media has been conducted, we still have the same problems shown in the findings of most studies. These mainly concerned two issues:

- Do children expose themselves to these programmes and this material, or are they wasted?

- Do we, as parents, have the right to select radio and television programmes and print material for our children?

These are the kinds of questions that need to be addressed by future research. It is very common at many Arab television companies to screen programmes at inappropriate times, for example while children are at school, and this leads to the children not seeing them.

The review of literature and analysis of findings have shown that researchers in the Arab world have given more attention to television than all other media. This may be due to the fact that television has been more influential on children than most other media have. Studies on children and radio were very few. Studies on children's use of other media such as cassette recorders were completely absent, although the use of the portable cassette recorder has become very popular across the Arab countries, especially among older children. Studies on use of video and video games were also rare. We believe that further research needs to be conducted on these last areas, and hope is placed on this future research. There is also a need to study children's use of modern media such as mp3 players, chat rooms and mobile phones.

The above review of findings has also shown that there is a real need for media education. Most studies have shown that mass media have a great deal of negative influence on children. These children need to be educated on how to deal with mass media. Families, especially mothers, also need to be advised on how to help their children deal with mass media.

During the 1980s, a number of departments were established at some Arab universities to qualify teachers for "educational media", but not "media education". In other words, these departments were concerned mainly with the media used at schools generally or in the educational process.

At the same time, beginning in the early 1990s, in most Arab countries schools were required by law to have "Multi-Media Laboratories". These are mainly computer laboratories, and most have access to the Internet. They are intended for use by children at schools for the sake of the educational process. These laboratories are more used in private schools than governmental schools.

Children use them mainly to go on line and work on their school projects. Media education at schools has been narrowed to the level of media use in the educational process.

Before 2002, there were no real workshops or conferences on media education. The first workshops were organized by UNESCO in Cairo and Tunisia in 2002.

As of today, the situation of media education has witnessed slight progress, which can be seen in the number of studies (especially PhD studies) being conducted on media education. This trend is very recent.

In sum, there is thus an urgent need for some kind of coordination between different organizations such as educational and mass media organizations to conduct joint research and work together. This will help, to a great extent, to improve the conditions of children's use of media. We also believe that there is a real need to conduct cross-cultural studies that can compare, for instance, the situation of children's use of media in the Arab world with that in other countries.

References

Amer, M.A. (1993) *Role of Children's Magazines in Simplifying Sciences: A Case Study of "Samir Magazine"*. Cairo: Child Studies Center.

Asran, S.S. (1998) *Role of Television Drama in Providing School Leavers With Social Values: A Study on a Sample of Egyptian Children Who Have left Education*. Egypt: Zagazeeg: Faculty of Arts.

Davies, M., et al. (1975) *The Hamlin History of the Cinema*. London: Hamlin Publishing Group Ld.

Dehny, S. (1993) *Television and Cinema Issues in the Arab World*. Damascus: Arab Writers Union Print House.

El Abd, A. (1993) *Children's Programmes on Oman Television: A Pilot Study*. Oman: Al Alwan Print House.

El Abd, A. (1988) *A Study of Children's Press in the Arab World*. Cairo: Arab Center for Childhood and Development.

El Abd, A. (1988) *Children's Cinema in the Arab World*. Cairo: Arab Center for Childhood and Development.

El Abd, A. (1988) *A Study of Children's Radio Programmes in the Arab World*. Cairo: Arab Center for Childhood and Development.

El Abd, A. (1988) *Children's Programmes on Television*. Cairo: Dar El Fekr El Arabi.

El Abd, A. (1988) *Children's Programmes in the Arab World*. Cairo: Arab Council for Children and Development.

El Aly, A.F. (1992) 'The Child on the United Arab Emirates, a Field Study', *Communication Research*, Vol. 7, (July 1992) pp. 51-79.

El Hadeedy, M., el al, (1994) *Children's Attitudes towards Their Radio and Television Programmes*. Cairo: Egyptian Television and Radio Union.

El Hadeedy, M., et al. (1990) *Children's Cinema in the Arab World*. Cairo: Arab Council for Childhood and Development.

El Hadeedy, M. et al. (1989) *Towards a Magazine for Arab Children*. Cairo: Dar El Hany Publishing House.

El Hadeedy, M.A.F. (1997) *Use of Children's Magazines*, Unpublished MA Thesis. Cairo: Cairo University.

El Keleeny, F.Y. (1995) Negative Influences of Video Games on Egyptian Child. Cairo: Ein Shams University, Childhood Studies Center.

El Keleeny, S. (1993) The Role of Television in Increasing the Egyptian Child's Environmental awareness. Cairo: Faculty of Mass Communication, Journal of Communication Research, Dec. 1993.

El Laban, S.D. (1995) *Physical and Psychological Dangers of the Use of Colors in Egyptian Children's Magazines: A Case Study on "Aladdin Magazine" During the Period of 1993 to 1994.* Cairo: Ein Shams University, Child Studies Center.

El Mishmishy, M. (1993) *Children's Programmes on Saudi Television,* Unpublished MA Thesis. Cairo: Cairo University.

El Sayed, L.H. (1996) *Children's Realization of the Televised Reality.* Cairo: Ein Shams University's Child Studies Center.

El Semary, H.B. (1995) *The Influence of Watching Television on Egyptian Children's habits of Reading.* Cairo: Childhood Studies Center, Ein Shams University.

El Shal, I. (1997) *Relationship of the Child with the Print and Electronic Media.* Cairo: Dar Nahdet El Shark.

Hassan, E.B. (1995) *Children's Attitudes towards Children's Programmes.* Cairo: Ein Shams University, Childhood Studies Center.

Hassan, E.B. (1989) *Local Media and Their Role in Providing Egyptian Child With Information,* Unpublished PhD Thesis. Cairo: Ein Shams University.

Hassan, M. (1998) *The Animation Films and Children's Cognitive Development.* Cairo: The University Press.

Hindy, S.D. (1998) *Influence of Mass Media on the Child.* Jordan, Oman: Dar El Fekr for publishing and distribution.

Ibrahim, A.F. (1994) The Portrayal of the Problem of Homeless Children in Egyptian Media. *Mass Communication Research Magazine,* Cairo: Al Azhar University.

Jaffar, H.A. (1998) *Use of Television in Spreading Health Awareness Among Egyptian Children: An Experimental Study.* Unpublished PhD Thesis. Cairo: Cairo University.

Jaffar, H.A. (1991) *Use of the Child in Television Commercials: An Analytical and Field Study.* Unpublished MA Thesis. Cairo: Cairo University.

Kaheel, A.A. (1995) *Values in Children's Advertisements in 'Aladdin Magazine' during the Period from August to December 1993.* Cairo: Child Studies Center, Ein Shams University.

Kamel, O.M. (1995) *Children's Perception of Personality Characteristics which are Portrayed in Children's Programmes.* Cairo: Ein Shams University, Childhood Studies Center.

Kamel, T.F. (1995) *Children's Translated Magazines: A Case Study of Mickey Magazine,* A Paper Presented to the conference of Egyptian Child between Danger and Safety, Cairo: April, 1994.

Kandeel, R. (1997) *The Egyptian Child and the Use of Book, Cinema and Theatre: Determinants of Children's Use of Mass Media.* Cairo: United Company for Printing, Publishing and Distribution

Kandeel, R.A. (1993) *Egyptian Child and the Use of Mass Media,* a Paper Presented for the First Scientific Conference of the Childhood Institute for Higher Studies, Cairo: Ein Shams University, Feb. 1993.

Labib, S. (1994) *The Child's Right in a Reasonable Media Coverage.* Cairo: UNICEF.

Lotfy, H.M. (1992) *Impact from Television Advertising and Arab Serials on the Egyptian Child,* Unpublished PhD Thesis. Cairo: Cairo University.

Mabad, I.K. (1995) *Trends in Scientific Imagination Stories Directed to the Egyptian Child.* Cairo: Ein Shams University, The Child Studies Center.

Reda, A. (1994) Impact From Televised Violence on Children's Behaviour. Cairo: Faculty of Mass Communication, *Journal of Communication Research,* July 1994.

Reda, M. (1990) *Role of Children's Programmes in Local radio Stations in Forming the Children's Concepts and Values,* Unpublished Master's Thesis. Cairo: Ein Shams University, The Child Studies Center.

Rezk, S.S. (1995) *The Role of Television Advertising in Forming Egyptian Children's' Values.* Cairo: Ein Shams University, Child Studies Center.

Sabry, H.A. (1995) *Mass Media and Cultural Security for Children.* Cairo: Childhood Studies Center, Ein Shams University.

Shokry, A. (1995) *Visual Drama.* Cairo: Al Araby.

Zeenada, A. and Beet El Mal, H. (1991) 'The Video: Its Uses and Effects on Saudi Children', *Communication Research,* Vol. 6, (Dec. 1991) pp. 100-118.

The Appropriation of New Media and Communication Tools by Young People Aged 12-18 in Europe
New Trends for Media Education

Evelyne Bevort & Patrick Verniers

Urgent Need for Applied Research

The starting point of media education is always based on knowledge of how young people use media. In the case of new media and communication tools, it is essential to know how these media are available to young people and what kind of appropriations they get of them. To foresee, complete or even modify their evolution in the future, it is imperative to analyse the habits of youths with regard to digital media.

The study of the appropriation of digital media is central in advancing and establishing critical thinking about them. New media education inevitably demands the observation of how the media are appropriated by youths, taking into account their specificities as well as unknown factors. Each develops his/her own process, following his/her path with the help of different people who are more or less agile. This appropriation is typically individualistic and personal.

How familiar are they with these media? In what context do they use them? What kind of relationship, of dependence do they establish?

All these crucial questions have been asked in Mediappro (Media Appropriation)[1], an applied research project focusing on the appropriation of new media by youths and funded by the European Commission. Between January 2005 and June 2006[2], a number of associations and foundations, universities and government ministries from nine European countries[3] collaborated on this project. A similar survey was also carried out during the same period in Québec, Canada in order to compare and gain a better understanding of the situation in Europe and North America.

The Mediappro study draws on the statements of young Europeans to elucidate and propose recommendations in the learning of new media, coherent with the modes of appropriation observed.

Research Axes and Question Fields

The principle axes of research cover four central areas of study:

1. The multi-media environment (access to media, context of use)

2. Knowledge and cognitive processes (knowledge of the Internet, perception or lack thereof of learning via the Internet)

3. The psychosocial dynamic (manner in which these methods of communication affect sociability, group belonging)

4. Capacity to imagine the future within a technical and democratic context

The questions asked were based on strategic topics for media educators:

*   Concerning representation: Spontaneously, what words do they associate with the Internet? In what register do they situate it?

*   On the use of these different media and within their different contexts (family, school, with peers) in order to ascertain where and how the Internet, mobile phones or video games are situated and to explore the relation with other media (press, television or radio) and spare time activities.

*   About their knowledge of the Internet through the Internet (What do they truly know about the Internet – how it works and functions? Where do they obtain this information? Do they consider themselves technically competent in terms of accessing content?

*   On how they consider the school's role and what they would like: Do they feel they need training? If so, in what aspect and by whom (school, family, others)?

*   In terms of their sociability, how do these techniques work? Do they feel they should always be available to communicate with others – "stay connected"? What exactly does this mean to them? From this perspective, do they have the impression of being a part of an open world or a restricted one? What respective roles do they attribute to blogs, SMS's, MSN, etc.?

How do they situate these new tools in the future? How do they imagine them to be? What changes do they foresee? What is the place for these new modes of communication in a democratic society?

Methodology

About 9,000 young people aged between 12 and 18 participated in the study (7,400 in Europe and 1,350 in Québec).

In order to construct a relevant sample at the international level, each national research team selected schools according to their geographical location and their social, economic and cultural setting.

Three school grades, representing three age groups, were defined: 12-14 (beginning of secondary school), 15-16 (middle of secondary school) and 17-18 (end of secondary school).

In using this sampling method, we were able to obtain a valid representation of the differences in young people's life contexts, reflecting national differences that exist across Europe.

The originality of the research method is based on two complementary steps to collect information from the young people:

First, a printed questionnaire was filled out anonymously, with closed-ended questions (administrated by a researcher).

Second, after mapping the appropriation profiles, the questionnaires were coupled with individual semi-directive interviews with a selected number of participants.

A Highly Developed Use of the Internet

If we look at the main results, it is clear that Internet use is almost universal across these countries for youths aged 12-18, though small numbers of non-users remain; these numbers vary across the countries.

Table 1.   Currently Use or Have Used the Internet (%)

Québec	100
Estonia	99
Denmark	98
UK	98
France	96
Poland	96
Portugal	96
Belgium	93
Greece	89
Italy	85

Nine of ten young people say that they use the Internet. The highest number of users is in Québec, where almost all the respondents report knowing and using the Internet. The lowest is in Italy where 78% say they use it, plus 7% who declare that they no longer use it.

The majority of young Europeans have used the Internet for a period spanning between one and three years (35%), or for four years or more (31%).

In several countries, the extent of Internet use correlates with levels of print literacy, suggesting that these two types of literacy might be usefully treated as being connected in educational practices.

Personal Communication, Search and Leisure Uses

Table 2. Activities on the Internet (sometimes + often + very often) (%)

	Search engines	E-mail	Instant Messenger	Chat rooms	Downloading
Belgium	95	74	81	28	58
Denmark	92	66	87	26	50
Estonia	90	69	88	33	73
France	94	67	69	32	49
Greece	81	46	39	41	65
Italy	86	59	49	33	59
Poland	91	62	75	34	67
Portugal	95	69	77	38	60
Québec	99	94	93	58	79
UK	98	81	78	20	60
Average	91	66	71	32	60

Analysing the distribution of uses by young people, we can observe that they are concentrated around personal communication, search for information and leisure.

• *Information and Search Engines*

Looking up information is by far the most common activity in all the countries: more than nine of ten young Europeans say they use search engines sometimes, often or very often (highest: United Kingdom and Québec, 98%; lowest: Greece, 81%). The French study[4] demonstrates that youths do not systematically use search engines for finding information, but for visiting sites they are already familiar with. The Danish study[5] underlines the fact that the youths in the sample group consider Google and search engines to be synonymous.

• *Popular Communication Tools*

Online communication remains very popular. Seven of ten European youths use instant messaging (for example MSN) and electronic mail. MSN Messenger is what they use most frequently: 42% use it very regularly as opposed to 23% for e-mail.

The study also reveals sensitive differences between countries. Instant messaging, (very closely linked to the availability of equipment, particularly the presence of a high speed Internet connection in the home) is used by 63% of Estonians, as opposed to only 12% of Greeks[6]: "Greek students ignore or are not interested in basic Internet functions, such as MSN, email, personal pages, blogs."[7]

In Québec, youths use electronic mail and instant messaging much more than in Europe: 80% and 90%, respectively, either often or very often.

More than half the participants stated that they wrote SMS messages often or very often (36% very often). Instant messaging is used, above all, to stay in touch with friends (62% of European youths, 89% in Québec) rather than one's family (14% claim to use this method of communication with their parents).

Instant messaging enables them to contact people of their choosing, and their address books can contain more than 50 names (30% of youths).

Instant messaging is an important vector of socialisation and represents the contentment of feeling connected to their network of friends, even from home.

• *Mobile Communication*

Table 3.   Declare to Have Their Own Mobile Phone (%)

Denmark	98
Italy	98
Estonia	97
Portugal	97
UK	96
Belgium	95
Greece	94
Poland	90
France	88
Québec	41

Ninety-five percent of young people have their own mobile phone (highest: Italy, 98%; lowest: France, 87%). It is very clear that they see the mobile phone as vitally important, something they would find it difficult to live without; a majority consider it important to be connected with their friends all the time. The situation is completely different in Québec, where only four of ten young people have their own mobile phone, and very few send text messages (22%).

Mobile phones are used mainly in Europe to communicate with friends, including planning events, telling someone they are thinking of them or gossiping. With the exception of Estonia, where calling is more popular than texting, youths are more likely to send text messages (79%) than to call (65%). One reason for this is financial: sending a text message is clearly cheaper than a phone call (72% of the young people agree with this affirmation). There is some evidence (as noted in the UK and Portuguese interviews, for instance) that they value the distance provided by texting, which makes difficult communication easier. The Danish interviews suggested that the older age group use phones for flirting, and also appreciate the distance afforded by texting to reduce embarrassment.

• *Other Activities*

If communication holds an important place in the habits of youths aged 12-18, they also frequently develop other activities:

- Downloading material from the Internet is widely practised. Sixty-one percent say that they download a range of material from the Internet sometimes (17%), often (18%) or very often (26%). Strikingly, 44% of the young people said that they download music even when it is forbidden.

- Music or online radio programmes are very popular: Sixty-seven percent of young people listen sometimes (21%), often (20%) or very often (26%).

- The number playing online or network games seems small: only 18% say that they play frequently or very frequently, though again this varied considerably between countries: for instance, 30% in Denmark and 26% in the UK, but only 11% in Poland). In Québec, more than one of two youths declare to be an online gamer.

- Creating their own content is less widely practised. For instance, 18% of young people say that they have a personal site, and 18% a blog. Blogs are quite popular in Belgium (38%), Québec (35%) and France (25%), while in some cases young people seemed uncertain as to what a blog was (a third of the Danish sample, for example).

Internet at School and at Home: a Growing Gap

It is within the home that the young people seem to have the most freedom to do what they want on the Internet. Their favourite activities are communicating with friends (via instant messaging), visiting websites, listening to music, playing games and downloading material. The use of search engines is also highlighted as a popular activity in some countries, especially the United Kingdom, Belgium, Poland and France.

Across all countries, including Québec, it is clear that the Internet is used far more at home than at school. Eighty-one percent of the young people say they use it at home (95% in Denmark and Québec vs. 64% in Greece). Thirty-eight percent use it every day – with huge differences between countries, from Estonia (65%) to Greece (8%) – and 30% use it multiple times a week. Sixty-seven percent of the young people say that they have a high-speed connection at home (highest: Estonia, 90%; lowest: Greece, 31%). The Estonian report[8] notes that "the private character of their activities may explain why respondents clearly prefer to use the Internet at home and use public access points as little as possible".

Generally, the use of the Internet seems to increase with age.

The home is where many young people claim to learn about the Internet, either through self-teaching or from siblings. Learning from parents also occurs, though from young people's point of view, parents do not seem to be great users of the Internet: Twenty-five percent use it sometimes, 25% often and 15% very often.

While home use of the Internet is extensive, it is equally clear that school use is severely limited and constrained in Europe as well as Québec. Although young people have physical access to the Internet at school in theory, in practice it is used much less than at home. Indeed, 22% (highest: Belgium, 42%; lowest: Denmark, 6%) of young people say that they never use the Internet at school during class, and 30% report using it rarely.

Table 4. Use Every Day + Several Times a Week (%)

	At home	At school
Belgium	69	9
Denmark	89	33
Estonia	83	30
France	57	10
Greece	38	25
Italy	56	7
Poland	68	45
Portugal	62	22
Québec	86	18
UK	79	56
Average	67	26

Students mostly say they use the Internet for their schoolwork, retrieving information. The most likely context for use cited in the interviews (in the UK, Portugal, and Poland) was for ICT lessons. The UK qualitative study[9] notes that "school uses were often talked of without enthusiasm compared with the zeal with which young people spoke about MSN, games, music and other home uses".

The interaction between the school or college and the young people does not seem developed in relation to the Internet. Explicit teaching about the Internet in schools seems to be seriously under-developed. Children in several countries say that they have learned more from friends and parents than from anyone else about Internet use.

While their experiences of the Internet in school are largely disappointing and constrained, the young people feel that the school should be an important resource, and consider it one that they need. While they report that their teachers do not talk to them about the Internet, they clearly believe that the teachers have the necessary skills.

95

Internet and the Other Media: A New Combination

Use of the Internet does not seem to have reduced the use of other media, with the exception of television (40% of the young people say that they watch less TV than before) and books (32% read books less often than before). The Polish report[10] mentions that "the Internet changes the behaviours at home and young people usually notice that fact. The Internet takes advantage over TV."

We can observe that Internet and new communication tools are combined with other media in new and unpredictable ways. Watching TV while communicating on MSN Messenger, listening to music while searching for information on the Internet – there is a tendency for young people to mix the different media in original ways.

Table 5.   Consequences on Cultural Practices (%)

	Less TV	Less reading	More music
Belgium	45	28	43
Denmark	33	28	49
Estonia	51	46	65
France	40	17	40
Greece	27	26	45
Italy	20	24	46
Poland	54	30	49
Portugal	36	35	48
UK	42	35	50
Average	36	23	45

A Dynamic Appropriation Process

What does the Mediappro study reveal about how and the extent to which the Internet is integrated in the daily habits of young people? The study aims not only to evaluate the impact and influence of these new practices in the daily activities of youths, but also to identify how young people adopt technology to meet their needs.

For instance, to what degree does access to the Internet modify, enhance or even alter social behaviour, learning techniques, habits in media and cultural consumption? What is the youths' level of awareness on these issues?

The appropriation of new media rests on two phenomena. Media is accessible by young people, who in turn modify its usage. Youths integrate these media in their own way according to their own interests and for their own purposes, in relation to other users.

The interaction between media and youths is continual and is a highly dynamic process. It is also very personal. Questioning the appropriation of new media leads to the identification of the uses and methods in terms of one's own chronology, practicalities, oversights and difficulties.

Studies demonstrate how youth movements are deployed almost instantaneously and spread extremely rapidly and contagiously. This necessarily leads to foreseeing what actually impacts youths: the influence of family background (attitudes regarding education, kinship, household organisation) and of friendship, shared values, representation, and access to these media through both technical and educational training.

By closely observing the "true" appropriation of these new media by youths, one must ask what elements are missing and how can youths gain a better grasp on media usage? While young people aged 12-18 are strongly interested in the Internet and use it frequently, many of these youths are not actually as competent as they think or say they are. They often lack the terminology and notions to explicitly describe and detail their habits, and as a consequence are unable to develop their own opinions on these media.

Their knowledge remains superficial, while in-depth savoir faire and insight are clearly needed. This also extends to the need for documented research despite the fact that schools have already taken this into consideration.

Law, Private Life and Critical Skills: A New Deal

As schoolwork is often delimited by the imperative of acquiring knowledge rather than acquiring skills, adolescents do not learn how to effectively use these new means of communication, particularly as it relates to legal or ethical issues, aspects of online communication and publication of media, particularly as related to legal or ethical issues. As a result, for instance, youths are not entirely clear on the notion of Internet anonymity. French youths are as numerous in believing that one can be identified even if a pseudonym is used as in believing the opposite, and only 44% of youths realise that anyone can access their personal blog.

On the other hand, many of these young people are quite aware of the laws and regulations regarding civic rights on the Internet, such as a person's rights to their image and royalties linked to downloading, as compared to other Europeans, who often have no clue concerning these issues.

In France, the protection of one's private life and rights to one's image are sensitive subjects on which much information is diffused, notably in school. But once again, young people's knowledge is often vague and does not prevent them from overlooking rules of which they have a very faint idea.

Some Europeans are quite critical regarding the information available on the Internet. This critical view increases with age, particularly amongst girls. The Québec study reports the same conclusion, though its authors point out that

Google and Wikipedia do not induce distrust but, on the contrary, evoke a sense of definite trust[11].

Finally, the majority of young people perceive electronic media as technologies in constant movement and rapidly adopt new tendencies. The Portuguese team,[12] however, points out that "Even though students are usually interested in new activities and new 'fashions', they tend to always do the same thing on the Internet, they follow a pattern." This undoubtedly results from inadequate and insufficient appropriation of the Internet. In this case, we could apply the metaphor of a young person who does not know his neighbourhood very well, walking through it several times a day but never thinking to take shortcuts or try new streets.

Even at the age of 17, youths do not have a clear idea on the societal impact of these media, and rarely have an educational outlet that allows them to reflect conceptually on the matter.

New Trends for Education

Perhaps the most striking conclusion of the whole study is the marked gap between home and school use of the Internet. Consequently, youths most often learn about the Internet without the help of adults, either with peers or individually through the process of trial and error.

From the responses obtained, we were able to understand that for the youths concerned, the Internet and mobile phones play a very minimal role in the world of education and that any interference between the two was weak.

It is equally clear that young people cannot adequately gain the skills that are needed. While in some countries they are sophisticated users of the Internet, with well-developed understandings of moral and cultural issues, there are areas in which they are much weaker, particularly in understanding any kind of legal question in relation to the Internet. Furthermore, there is evidence in all the countries that the youths over-estimate their own ability to evaluate.

While the creative potential of new media is much discussed in academic literature, the evidence here was that creative work was limited, with a minority of young people developing their own websites or blogs.

Except in Québec, phones emerge as being vitally important to young people's lives: they are used to develop and cement relationships, to attain independence (though also to retain safe contact with parents), and to finely discriminate between different degrees and levels of social proximity. Again, it seems that schools have not properly considered the educational potential of phone uses. Games seem to be rather less important to these young people than popular wisdom often suggests, but they are still an important leisure and cultural medium, and it may be that online gaming, while still used by a minority, is growing.

Finally, with respect to questions of safety, the study shows that young people extremely rarely report being in dangerous or even uncomfortable situations.

However, all of these issues would benefit from further research, particularly longitudinal study.

An Emerging Digital Culture

The findings that have resulted from the Mediappro study should not be interpreted as pessimistic. On the contrary, there is much building to do.

The study demands an actualisation of the field data and of the habits and expectations of youths. Moreover, considering the actual "true" skills of youths, as opposed to their "perceived" skills, demonstrates the necessity of providing a structured framework, of re-defining certain terms, of conceptualising certain fields and initiating the thought process on the current socio-economic evolution as well as its impact on society.

Schools could play a much more important role. Young people could have the opportunity to shed their tentative approach and effectively learn how to master their use of the Internet and future new media. Indeed, the youths could potentially elaborate a true digital culture.

With regard to appropriation by youths, it is certainly a question of either indifference or a complete lack of knowledge, but rather of a dependence on the structures and organisations that govern the Internet. Youths mostly know how to use the Internet through intermediaries, and the way they use it has usually been imposed by the Internet itself.

Digital culture is a work in progress. Media education has to deal with this emerging culture, built on a dynamic process between the young citizen, media and society. It is an indispensable factor in societies of knowledge and in turn demands that its appropriation be reflexive, creative and supported by true critical thinking.

Notes

1. Full research published on http://www.mediappro.org.
2. The research was co-ordinated by Professor Thierry De Smedt, University of Louvain-La Neuve, Belgium.
3. Belgium, Denmark, Estonia, France, Greece, Italy, Poland, Portugal and the United Kingdom.
4. Bevort, E., Bréda, I. (2006) Mediappro, Appropriation des nouveaux médias par les jeunes: une enquête européenne en éducation aux médias. Retrieved April 1, 2007, from http://www.clemi.org/international.html.
5. Tufte, B., Rasmussen, J., Christensen, O. (2006) The Appropriation of New Media by Youth. Mediappro final report.
6. Source: http://epp.eurostat.cec.eu.int.

7. Aslanidou, S., Ikonomou, A. (2006) The Appropriation of New Media by Youth. Mediappro final report.
8. Ugur, K., Ollivry, J.-P. (2006) The Appropriation of New Media by Youth. Mediappro report.
9. Burn, A., Cranmer, S. (2006) The Appropriation of New Media by Youth. Mediappro report.
10. Wenglorz, J. (2006) The Appropriation of New Media by Youth. Mediappro report.
11. Piette, J., Pons, C. M., Giroux, L. (2007, March) Les Jeunes et Internet: 2006 – Appropriation des nouvelles technologies. Final report to the Ministry of Culture and Communication, Quebec Government.
12 Reia Baptista, V., Balthazar, N., Mendes, S. (2006) The Appropriation of New Media by Youth. Mediappro report.

IV. Education and Media Culture in the Context of Media Literacy

Media Literacy
New Conceptualisation, New Approach[1]

José Manuel Pérez Tornero[2]

Media literacy is the term used to describe the skills and abilities required for conscious, independent development in the new communication environment – digital, global, and multimedia – of the information society. Media literacy is taken as the outcome of the media-education process.

However, the concept is polysemic and competes with other terms such as audiovisual literacy, digital literacy, and so on. Therefore, a clear definition should be given and, more importantly, the various approaches to media literacy through different policies should be considered.

In this article we shall see how, from the UNESCO and European Union definitions of media literacy, as well as other European initiatives, a conceptualisation can be framed that, besides delineating the field of media literacy, illustrates its different areas and aspects.

We need to move closer to a general understanding.

Media Education in the International Context

Media education and its outcome *media literacy* have been described and defined in an international context by UNESCO, as part of an initiative that began in 1982 with the conference in Grünwald (1982)[3], and continued with conferences in Toulouse (1990)[4], Vienna (1999)[5] and Seville (2002)[6].

UNESCO's work focuses on what is known as media education, which is the immediate predecessor of media literacy in its broadest sense.

In Europe, at the start of the 21st century, *the term media education was used with that of media literacy*, doubtlessly in an attempt to include and expand digital literacy, which has been a large part of movements to promote the development of the information society and narrow the digital divide.

This work has been carried out with the support of the Council of Europe[7] and the European Commission – which throughout 2006 and 2007 has supported a Group of Experts in the field of media literacy and has launched a public consultation on the subject[8]. The work has also been supported by the *European Media Charter*[9] and a number of public media regulation authorities, such as the United Kingdom's OFCOM[10].

Using all of these proposals, and in particular following the headway made by UNESCO and European Commission on the topic, we shall draw up a comprehensive concept map.

There were four stages in UNESCO's formalisation of the concept of media education.

The first, captured in the Grünwald declaration of 1982, was the creation of the field of media education, which focused attention on the impact of the media on training and education.

The second, brought forward by the 1990 Toulouse conference was the systematisation and more precise definition of the field.

Thirdly, the 1999 conference in Vienna,[11] took a new look at media education in the context of digital advances and the new communication era that came about as a result.

The fourth was the UNESCO Seminar in Seville held in 2002[12], which adopted the definition of the field developed in the Vienna conference and highlighted the need for action through active promotion policies in four areas: 1) Research; 2) Training; 3) Co-operation between schools, the media, NGOs, private business and public institutions; 4) Consolidation and promotion of the public sphere of society and its relationship with the media.

We shall now look at European contributions.

The most basic definition of media literacy is provided by OFCOM, which states that media literacy consists of 'the ability to access, understand and create communications in a variety of contexts'[13].

According to the *European Charter of Media Literacy*[14], there are seven *areas of competence* (or know-how) related to media literacy:

- Effective use of media technologies to *access, store, retrieve and share* content to meet individual and community needs and interests;

- Accessing and making *informed choices* about, a wide range of media forms and content from different cultural and institutional sources;

- *Understanding how and why* media content is produced;

- *Critically analysing* the techniques, languages and conventions used by the media, and the messages they convey;

- *Creative use of the media* to express and communicate ideas, information and opinions;

- *Identifying, avoiding and/or challenging*, media content and services that may be unsolicited, offensive, or harmful;

- Making effective use of media in the exercise of *democratic rights* and *civil responsibilities*.

Meanwhile, according to the European Commission, media literacy involves a variety of skills and abilities related to the media, its images, language, and messages: "Media Literacy may be defined as the ability to *access, analyse* and *evaluate* the power of images, sounds and messages which we are now being confronted with on a daily basis and which are an important part of our contemporary culture; as well as to *communicate competently* using available media, on a personal basis. Media literacy concerns all media, including television and film, radio and recorded music, print media, the Internet and other new digital communication technologies". This definition is complemented with a series of broader considerations, which we shall look at below[15].

On the one hand, the *media concept* (with the corresponding *messages* and *languages*) refers to all means of communication that form part of daily life and incorporate contemporary culture, independently of the specific nature of the medium (image, sound, written word...)[16].

On the other hand, the skills related to media literacy can be summarised in four areas of ability: *access, analysis, evaluation* and *creative production*[17]. All of these skills boost aspects of personal development: *consciousness, critical thinking*[18] and *problem-solving abilities*.

When considering other elements that help to define the field of media literacy conceptually and thematically, one must remember that it is the outcome of a learning (and teaching) process in any given context, but particularly in formal, informal, social, family, and media settings. This multi-contextual process leads to the acquisition of specific abilities and competences, in addition to attitudes and values. The process is termed *media education*[19].

Media literacy should not be treated as an isolated or independent skill. On the contrary, it is a skill that involves and encompasses other skills and forms of literacy: *reading and writing literacy, audiovisual literacy* (often referred to as image or visual literacy) and *digital or information literacy*[20].

Furthermore, media literacy is a necessary part of *active citizenship*[21] and is key to the full development of *freedom of expression* and the *right to information*. Therefore, it is an essential part of *participatory democracy*[22] and *intercultural dialogue*. "Today, media literacy is as central to active and full citizenship as literacy was at the beginning of 19th century," DG INFSO Commissioner Viviane Reding (Press release IP/06/1326, Brussels, 6 October 2006).

These concepts can be linked to, and complemented by, different terms and areas involved in media literacy.

The following chart is a conceptual map that gives a visual representation of the relationships between these concepts.

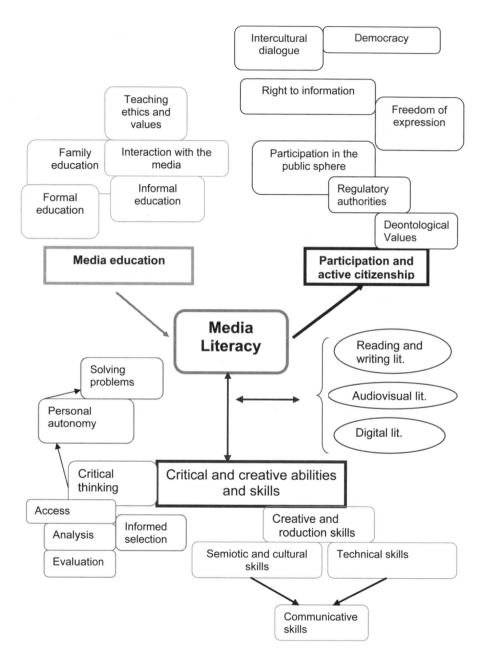

In the centre, media literacy appears as the result of a process, "media education" which is described through different concepts in the upper left of the chart.

Concepts related to "participation and active citizenship" are located on the upper right hand side.

In the lower part, elements that make up media literacy are divided into two main areas, one related to critical thinking, and another related to creation and production skills.

Finally, the three types of literacy that make up media literacy – reading and writing, audiovisual and digital literacy – are positioned to the right of media literacy.

The sole aim of the chart is to illustrate the different concepts related to media literacy and show how they are interlinked.

Areas of Media Literacy

For a complete definition of an operative model of media literacy, it is important to consider the competence areas into which the necessary skills are divided.

The following areas can be identified from the European Commission's definition:

- *Access*: This refers to the opportunities for using media. We shall make a distinction between a) physical access to media and to the contents of the media; and, b) the *ability – both cognitive and practical – to use such media* properly[23]. To cover both aspects, we shall talk about *conditions of access*.

    In this way, it will be possible to consider different conditions of access that exist among individuals, age and gender groups, social and cultural groups, and according to geographic contexts, and disabilities. A distinction can also be made between different conditions of access to electronic media (film, radio, television, and telephone) and digital media, such as the Internet. Access conditions will obviously vary according to the *physical availability* of instruments and tools, the *social and institutional rules and regulations* governing the use of media, and the different kinds of capabilities or disabilities.

- *Analysis and Evaluation*: This refers to a) the ability to read[24] *understand*[25] and *evaluate*[26] media content[27] and, b) the ability to sense and understand the conditions and possibilities of the media as tools.

There are several sub-areas to reading, understanding, and evaluation: 1) the ability to seek, locate, and select information to suit the individual's needs; 2) the individual ability to evaluate the information according to parameters such as truthfulness, honesty, interests of the broadcaster, etc.

Analysis and evaluation involve the most sophisticated abilities and skills such as *critical thinking* and *personal autonomy*.

- *Communicative competence:* This is the set of abilities that allow individuals to create messages from different codes – and produce and distribute them using the different media available. Therefore, it includes creative, technical, semiotic, and social skills.

The theory of communicative competence goes back a long way. Originally, it referred to the ability of speakers to use their linguistic abilities adequately, according to the target group and the context (Noam Chomsky[28]). In other words, it is a pragmatic skill. Jürgen Habermas[29] redefined it as a universal pragmatic skill that allows interaction between people and is based on rules. This is the skill, which should be normally widespread, that allows citizens to be active and engage in the public sphere. It is precisely in this light that it should be seen as a skill for civil communication.

New media have greatly improved people's skills for creating and producing messages, and have produced a qualitative leap ahead from the previous model of mass communication. Media literacy is tightly bound up with this new context and introduces a new framework for the development of communicative skills.

Elements of Media Literacy

The concept map from the previous section, can serve to improve the design of a general conceptualisation for the analysis of the process of media literacy, highlighting the contexts and the role of all the different players.

We shall evince the distinction between contexts, players, competences, and areas.

Our objective is to interconnect the theoretical models with empirical policies aimed at promoting and driving literacy.

To create an operational chart on media literacy, the following essential elements must be highlighted:

- *Contexts*: Physical and institutional spaces in which certain players interact in order to achieve a functional objective. A distinction is made between the *personal context* – which relates to the individual activity of a person as part of his/her private and personal life; *family context*, at the heart of family relationships, and generally in a family setting; *educational context*, corresponding to institutional spaces, schools, and formal teaching; *media context*, a space created by the interaction of individuals with the media, its messages and its uses; and *civil context,* in which citizens perform their public activities in accordance with their rights, duties, and responsibilities. Each context determines specific conditions of access and use, and occasionally, regulation, of the media.

- *Players*: People, groups, institutions with a particular status and specific role in a given context. These players are defined by different parameters: the attributes of the person, roles, situation and institutional characters and their social function.

- *Competences*: Set of skills and abilities that enable particular players to perform a specific function. There are specific skills for each player and area.

- *Processes*: Activities linked to all the above elements.

- *Areas*: Areas of activity and processes that, in a given context, bring together different actors with specific aims.

The table below illustrates how all these elements interrelate:

Contexts	Actors	Competences	Conditions and processes
Personal	Adults	Personal training and skills	• Conditions of access and use • Self learning • Tutoring and accompaniment • Media production activities
	Children and young people		
Family	Parents and tutors	Skills of parents and tutors in media education and media literacy	• Conditions of access, use and accompaniment of media and ICT in the home
	Children and young people	Media skills of children and young people	• Family media education activities • Media production activities
Educational Media Civil	Authorities	Skills in media education policies	• Conditions of access, use and accompaniment of media and ICT in educational centres
	Teachers and educators	Skills in media education of teachers, parents and tutors	• Curriculum: Objectives, contents and activities related to media and ICT
	Parents and tutors		• Media education and ICT-related activities in the curriculum
	Students	Students' media literacy skills	• Media production activities
	Authorities[30]	Skills in media literacy policies	• Conditions of regulation and media participation
	Businesses	Skills in media literacy	• Media literacy activity of regulatory authorities
	Professionals	Training and skills in media literacy policies	• Media literacy activity of the media • Media literacy activity in businesses • Media literacy activity of professionals
	Audiences	Media literacy	• Audience training, skills and participation
	Associations[31]	Skills in media literacy	• Conditions of media regulation and participation by citizens
	Communities[32]	Skills in media literacy	• Media literacy activity of public authorities • Media literacy activity of associations • Media literacy activity of communities • Training, skills and participation of individuals

Possible Approaches

This general model shows the main variables that can define approaches to media literacy.

Depending on the different needs and demands, there are projects and activities that require different strategies, contexts, players, and skills, with particular emphasis on specific abilities and subjects.

Although there are several ways of combining the various elements, we shall link and define some of the most important possible approaches to media literacy:

- *Government (or government-related) policy activities*: Those developed by <u>government</u> and <u>institutional authorities</u> aimed at promoting media literacy. They include investment, subsidies, support, rulings, control, vigilance, etc.

   Ordinarily, the purpose of such undertakings is to establish methods and improve conditions to facilitate action from other citizens' groups aimed at meeting specific objectives.

   <u>Some examples:</u> Moves made by the education ministries of various European countries to establish an educational curriculum related to media literacy; the work of centres such as Spain's CNICE; the Bundesprüfstelle für jugendgefährdende Medien: BPjM (Federal Department for Media Harmful to Young Persons) in Germany; the Ministero delle Comunicazioni, Italy; or the Landesbildstellen in Austria; CLEMI in France and Belgium's Conseil de l'éducation aux médias, etc.

- *Family activities:* The leading players are family members – both individually and as a group – although other entities are often involved in these processes to provide stimuli and frames of reference. In general, they are intended to promote exchanges, actions, and co-operative tasks to encourage the use of – and access to – communications, thereby promoting family and personal use of the media.

   The objective of many of these elements is to promote dialogue between family members; establish objectives, rules, and guidance for media use; and promote individual autonomy and group consensus in a family setting.

   <u>Some examples:</u> APTE. Les écrans, les médias et nous in France ; Collectif interassociatif Enfance et Media (CIEM) ; the Family Friend Festival in the United Kingdom; Movimiento Italiano Genitori (MOIGE) in Italy; etc.

- *Civil participation:* This is the participation of citizens in activities related to media literacy involving different authorities in the media (generally, public media) domain. That is, participation in consultative or debating forums; in spaces provided by the media for response or discussion; in spaces for evaluation and criticism of media contents; and in spheres that have been instituted by law in various countries for the active participation of citizens.

Some examples: R.A.P. (Association résistance à l'agression publicitaire) and casseurs de pub in France ; CMA (Community Media Association) and Community TV Trust (CTVT) in the United Kingdom; Media Hungaria Konferenciairoda in Hungary; Agrupación de Telespectadores y Radioyentes (ATR) in Spain; Associazione Spettatori Onlus (AIART) in Italy; ŠKUC in Slovenia.

- *Educational and training activities:* Based on the promotion of teaching and learning processes. They can take place in educational, school-based, formal, or informal settings; can be aimed at children, young people, or adults; and can involve professionals from education and lifelong training, the media, or other areas.

  The objective of these activities is the acquisition of new knowledge, attitudes, or skills. They require the establishment of a basic curriculum, specific resources, and certain institutional conditions.

  Some examples: Centre de liaison de l'enseignement et des médias d'information (CLEMI) and Délégation aux usages de l'Internet in France; The Hiiripiiri Project in Finland; CNICE and Grupo Comunicar in Spain; Media Education (MED) in Italy, etc.

- *Campaigns:* These are the orchestrations of various actors, media, and resources to achieve specific objectives. They are generally intensive and short-lived. Media-literacy campaigns can aim at promoting specific information, causing changes in attitude, or heightening public awareness.

  Some examples: La semaine de la presse dans l'école (Press Week in Schools) and La semaine sans 100 télés in France; *"First Writes"* in the United Kingdom, etc.

- *Media activities:* Through their content, activities and suggestions, the media promote the acquisition of new skills and competences. Simple user guides or the distribution of programming and content guides are already, in themselves, instruments for the promotion of new uses and skills, and provide opportunities for the promotion of media literacy to a certain extent. However, the media could do much more systematic and sustained work with a marked impact on this promotion.

  Some examples: BBC Learning Resources and Channel 4 Learning. Online educational products in the United Kingdom; El País del estudiante in Spain; France 5 and ARPEJ in France, etc.

- *Mediation activities:* These are carried out through stable links between different players involved in a given process. In the case of media literacy, mediatory activities generally involve producers and consumers; the media and users; citizens and authorities, etc. Entities involved in readers' rights that own publications or citizens' forums that establish independent regulatory organisations of the media are examples of this type of mediation.

Some examples: Oficina del Defensor del Telespectador y del Radioyente de RTVE and the Oficina del Telespectador de Antena 3 in Spain; the Consiglio Nazionali per l'Utenti in Italy; the Foro de Entidades de Personas Usuarias del Audiovisual (forum of users' entities) in Catalonia,(Spain); etc.

- *Regulatory activities:* The purpose of these is to promote standards of conduct – formal and informal, obligatory or discretionary, etc. – for the use and enjoyment of media and technologies. These codes can be established to cover different contexts (personal, family, educational, civil, legislatorial, etc.) and can be organised and set out in codes of conduct, standards, guidelines, etc.

Some examples: OFCOM in the United Kingdom; the Conseil supérieur de l'audiovisuel (C.S.A.) in France; the Autorità per la garanzie nelle comunicazioni (AGCOM) in Italy; the Consell Audiovisual de Catalunya in Spain; etc.

- *Professional and business activities:* These are media literacy initiatives organised, led, and carried out by business or vocational sectors. The activities are prompted by industrial or professional criteria.

Some examples: Media Smart and MindTrek Media Week in the United Kingdom; Internationales Zentralinstitut für das Jugend – und Bildungs- fernsehen beim Bayerischen Rundfunk (IZI) in Germany, etc.

- *Production-skills activities:* Production-skills activities focusing on critical acquisition of media literacy and available to the general public. They can take place in different settings: schools, museums, cultural centres, the Internet, etc. They combine educational and development activities with activities in expression and communication.

Some examples: First Light Movies, Film Education, London Children's Film Festival and Showcomotion in the United Kingdom; Association Régions Presse-Enseignement Jeunesse (ARPEJ) in France; Idea Video Exchange Network (IVEN) in Hungary, etc.

- *Orientation and reference activities*: These centre on providing resources and criteria for the development of activities related to media literacy. They include the creation and provision of material resources, assistance systems, and consulting mechanisms; guidance and consulting for specific activities and subjects; introduction of codes of conduct and standards, etc.

   The goal of these activities is to help, guide, advise, support, and strengthen the various work undertaken in the area of media literacy.

Some examples: Mediamanual.at in Austria; Informationssystem Medien- pädagogik ISM in Germany; OMERO in Italy; Éducaunet in France; Hungarian Moving Image and Media Education Association in Hungary; etc.

- *Exploratory, experimental, investigative, and evaluation activities*: These activities are aimed at opening new avenues for the development of media literacy through the experimentation and investigation of new models and uses, and the evaluation of experiences.

  They contribute to innovation, change, the search for precise objectives, and the evaluation of specific policies.

  Some examples: Éducnet in France; Institut für Medienpädagogik in Forschung und Praxis JFF in Germany; Hans-Bredow-Institut für Medienforschung HBI (Institute for media research); Observatorio de la sociedad de la inforamción (de Red.es) and the Gabinete de Comunicación y educación de la UAB in Spain; Centre for the Study of Children, Youth and Media in the United Kingdom; L'Osservatorio sui Diritti dei Minori and EURISPES in Italy, etc.

The possible links and complementarity between these activities are illustrated in the chart below.

The balance and complementarity between all of these activities ensure efficient functioning of media literacy and create the optimum conditions for their performance.

Notes

1. This text that originated from the *European Commission* is one result of the *Study on Current Trends in, and Approaches to, Media Literacy in Europe*. It seeks to provide a general understanding of media literacy in Europe. Hence, all examples are drawn from Europe.
2. Professor at the Universidad Autónoma de Barcelona. Head of the communication and education department (Gabinete de Comunicación y Educación).
3. International Symposium on Media Education at Grünwald, Federal Republic of Germany. http://www.unesco.org/education/nfsunesco/pdf/MEDIA_S.PDF
4. 'New Directions in Media Education" UNESCO International Media Literacy Conference in Toulouse   http://portal.unesco.org/ci/en/ev.php-URL_ID=5680&URL_DO=DO_TOPIC&URL_SECTION=201.html
5. "Educating for the Media and the Digital Age" 18-20 April 1999 Http://www.nordicom.gu.se/clearinghouse.php?portal=linkdb&main=reconedu.php&
6. Youth Media Education Seville, 15-16 February 2002 http://portal.unesco.org/ci/en/ev.php-URL_ID=5680&URL_DO=DO_TOPIC&URL_SECTION=201.html
7. Cf. http://ec.europa.eu/avpolicy/media_literacy/docs/coe_fr.pdf
8. Cf. http://ec.europa.eu/avpolicy/media_literacy/index_en.htm
9. Cf. http://www.euromedialiteracy.eu/
10. Cf. http://www.ofcom.org.uk/consult/condocs/strategymedialit/strategymedialit/
11. "Media Education
    – deals with all communication media and includes the printed word and graphics, sound, the still as well as the moving image, delivered on any kind of technology;
    – enables people to gain understanding of the communication media used in their society and the way they operate and to acquire skills in using these media to communicate with others;
    – ensures that people learn how to:
      • Analyse, critically reflect upon, and create media texts.
      • Identify the sources of media texts, their political, social, commercial and/or cultural interests and their contexts.
      • Interpret the messages and values offered by the media.
      • Select appropriate media for communicating their own messages or stories and for reaching their intended audience.
      • Gain, or demand access to media for both reception and production.
    The Media Education is part of the basic entitlement of every citizen, in every country in the world, to freedom of expression and the right to information and is instrumental in building and sustaining democracy. While recognising the disparities in the nature and development of Media Education in different countries, the participants of the conference "Educating for the Media and the Digital Age" recommend that Media Education should be introduced wherever possible within national curricula as well as in tertiary, non-formal and lifelong education.
      • Media Education addresses a wide range of texts in all media (print, still image, audio, and moving image) which provide people with rich and diverse cultural experiences.
      • In countries moving towards the introduction of new technologies, Media Education can assist citizens to recognise the potential of the media to represent/misrepresent their culture and traditions.
      • In situations where access to electronic or digital technologies is limited or non-existent, media education can be based on available media texts in that context.
      • Media education should be aimed at empowering all citizens in every society and should ensure that people with special needs and those socially and economically disadvantaged have access to it.
      • Media education also has a critical role to play in, and should be responsive to, situations of social and political conflicts, war, natural disaster, ecological catastrophe, etc."
12. Seville Seminar Cf. http://portal.unesco.org/ci/en/files/5680/10346121330Seville_Recommendations.rtf/Seville+Recommendations.rtf.

13. Cf. http://www.ofcom.org.uk/advice/media_literacy/of_med_lit/whatis/
14. Cf. http://www.euromedialiteracy.eu/index.php?Pg=charter
15. The aim of media literacy is to increase awareness of the many forms of media messages encountered in our everyday lives. It should help citizens recognise how the media filter their perceptions and beliefs, shape popular culture, and influence personal choices. It should empower them with the critical-thinking and creative problem-solving skills to make them discerning consumers and producers of information. Media education is part of the basic entitlement of every citizen, in every country, to freedom of expression and the right to information; it is instrumental in building and sustaining democracy. Today, media literacy is indeed one of the key pre-requisites for active and full citizenship and is one context in which intercultural dialogue needs to be promoted. Furthermore, media education is a fundamental tool to raise awareness about IPR issues among media users and consumers.
16. The European definition is inspired by UNESCO's Grünwald declaration, according to which media education should cover each and every means of communication.
17. As in UNESCO documents, the European Union's public consultation on media literacy has emphasised creative production: "The most commonly expressed concern among the respondents was the importance of adding to the definition the ability to *create and communicate messages*, as this aspect of media literacy is viewed as fundamental in empowering people to become active and informed consumers of media. Moreover, the communicative aspect of media literacy is considered essential for enabling people to make effective use of media in the exercise of their democratic rights and civic responsibilities".
18. The concept of "evaluation" can be enriched – as called for by several experts in the European Union's public consultation on media literacy – with the idea of "critical literacy": Several respondents also stressed the importance of including *critical literacy* as part of the definition. Again, this aspect of media literacy is regarded as crucial in the formation and of an active and discerning citizen. "We would also stress the importance of critical literacy as part of the evaluation component of the definition, for accessing and analysing media messages are not effective if one cannot also critically evaluate those messages, distinguishing the honest from the deceptive, the public interest from commercial persuasion, the objective and trustworthy from the biased or partisan". (Sonia Livingstone, London School of Economics, and Andrea Millwood Hargrave, UK Media Literacy Task force. Also: "There exist many definitions of media literacy around the world. More and more often they include the ability 1) to access the media, 2) to understand/critically evaluate different aspects of the media and media contents, and 3) to create media contents/participate in the production process. It is not unusual that the definitions also include aspects of learning to use the media in order to participate in the process for social change, for development, towards increased democracy." (Cecilia Von Feilitzen, The International Clearinghouse on Children Youth and Media, Nordicom, Göteborg University).
19. According to John Pungente, media education "is concerned with helping students develop an informed and critical understanding of the nature of the mass media, the techniques used by them, and the impact of these techniques. More specifically, it is education that aims to increase students' understanding and enjoyment of how the media work, how they produce meaning, how they are organized, and how they construct reality. Media literacy also aims to provide students with the ability to create media products." We see media education as a process and media literacy as the outcome of this process.
20. Digital literacy is a natural consequence of the spread of digital technologies and the promotion of the information society. For a definition of digital literacy Cf. Pérez Tornero, José Manuel: *Promoting Digital Literacy*, European Commission.
21. "Media literacy, like print literacy before it, should be recognized as a key means, even a right, by which citizens participate in society and by which the state regulates the manner and purposes of citizens' participation" (Sonia Livingstone, "What is media literacy?" *Media@lse*, (http://www.lse.ac.uk/collections/media@lse/pdf/What_is_media_literacy.doc)

22. "Media education is a part of the fundamental right of each and every citizen of any country in the world to freedom of expression and the right to information, and is a tool for building and maintaining democracy". UNESCO: ibid. According to Sonia Livingstone, "Indeed, literacy is a concept grounded in a centuries-old struggle between enlightenment and critical scholarship, setting those who see literacy as democratising, empowering of ordinary people against those who see it as elitist, divisive, a source of inequality. Debates over literacy are, in short, debates about the manner and purposes of public participation in society. Cf., "What is media literacy?" *Media@else*, (http://www.lse.ac.uk/collections/media@lse/pdf/What_is_media_literacy.doc)

23. "Access has two dimensions. It is, firstly, about physical access to equipment, in a setting where it is possible to use it in an unrestricted way. However, it is also a matter of the ability to manipulate technology (and related software tools) in order to locate the content or information that one requires" David Buckingham et al. "The Media Literacy of Children and Young People: A Review of the Academic Research" (London: Ofcom, 2005)

24. "Reading" is the ability to decipher a message with relation to a specific code and a particular communicative situation.

25. "Understanding" means the ability to link a meaning – previously decoded – to a specific personal context. It implies meaningfulness; that is, the ability to add meaning to the knowledge and interests of the person decoding the message.

26. "Evaluation" is the process whereby the contents of a message are classified and categorised in relation to previously acquired value scales.

27. Several traditions related to this subject have enriched the concept of media literacy. In Europe, the most powerful have been, and still are: firstly, the tradition of semiotic analysis, with important contributions by France and Italy, thanks to authors such as Barthes, Morin, Metz, Greimas, Umberto Eco, and Fabbri; and secondly, the tradition of British cultural studies by R. Hoggart, Raymond Williams, and Stuart Hall (assembled and disseminated in the field of media education by Len Masterman, A. Hart and others).

28. Cf. Noam Chomsky *Aspectos de la teoría de la sintaxis*, Barcelona, Gedisa, 1999.

29. Cf. Jürgen Habermas, *Teoría de la acción comunicativa*: I. Racionalidad de la acción y racionalidad social, II. Crítica de la razón funcionalista, Madrid, Ed. Taurus, 1981.

30. Government or public institutions involved in the intervention, regulation or control of the media system.

31. Formal groupings of citizens with recognised legal status

32. Active grouping of individuals who have functional objectives, but no legal status or formal regulation.

A European Approach to Media Literacy*

Matteo Zacchetti & Philippos Vardakas

We become what we behold. We shape our tools and then our tools shape us.
Marshall McLuhan

Big brother isn't watching. He's singing and dancing. He's pulling rabbits out of
a hat. Big brother is busy holding your attention every moment you are awake.
Chuck Palahniuk

Some 50 years ago, 6 European countries (Belgium, France, West Germany,
Italy, Luxembourg and the Netherlands) signed the Treaty of Rome[1] creating the
European Economic Community. The idea was for people, goods and services
to circulate freely across borders. But the real concern was bringing together the
nations and people of Europe. We should never forget that the historical roots of
the European Union lie in an overwhelming tragedy: the 2nd World War. Europeans
decided they would do anything to prevent such killing and destruction from
ever happening again. Now the European Union embraces 27 countries from
Portugal in the very west of the continent to the new Member States, Romania
and Bulgaria, from the polar circle to the coasts of the Mediterranean Sea. Europe
has almost half a billion citizens with many different languages, cultures and
traditions but also with deeply shared values of democracy, freedom and social
justice. Europe is against any discrimination based on ethnic origin, sex and
philosophical belief. In its relations with international partners, the EU projects
the values that have contributed to its own success. The prosperity of the EU has
grown out of a particular form of regional cooperation, which has developed
hand in hand with a deeper political commitment to democracy, human rights
and the enhancement of citizenship.

Today, we are witnessing an unprecedented technological revolution. The
meaning of "wealth" has shifted towards ownership of knowledge and information. Technological change makes it possible for virtually all people to become

not only creators but also consumers of media content. The media have become an increasingly powerful economic and social force and are accessible instruments for European citizens to better understand the societies in which they live and participate in the democratic life of their community. In this context, at the Lisbon European Council[2] in March 2000, Heads of State and of Government set an ambitious objective for Europe: to become a more competitive knowledge economy and at the same time a more inclusive knowledge society. A higher degree of media literacy would definitely help our societies to fulfil this ambitious objective.

Audiovisual and Media Policy

The audiovisual sector directly employs over one million people in the European Union. In addition to its economic importance, it also plays a key social and cultural role: television is the most important source of information and entertainment in European societies, with 98% of homes having at least one television set, and the average European watching more than 200 minutes of television per day[3].

The EU's landmark piece of audiovisual legislation is the "Television Without Frontiers"[4] Directive which in 1989 set the conditions for the transmission of television broadcasts within the European single market. The aim was to come up with some minimum standards applicable in all Member States. Europeans could finally profit from watching TV channels from all over Europe just as they were able to buy goods and services in any EU country. The Directive was revised in 1997 further to developments in the audiovisual sector and has been re-shaped and re-named (Audiovisual Media Services Directive[5]) in 2007 in order to take account, inter alia, of the impact of multi-channel digital broadcasting and the introduction of new electronic media. Media literacy made also its way into the text of the Directive. The recently approved text contains a recital referring to media literacy[6]. Moreover, Article 26 of the Directive provides that "The Commission shall report....on levels of media literacy in all the Member States."

With the development of new technologies and the presence of internet in almost half of European households[7], it seems obvious that technological understanding of Information and Communication Technologies (digital literacy[8]) is not sufficient to get the best out of these new opportunities. Also for these reasons, the need to study the media in a critical and coherent way has become increasingly important in recent years, as they have taken up a central position in our cultural, social and political life. Virtually all we know – or think we know – about the world beyond our immediate experience comes through the media. It is not surprising, therefore, that we now study the media; it is only surprising that it has taken so long.

Media Literacy

Media literacy may be defined as the ability to access the media, to understand and critically evaluate media contents and different aspects of the media and to create communications in a variety of contexts. This definition is the result of the work of many different people (institutions, media professionals, teachers, educators) and it is built on three main elements: 1) access to media and media content; 2) critical approach, ability to decipher media messages, awareness of how the media work; 3) creativity, communication and production skills. Media literacy relates to *all media*, including television and film, radio and recorded music, print media, the Internet and other new digital communication technologies.

Media literacy is an extremely important factor for *active citizenship* in today's information society, a real key pre-requisite just as literacy was at the beginning of the twentieth century. It is a fundamental skill not only for the young generation but also for adults (elderly people, parents, teachers and media professionals). As a result of the evolution of media technologies and the presence of the Internet as a distribution channel, an increasing number of Europeans can now create and disseminate images, information and contents. In this context, media literacy is viewed as one of the major tools in the development of citizens' responsibilities.

Media literacy relates to *European audiovisual heritage and cultural identity*. The audiovisual production sector is an essential instrument of expression of our cultural and political values. It is a vector for European citizenship and culture and plays a primary role in building a European identity. Media-literate people will be able to exercise more informed choices also with regard to the audiovisual content market. Citizens would therefore have a higher degree of freedom as they will have the instruments to choose what they want to see and will be able to better evaluate the implications of their choices.

Finally, media-literate people will be better able to protect themselves and their families from harmful, offensive or undesired content. Media literacy refers also to the skills, knowledge and understanding to enable citizens to use media effectively. It should empower them through critical thinking and creative problem-solving skills to make them informed consumers and producers of information

The European Commission Strategy – State of Play

Since November 2000, in the framework of the Lisbon Agenda, the European Commission has taken specific initiatives in the field of media literacy and has integrated media literacy aspects into existing programmes

1. Media literacy projects have received European financial support in 2002 and 2003[9] under the eLearning Initiative[10] with the objective to:

- analyse media representations and media values in a multimedia perspective;

- encourage the production and distribution of media literacy related content;

- stimulate the use of media in order to improve participation in social and community life;

- intensify networking around media education-related issues;

- concentrate on the implementation of media literacy initiatives bridging the media industry and the education world, in a "hands-on" approach.

Financial support came to an end in 2005. Analysis and evaluation of the projects, which was carried out by the Grenoble School of Management prove that these projects had a positive impact in particular as regards innovation, development and reinforcement of European collaboration in media literacy.

2. Implementation of *MEDIA 2007*[11] objectives related to media literacy (the education and creation of an audience for European cinematography). The MEDIA 2007 proposal underlines the importance of media literacy and image education initiatives and in particular those organised by festivals for a young public, in close cooperation with schools and other institutions. New guidelines were approved by the MEDIA Committee in April 2007.

3. The *SAFER INTERNET PLUS*[12] programme aims at empowering parents and teachers with internet safety tools. It also covers other media, such as videos, and explicitly addresses the fight against racism and "spam". It focuses more closely on end users: parents, educators and children.

4. A *"Media Literacy Expert Group"*[13] composed of a number of European personalities, with a mix of different competences and from various backgrounds, has been setup by the Commission with the aim to analyse and define media literacy objectives and trends, to highlight and promote good practices at European level and to propose actions in the field. The group met three times in 2006 and is pursuing its work in 2007.

5. In the last quarter of 2006, the Commission launched a public consultation in order to nurture reflection on media literacy and gain from the experience of all those concerned with this issue. The response to the consultation was extremely satisfactory both in quantitative terms and in the quality and variety of the respondents (replies received included media organisations and industry, formal and non-formal education institutions, content providers and producers, research and cultural institutions, regulators and citizens' and consumers' associations). A report on the results of the public consultation on media literacy has been drafted and is available to the general public[14].

6. A *study* on "Current trends and approaches to media literacy in Europe" has been commissioned recently with UAB (Universidad Autonoma de Barcelona). The objective is to map current practices in implementing media literacy in Europe. The study will cover the 27 Member States of the European Union, the EEA Member States (Norway, Iceland and Liechtenstein). The end result is to provide a concise evaluation of the emerging trends in the field of media literacy as it already exists throughout Europe. It should also further provide recommendations on measures to be implemented at Community level to help foster and increase the level of this new form of citizen awareness. Finally, it should briefly outline the possible economic and social impact of an EU intervention in this field.

The European Commission Strategy – Next Steps

In the last quarter of 2007, the Commission intends to publish a *Communication on media literacy*. This document will represent an important step as it would add a further building block to European audiovisual policy under the overall i2010 initiative[15]. By its very nature, media literacy issues can be addressed in many different ways at different levels. It is the firm intention of the Commission to respect the subsidiarity principle. It is of course the authorities in Member States who bear the primary responsibility for discussing and possibly supporting the inclusion of media literacy in school curricula at all levels. The role played by local authorities is also very important since they are closer to the citizens and support initiatives in the non-formal education sector. On the other hand, European action in this field could help and strengthen a European identity and foster awareness and exchange of experience. The Communication will include a stocktaking exercise on the development of media literacy in Europe and will analyse and define media literacy objectives and trends. Its main objective will be to highlight and promote good practices in media literacy at European level and propose possible actions in the field. Also, it will build on the results of the work of the Media Literacy Expert Group and on the findings of the public consultation which was launched in October 2006. The Communication will focus on three priority areas: commercial communication literacy, media literacy for audiovisual work and media literacy in the online environment. Action in these areas can build on the existence of existing instruments and programmes. Evaluation of these actions will enable the Commission to assess whether and where broader action might be necessary to be implemented with new tools.

Conclusions

The following conclusions emerge from the work carried out until now:

1. Media literacy is a life-long skill not only for the young generation but also for adults (elderly people, parents, teachers and media professionals), giving them the opportunity of being critically aware of the information they are confronted with on a daily basis. In this respect, it becomes an extremely important factor for citizenship in today's information society.

2. Currently, there are different practices and different levels of media literacy throughout Europe.

3. It is important to analyse, highlight and spread good practices in the field throughout the European Union.

4. There are no agreed criteria or standards for assessing media literacy, and there is an urgent need for larger-scale, longer-term research to establish a body of evidence, on which such criteria could be based.

5. Partnership between public and private, civil society and media industry is extremely important.

6. All forms of political support and recognition given by the European Institutions and the Member States to media literacy campaigns, conferences, manifestos, competitions, public commitments and institutional agreements are extremely important as they would help create more public awareness of media literacy

Finally, it has to be stressed that if European societies are not able to properly support the development of media literacy competencies, they will pay a very high price in terms of response to the opportunities offered by the information society.

Notes

1. http://www.treatyofrome.com/treaty.htm
2. http://www.europarl.europa.eu/summits/lis1_en.htm
3. Souce: European Audiovisual Observatory
4. http://ec.europa.eu/avpolicy/reg/tvwf/index_en.htm
5. http://ec.europa.eu/avpolicy/reg/tvwf/modernisation/proposal_2005/index_en.htm
6. recital 25a : Media literacy refers to skills, knowledge and understanding that allow consumers to use media effectively and safely. Media-literate people will be able to exercise informed choices, understand the nature of content and services and take advantage of the full range of

---

* The views expressed are those of the authors and do not necessarily represent the official view of the European Commission on the subject.

opportunities offered by new communications technologies. They will be better able to protect themselves and their families from harmful or offensive material. Therefore development of media literacy in all sections of society should be promoted and monitored."

7. Source: Eurostat
8. http://ec.europa.eu/information_society/edutra/skills/index_en.htm
9. A list of the media literacy projects supported by the European Commission is available on: http://ec.europa.eu/education/programmes/elearning/projects/022_en.html http://ec.europa. eu/education/programmes/elearning/projects/031_en.html
10. The eLearning initiative of the European Commission seeks to mobilise the educational and cultural communities, as well as the economic and social players in Europe, in order to speed up changes in the education and training systems for Europe's move to a knowledge-based society. See: http://ec.europa.eu/education/programmes/elearning/index_en.html
11. Since 1991, the MEDIA programme is supporting the European audiovisual industry, its main aim being to strive for a stronger European audiovisual sector, one that is reflecting and respecting Europe's cultural identity and heritage. With a budget of 755M for the period of 2007 to 2013, it is acting on the following fields: training of professionals, development of production projects and companies, distribution of cinematographic works and audiovisual programmes, promotion of cinematographic works and audiovisual programmes, including the support for cinematographic festivals and the support of pilot projects.
12. http://ec.europa.eu/information_society/activities/sip/programme/index_en.htm
13. For a list of experts and explanation of the activities carried out by the group, see: http://ec.europa.eu/avpolicy/media_literacy/expert_group/index_en.htm
14. http://ec.europa.eu/avpolicy/media_literacy/consultation/index_en.htm
15. http://ec.europa.eu/i2010/

Educational and Mass-Media Cultures
Integration or Contradiction

Saeed Abdallah Hareb

Culture is the result of humanity's achievements. Through it, values and concepts are determined in a society. Culture is strongly linked to human existence; this link has developed with what human beings have created and produced in different fields. Culture is the "complicated structure" that includes languages, beliefs, knowledge, arts, instructions, laws, constitutions, ethical criteria and values. It also includes the norms, habits, social traditions and skills owned by people in a given society (Reda, 1996: 26).

Culture is still the main engine for any human action. The measure of a nation's development and progress is fully linked to its cultural progress. Today, advanced nations are those that have managed to take into consideration their cultural heritage and transfer it into public action, which helps to achieve more progress than others.

This indicates that societies are cultural images, as expressed by Thomas Elliott in his definition of culture. Thinkers and writers have disagreed among themselves about a general definition of the term. Thompson defines culture as characteristics of a group that include values, beliefs and behaviour patterns, which vary from one group to another and distinguish one group from the other. Omrod (2004) defines culture as "the behavior and believes system which distinguish one societal group". At the same time, Arends asserts that culture shows a group's lifestyle with its history, attitudes and values. Culture is not fixed; it is constantly changing. Arends also sees culture as not representing groups but instead existing before them (Reda, ibid: 24).

Arab and Muslim scientists were pioneers in studying the correlation between culture and society, many ages ago. The first of these Arab scientists was the sociologist Ibn Khaldoon. Many others followed him, such as the Algerian Malik Ibn Nabi and sociologist Aly El Wardy, among others.

The correlation between culture and society is strong. We can never understand a society without understanding its culture. Conversely, we cannot understand the culture of a given society without understanding the society itself, whether from its fixed pillars such as religion and ethical values or from its changeable aspects such as creativity, the arts, literature, scientific production and other changing and developing cultural actions.

The social role of culture is assured through:

1. Values, ethical and behavioural influence of culture on the individual's life, his actions and behaviour.

2. Its important role in continuity across history.

3. An increase in the perception of its role in changing trends in local and world public opinion through the indirect effect of culture on people's lives.

The role of culture has increased dramatically during the past few years through the formation of many global and regional cultural organizations and institutions. The United Nations Educational, Scientific and Cultural Organization (UNESCO) is at the fore of all these organizations. At the regional level in the Arab World is the Arab League Educational, Scientific and Cultural Organization (ALESCO).

As culture holds this importance and value in the lives of nations, peoples and societies, education and mass media are the two gates through which it is transferred to individuals. Education is very close to culture, and they have a mutually influential relationship. Mass media has the same importance. It is also an important channel for transmitting culture; even the media content has a cultural element. The fast development of mass media and the new communication technology have helped a great deal in reinforcing the role played by mass media in this respect.

In brief, educational institutions and mass media are the major channels that transmit culture to individuals. Educational culture is "the cultural contents that the individual or group receives from educational sources. These contents form their beliefs, images, understandings and values, which affect their behavior, habits, traditions and lifestyles". Mass-Media Culture: is "the cultural contents that the individual or group receives from the mass media and that form their beliefs, images, concepts and values, which influence the formation of their behavior, habits, traditions and lifestyles".

If educational institutions provide children and young people with educational plans and programmes as these programmes help students to learn, there are other channels that are equally important. These are the educational cultural sources that include the family, school, friends and others. In the following lines, different sources of educational and mass-media cultures in the United Arab Emirates as well as in the Arab World will be discussed.

I. Sources of Educational Culture

These sources include the family, the teacher, the educational libraries, the friends and other societal institutions. These different sources will be handled in the following lines.

1. The Family

Caring for the family means caring for the whole society. If families are built and furnished with good values and ethics, this provides good roots. If a family neglects its role in education and socialization, then individuals from this family will not be able to help in society and will instead destroy it.

Special care and attention has been given to the family so that it can produce good members of society. The family's most important role in forming educational culture is reflected in the care it takes concerning ethical and behavioural aspects, and in teaching children good values and ethics. There is no other organization in society that plays a role as vital as that of the family.

The role of the family is also reflected in the attention it must give to the social behaviour, as individuals live in a specific human environment and must know and understand this environment so that they can live in it. The development of cultural aspects is another role the family plays. A human being must have a culture and knowledge, which he learns at an early age and grows up loving. The family is and will always be the ultimate source of culture.

2. The Teacher

The teacher is the focus for the educational process. Other factors such as the book, the curriculum, and supporting methods cannot affect or develop the educational process without passing through the teacher. He forms the thinking methods of children and is the leader and motivator for the educational process. The profession of education is, as expressed by Chandler, "the mother profession" and "the main source for other professions" (Chandler, 1971).

The global trend in modern education seems to give the teacher more roles than merely that of transmitting material. The teacher must teach the students the educational method and not only the material, and is also required to develop himself.

3. Educational Libraries

Generally speaking, libraries are still the main source of educational culture for students. The library is a supportive source for curriculum where students find their references and the research support they need. All educational institutions aim at providing teachers and students with what they need, and therefore develop and upgrade their libraries, providing them with new books and references as well.

But if we follow the role of libraries as a source of educational culture, they are still limited in most of the Arab countries. This may be due to the following reasons:

- A lack of awareness on the side of students about the role of culture as an important factor in their personal life

- A very limited rate of reading among students

- A lack of desire among student to educate themselves

A lack of reading and of the desire to read generally lead to the fact that students read less. The percentage of students who read books outside their curriculum is very small. A study was conducted during the academic year 2003/2004 on a sample of students from Dubai (the United Arab Emirates) to examine their general reading habits. It was found that those who read one to two books during the school year represented 37.5% and those who read three to four books represented 29%. Those who read five books or more made up only 25% of the students. The above findings indicate that students' general interest reading is limited (Al Any, 2005).

4. Friends

Friends form an important source of educational culture, especially for those who lack answers to their questions. Many peer groups have more influence on the individual than other influences do. At the same time, integration of individuals into the groups occurs easily and freely. Belonging to a peer group gives the individual a feeling of freedom and independence, as he is the one who selects one group of friends or another. Though there are some negative influences from friends on the individual, friends are still an important source of culture and knowledge for peer group members.

New communication channels such as mobile phones have led to the greater importance and influence of peer groups. In a study conducted on a sample of young people from the Gulf area (Al Hamoud et al., 2007), more than one-third of the sample (35%) said that they meet their friends on the Internet all the time. Twenty-five percent said that they do so sometimes. When the interviewees were asked about the role of the Internet in increasing their general knowledge, 26% said that these meetings on the Internet help to a great extent, 47% said they help sometimes and the remainder said that they did not help. This indicates the importance of new communication technology in reinforcing the role of friends in this respect.

128

5. Societal Institutions

Students come to educational institutions with a certain number of cultural values, which they have usually received from the other institutions in society. These values follow them throughout their educational life, and become stronger through what the students receive at school/university from their teachers.

In the United Arab Emirates as well as in other Arab countries, the strongest institutions for culture are the religious ones. The role of these religious institutions has become stronger, especially with the use of new communication channels to transfer cultural values to young people such as CD, the Internet, mobile phones, etc.

Many students form their opinions and attitudes in accordance with what they learn and take from these religious institutions.

Other societal institutions include cultural centres and social societies, which are common in most Arab countries. These clubs form an important source of culture for students and all individuals in society. Their main activities include meetings, lectures, seminars, etc. Cultural values are transferred through these activities. These institutions also publish books, magazines and other periodicals, which all aim at spreading cultural values among people.

In sum, societal institutions have an important role to play in educational culture and there is a need for integration between these institutions and other educational institutions.

II. Sources of Mass-Media Culture

Mass media are the most influential forces in shaping public opinion and determining its trends, and have become an important source of public culture for the whole society. They have an effect on all members of society through the wide variety of programmes. The use of new communication technology has also greatly helped and reinforced this effect. At the same time, mass media are seen as the most important challenges to culture, as mass-media culture is formed by these sources, which include electronic, new communication and print media. In the following lines, these sources will be handled in some detail.

1. The Electronic Media

Radio and television are the most important sources of mass-media culture, especially when we take into consideration satellite transmission. The danger of this is that we can never control the negative influences of these media. Although also have positive influences in society, the negative influences are more numerous than the positive ones. In many cases the content screened on television contradict what the individuals receive from the educational content. The danger of the situation emerges if we consider that those who are most influenced by mass media content are young people.

The findings of most studies indicate that mass media have a great deal of influence in forming an individual's culture and behaviour, especially the negative behaviour of young people. There are more than 140 satellite channels watched by people in the Arab World. In a recent study (*Al Bayan Magazine*, Issue 186), it was found that 69% of the Arab audience watch satellite channels four hours a day, 31% for three hours, 34.5% for two hours and 15% for only one hour. The yearly increase in satellite dish owners is 12%. It is also worthy of mention that 40% of the Arab satellite channels are owned by governments and the remainder are privately owned. News programmes represent only 5% of the total number of programmes on these satellite channels. It was also found that 57% of parents and 65% of children in Saudi Arabia, Kuwait and the United Arab Emirates watch video clips, which are mainly musical programmes (op. cit). Many of these video clips are seen are having scenes that contradict Islamic and Arab cultures.

Cultural influences on young people are due to the fact that we live in a world with open skies. It is no longer possible observe or control what children and young people watch, especially if we take into account the low level and weakness of programmes and materials screened on the national and governmental television channels. This causes audiences, especially young ones, to seek better programmes on satellite channels. It was also found that more than half (53.3%) of the audience do not trust their governmental media. This indicates that children and young people in our society do not receive culture from official and governmental institutions. At the same time, what they receive from other, nongovernmental, media outlets may not necessarily match the common culture in society. This in turn may lead to bad habits that contradict our culture.

The findings of another study (El Bayaty, 2005) on young people's exposure to television in the United Arab Emirates show that 21% of the viewers in the United Arab Emirates watch TV for one hour every day, 27.5% for two hours, 22.3% for three hours and 29% for more than three hours. Regarding preferred programmes, it was found that musical and song programmes were the most mentioned (26%), followed by action programmes and movies (19%), sports programmes (14%) and religious programmes (10.4%). Other programmes such as news, soap operas and educational and cultural programmes were mentioned less.

When the interviewees were asked about television's influences in society, 57.5% mentioned that television weakens relationships within the family, that it has more effects on young people in the family (51%) and that it has negative influences on young people's habits and traditions (66%). An amazing finding of studies in the Gulf area is that when today's children reach the age of 70, they will have spent 27 years in front of the television screen.

If these are the negative influences of television, one should also mention that television has positive influences as well. The most important of these are the increase of children's and young people's perception and an availability of information that they can use in their education. At the same time, watching television may increase children's ability to remember and understand. Watching television also can help build a child's personality.

2. New Communication Media

The new information technology has opened the door on a new era, which can be compared to the Industrial Revolution in the changes it has brought to bear on human activity. This "Information Revolution" has created a new horizon for knowledge and culture. The individual is now able to communicate with others very easily and freely, without barriers. At the same time, the number of sources of knowledge has become great. When we talk about the new communication media, the most important of these is the Internet, as well as email and mobile phone messaging.

The Internet, for instance, has become an important source of general and specialized information. It is also an easy and fast medium. The amount of information available on the Internet increases every day. Any researcher can go on the Internet and see literature and research in their field. Among the beneficiaries of the Internet are students, who are lucky enough to receive education and training that enables them to easily deal with the Internet. Therefore, we can see a great difference between the children of today and their parents in this regard.

In a study on the use of the Internet (Al Any, ibid) by a sample of young people in Dubai, it was found that 75.4% use the Internet for an average of one to two hours dailyand 17% for two to three hours daily. In another study (Al Hamoud et al., ibid), it was found the heavy use of the Internet among young people is due to its wide availability at universities, homes, Internet cafés and other public places. Access to the Internet has become very easy for most young people in the United Arab Emirates as well as in other Arab countries.

The value and importance of the Internet has also increased with the use of email, which has become the fastest and cheapest medium of communication and overcomes problems of distance. It has become a method of communication among teachers and their students. It also enables students to register the courses they wish to attend and even see the results of their exams. The new information technology has caused an important shift in the educational process, and is helping to develop the administrative and education systems. It is a wide-open window onto the world for people.

Short messaging via mobile phones has also become another tool that Arab young people use heavily, even for educational purposes.

3. Print Media

Print media represent the third corner in the triangle of sources of mass-media culture. Newspapers and magazines are t he least important mass media for young people, especially those who are still at different stages of their education. Their interest in what newspapers publish in terms of politics and current affairs is very limited. Those who do read mainly read social and artistic magazines, sport magazines, women's magazines, car magazines, etc.

In a study conducted on the United Arab Emirates young people's reading habits , it was found that 20% of the respondents read newspapers on a daily basis, 28% once a week and 14% once a month. One-third of the respondents mentioned reading occasionally (Watfa, 2006).

The findings of another study have shown that only 34% of young people in the Gulf countries read daily newspapers, while 61% read them sometimes and 5% never do.

Conclusion and Recommendations

There is no doubt that the relationship between educational culture and mass-media culture will always be an essential societal issue. It will always be the topic of research and study, as this issue has important effects on the educational process and the whole society. The relationship between the educational and mass-media cultures is not entirely simple, but is rather a very complicated one. There are many reasons and factors that cause this relationship to be neither completely integrated nor completely contradictory. Those who examine the nature of this relationship are divided among themselves. Educationalists see mass media as an influencing force in the educational process through their interesting and exciting contents. Despite the fact that many mass-media messages are used to serve educational goals, the argument is still not yet settled about the role of mass media in the educational process. This leads to a wider gap between the education and media people.

A second aspect related to this relationship is the fact that mass media have a great deal of influence in society due to their capacities, the use of modern communication technology, and the variety of mass-media messages. All this leads to a view of the mass media as being very near the individual, his needs, his aspirations, etc. It also leads to a view of the mass media as being more influential, especially as they address all the human senses. There is also a kind of excitement in their contents.

In sum, therefore, one may conclude the following:

1. Studies on the relationship between educational culture and mass-media culture must be encouraged and well prepared. Findings from these studies will help narrow the gap between the two cultures, for the sake of

building the good individual in society. This will help, to a great extent, in minimizing the negative effects of the mass media, especially on young people, who are the groups that are the most vulnerable to these negative effects.

2. Sources of educational culture must be constantly updated to match recent changes in education as well as mass media, especially with the introduction of new communication media (e.g., the Internet) and the use of these channels in the educational process.

3. There is a need for some kind of cooperation between educational and mass-media institutions. For instance, some mass-media materials/programmes may be prepared and produced in cooperation with educational institutions. This will help a great deal in supporting the positive influences of the mass media.

4. The family and the school have important roles to play in the educational process of children. They must be seen and dealt with as two important approaches in building basic aspects of a child's personality. Therefore, they must be helped and encouraged to carry out their complimentary tasks.

5. Change in the Arab educational environment, as well as the introduction of modern communication technology and the new satellite channels, may necessitate making full use of these facilities in a correct and good direction, so that young people can make also full use of them, for sound educational reasons.

6. More transparency and freedom are needed for the media organizations in most Arab countries, especially those owned by the governments. This will help in improving their contents and will consequently benefit the media audiences.

7. The educational process must make full use of mass media to serve the student and the educational process as a whole. Mass media have a great deal of potential to aid the educational process.

8. Codes of conduct and ethics between educational and mass media institutions will help, to a great extent, in converting their relationship from one of contradiction to one of integration.

References

Al Any, W.T. (2005) *Contemporary Cultural Interests of Young People*, a Paper Presented for the Conference on Children and Young People in the Middle East and North Africa, Dubai, May 16-18.

Al Bayan Magazine, Issue 189, Dubai: UAE.

Al Bayaty, Y.K. (2005) *Potential Social Effects of Television on Young People*, Dubai.

Al Hamoud, M. et al. (2007) *Trends of Young People in the Gulf Towards Mass Media*, a Paper Presented for the Gulf Development Forum, Feb. 7.

Chandler, B.J. et al. (1971) *Education and New Teacher*. N.Y.: Modd Mead Company).

Office of Arab Education for Gulf Countries (2002) *Education and Electronic Government*. Riyadh, S. Arabia.

Reda, A.T. (1996) *Culture: Competition between the Paper and Screen*. Riyadh: Office of the Arab Education for Gulf Countries.

Watfa, A. (2006) Attitudes of Young People towards Mass Media. Dubai: *Social Affairs Magazine*, Issue 49.

I, Myself and The Other

In the Light of Educational Culture and the Media Culture:
Integration or Contradiction?

Essmat Sweedan

Media's progressive role in society has a great impact on educational activities in general, and the systematic ones in particular. Media content vigorously affects Western organizations, particularly political, cultural and educational aspects, by enticing and marketing the ideas of the West that conclude that other (non-Western) cultures are archaic and should be replaced by modern ones. The idea of replacing religious values with secular ones is very apparent. It does not call for improving or upgrading the current cultures but instead for replacing them with the Western culture. This replacement would include all aspects of life, even excluding religion from people's lives and separating them from their surroundings. Such ideas have impacted Western society so strongly that they have achieved both progress and destruction at the same time. The West has employed globalization (through satellite broadcast) to achieve their goals in the world, particularly in Muslim communities. Unexpectedly, the ideas they call for include the *freedom of expression* principle, which has undermined the Western culture from within.

The importance of "Media education" versus the "Culture of the Other" is crucial for the international community. The first ever international conference on media education has raised awareness concerning the "ego/audience" of media content and its indirect and underlying messages, especially those based on the Culture of The Other.

The difficulties facing systematic education in Muslim countries has given the media an opportunity to win people's hearts and minds. This was the easiest and most effective way for many communities to learn about different aspects of life, especially the materialistic ones. Audiences would see the media as presenting the latest inventions and theories for them to follow, so that they would be up-to-date and modern with regard to human, romantic and financial relationships, regardless of the ideas and tendencies of the broadcaster.

This article attempts to answer the following questions: What is culture? How it is related to the entity of "I, Myself and The Other"? What is the relationship between society and the educational culture? What is the relationship between society and the media culture? What are the results of integrating or disintegrating the media and educational cultures? This article includes an example, "I, Myself and The Other and the Culture of Ya'qobian's Apartment Building (Film)".

First Axis: Culture and Society – Integration or Contradiction?

Culture and society: Culture is a collection of factors interacting to produce specific features in the human being, which is what distinguishes him from other creatures. These factors can be natural, geographical, environmental, social and economic, as well as religious.

What is meant by "Culture"?: According to Arabic morphology the term *"Thaqa-fa"*, meaning "Culture", is derived from the root *"th-qa-fa"* which means "became skilful, clever, and smart". To "tha-qa-fa" someone means to "cultivate, educate and enlighten" him. Finally, "tha-qaa-fa – culture" means"sciences, knowledge and arts required to be skilful, clever and smart". Accordingly, "Thaqafa – culture" is the resultant texture of the theories, thoughts, beliefs, customs, traditions, principles, trends, tendencies of thinking, work, typical behaviour and all that is based on these factors such as new inventions, devices and tools, in addition to heritage, which can be adopted as is or updated to fit present lifestyles.

Culture Components: The materialistic and moral aspects of a culture that include its concepts, beliefs, values, social institutions, hopes and means of communication, which form the culture's national entity and distinguish it from other nations. In addition, one's "cultural entity" can greatly influence one's "personal entity".

Culture types and their sources – Indirect (unsystematic education): Acquired knowledge, skills and moral values through the five senses. They are neither restricted by place/time nor clash with censorship in quantity or quality. Upon the development of societies, more systematic education systems evolved to teach individuals through educational institutions that represent the second method of acquiring culture.

Importance of culture to society: It plays a vital role in preserving the unity of a society and putting its social life in order by providing it with commonalities that facilitate interaction and communication among its citizens.

Culture is the basis upon which a society's civilization is built. Civilization refers to "town and village-dwelling" as opposed to "nomadic", and is a high level of development and indicates scientific, literary and social progress in the urban lifestyle. Hence, the educational and social sciences have paid close attention to the concept of "culture" and the factors influencing it.

In conclusion, culture is the most important factor in societies' existence over time.

Second Axis: Educational Culture and Society
– Integration or Contradiction?

Education and Culture: Education is the second method for acquiring culture. Noury and Abboudy state, "Education is merely a cultural process". Education has nine constituents, which are well known to educators. The most important of these is the "education policy", which determines the goals, destination, and outlines of the process as well as planning for its establishment.

Habanka Al-Meidany said, "Educational policy is defined and set by the beliefs or the personal as well as the national interest of those who are in charge of it."

Abbody and Noury say, "The concept of 'raising' and the concept of 'education' are inseparable." "Ta'-leem" is derived from "A'-li-ma", meaning"knew". The comprehensive meaning of "Ta'-leem – education" is "Gaining and acquiring knowledge, skills, beliefs, values and lifestyles". Any social system seeks for the individual to learn and acquire what would be in accordance with the social philosophy of the ruling class at any given time. Accordingly, the entity of the social system is reflected in the educational system in one way or another.

According to the above presentation, "raising" is not a synonym for "education" as it is more comprehensive than "education", which only deals with information and sciences. "Raising" is rather concerned with the materialistic and moral aspects of an individual's life. So, every society is keen on preparing an educational policy based on its culture, intellectuality and view of the nature of existence.

Based on the above, we would define the educational culture as: the content of a society's cultural being intentionally passed to the members of that society through a prepared process based on a well-defined plan that aims at preserving the society's constituents and heritage, as to develop them, and expressing the hopes and vision of the society for the future.

Conclusion: If the source of the educational culture is the society itself then they integrate, and vice versa.

Third Axis: Media Culture and Society
– Integration or Contradiction?

Firstly, Media – Arabic and non-Arabic references did not agree on a single definition.

French sources define media as "information" due to the word's precise, comprehensive and consistent nature, which goes hand in hand with scientific and technological progress. The American sources insist on the term "Media of Mass Communication", although this does not cover all the meanings included in the process. In Arabic, the meaning conveyed by the term "*I'lam* – informing" is not any better than the American one, as it expresses only the last phase of the process that involves sending information, and overlooks the first phase that represents receiving the information. "Al-I'lam – Informing" is "reporting the information, knowledge, manner and intellectual culture in a specific method via tangible and intangible tools, be it real or legal persons with the intention of affecting people's minds and/or natural impulses.

Media Corp: The institutions of journalism, radio broadcasting, public or private cinema, whose activities include collecting and publishing news and/or opinions. This process is based on two main theories: Control and Freedom of Speech. Media function in conveying the news/opinions directly or indirectly, to targeted audiences or an indiscriminate mass public. Media can also rely heavily on one sense more than others such as listening or watching, or on both.

Linguistic Message in the Media: Language has always been one of the most effective factors in a culture. It is the most important communication tool among individuals, and between individuals and groups in all combinations. Language is simply a set of acoustic signals that emerges and develops together with the history of its speakers. The most prominent use of a language is to enable a group to converse with one another, and media language is no exception. Media language is an indirect type as it is conveyed through media sets and is intended for a larger audience than is the case with individual communication. Moreover, media language instantly reaches its audiences through live broadcast. Media materials aim at forming and guiding an audience at an average level of culture in a particular direction and establishing a special relationship between the producer and the audience. As a result, the response of the audience would vary from one to another due to the different vocabulary used in the material of the message. Therefore, the relationship between audience and message is not constant but rather dynamic. As a conclusion, we submit the sound saying of the Arab scholars: "For every situation a saying, and for every saying a situation"

Based on the discussion above, this research concludes that "media culture" is: The cultural vocabulary/items included in the directed message and its content. This vocabulary/these items could be news, a thought, or a call for behavioural change or cultivation. They are produced by a human being (sender) via mass communication media in order to achieve particular impact or response to the vocabulary/items in accordance with the context of the situation and message. Therefore, media culture would integrate with society's culture if the media's cultural content emerges from *I Myself* (the society) and addresses the same cultural vocabulary of its individuals. On the other hand, if the media content and vocabulary are different from the cultural vocabulary of the society, then they represent *The Other's* culture, which makes it contradictory to the culture of *I Myself*.

The social impact of media content and how it is related to social movements and modernization: Media, without a doubt, have enormous effects on any society. Their role includes, but is not limited to: acting as a resisting force to ignorance, tyranny and superstition; enhancing the human conscious and becoming an integrating part of society as are family, Mosque, friends and the like. In addition, media are employed to support and strengthen political regimes. Otherwise, media alone would not have the overwhelming effect some believe it does. Dr. Samiya says, "The concept of social development indicates the process through which the transformation in the social system and its role occurs". An example of this is could be a national revolution or the invention of a new industrial process. The process of social transformation is represented in three steps: First is invention, the creation of a new idea(s) or upgrading old one(s). The second step is distribution, the process of delivering the new ideas to the society through its system. The final step is the result, which is the resultant change inside the social system that has occurred as a result of the adoption of some of the new ideas, or their rejection. The evidence of the relationship between the media and development and modernization is that the conducted studies, especially those in developing countries, have shown a direct relationship in their societies, such that the individual's traditional attitude would experience changes especially with regard to the technological aspect, which itself is characterized by speedy changes.

Fourth Axis: Application of I, Myself and The Other and the Culture of *Ya'qobian's Apartment Building* (Film)

I, Myself

Ya'qobian's Apartment Building is a recent film based on an Arabic novel that has been translated into seventeen languages by unknown sponsors. Its direct intellectual content targets young men and women, in particular, to weaken their struggle between *I Myself* and *The Other*. It also shows the gap between the educational culture and the media culture. This work reveals how the culture of *The Other* affects the Egyptian social culture. The vocabulary of the film is channelled into many areas including the political, economic and social domains. It seems like the film is based on the prevailing/dominant culture in Egyptian society. The degradation of humanity is apparent. In the film, the lowest level of human nature has been reached. The natural instincts of motherhood, protection and guidance, have diminished and the concepts of friendship and sincerity have collapsed, destroying the institution of marriage. Many other cultural components are introduced to *I Myself*. All these scenarios question whether the educational and media cultures are integrated or in contradiction.

Glossary

I Myself: (Audience, individual, society) Which of these is meant will be mentioned at the point of the discussion. *I Myself* is a person in the film or the audience.

The Other: (Broadcaster) The sender of the cultural vocabulary/components. This can be found in two flavours: one character addressing another in the film, or indirectly, through the audience's watching and/or listening to it.

Individual Direct Communicative Cultural Content: The cultural vocabulary/components mentioned during the dialogue in the film/novel (*Ya'qobian's Apartment Building*).

Beyond-the-novel Community Communicative Cultural Content: All the cultural vocabulary/components presented by the dialogue of the work being analysed.

Media Culture: The cultural vocabulary/components of the linguistic message of the broadcaster via the means of media, whether directly or indirectly.

We will present some situations presented by *The Other* to *I Myself* with the hope of changing its behaviour, way of thinking and beliefs. However, *The Other* does not direct *I Myself* to change its environment! *The Other* does not forcibly impose its message, but rather employs only the power of the word.

We will review how the camera tells us about the features and characteristics of *I Myself* and *The Other* during the dialogue. It is worth noting that this paper is not meant to be a professional literary analysis or criticism, but instead attempts to examine the way and the extent to which *The Other's* culture influences *I Myself's*.

First Example – Normal human relationship: *I Myself* (Butheina) and *The Other* (Mother and Friend)

Scene 1: We see the struggle between *I Myself's* chastity and the modern concept of success in *The Other's* words – represented by the mother. A mother would naturally address her daughter as "Daughter/Sweetheart", to show compassion, truthfulness and their special relationship. We find that the mother uses the word "Sister" instead, so as to shake the daughter-mother relationship. The mother then advises her daughter in words that are characterized by seriousness and modernization and that include phrases like "The clever mature young woman would know how to preserve her chastity without upsetting anyone!" The mother's words reflect her confusion between holding fast to her culture as well as the new additions to the very same culture. Moreover, the modern understanding of freedom shows in her words: "Everyone has the right to choose whether to have their clothes on!" and also: "What matters is that your clothes stay on"; moreover, she encourages her daughter to satisfy others' desires, provided she preserves her virginity. Then comes the girlfriend, who is supposed to be truthful, to approve the mother's advice and adopt the culture of *The Other* by saying: "Do it by measures, one can yield sometimes" and "As to some other matters, No; STOP" and using the foreign vocabulary of *The Other's* culture, "STOP". She also says, "That all depends on how clever and mature the girl is". Is this not a clear invitation to practice immoral acts? The girlfriend is also being sarcastic about the girl's beauty by saying: "If you are pretty, there is prettier out there". She adds to this, talking to her very lightly and describing her with words like "you idiot" and "inexperienced". No value is placed on an educational degree, since they consider it to be not worth more than teaching people to beg people in the streets, saying: "You obtained a diploma like others have done, and can't do more than beg people in the streets with it". Admitting and accepting that all men stare lustfully at other women, she says "Is there any man who doesn't stare at other women?". Being vulgar about committing acts of shame, she says "Everybody knows we used to practice sexual activities with our clothes on!", and "Why doesn't everyone watch what she does first? Why?". What the girlfriend is saying implies society's acceptance of such acts, overlooking any incidents of sexual harassment as if it were normal and an acceptable component of *I Myself's* culture to the extent that she expects that the time will come when she must be a prostitute and that it is only a matter of time. This is reflected in *The Other's* cultural vocabulary and understanding of the phrase "The clever and mature girl/young woman" is to become a prostitute!

Second Example – Human relationship: The culture of *The Other* (Hatim Rashid) and *I Myself* (his friend, Abd Rabbuh)

Since their first meeting, we realize the methods used to pull Abd Rabbuh's leg, starting with staring lustfully at him and asking him "Do you still stand all night?", in order to learn how patient and strong he is. Then, Hatim starts praising him without real premise by saying: "You look like a very good man, and from a good family", until he starts taking advantage of his bashfulness (by holding his hands and taking a few steps together), to the level of examining Abd Rabbuh's inexperience and weakness, and encouraging him by saying "Nobody is there to see us". Hatim then offers him money without obvious reason, while criticizing his shyness: "Here you are, take it, are you being shy!?" and uses other statements to make fun of his heritage, shows hospitality by offering him liquor, and the possibility to indulge in physical pleasure by sleeping with other women despite the fact that they are married. All this vocabulary of *The Other's* culture is dangerous to *I Myself's* culture and beliefs. When Hatim addresses Abd Rabbuh with "Sweetheart", *The Other's* vocabulary alternates the name of the vice of the people of Lut to be "love" and says nothing is wrong with practicing homosexuality: "Why are you aware of your Lord? Are you doing something that is taboo?". Here we see that the culture of *The Other* states that "adultery" is committed only if the woman is married and even so, in case of pregnancy, she can claim her husband as the father! Furthermore, sex between men will not result in pregnancy so it is safe and fine to practice under the cloak of love.

The content of the culture of *I Myself* is small, weak and confused by that of *The Other*. This is obvious when he accepts the money without a legitimate reason, and when he changes his clothes in front of Hatim, while Hatim is staring at his body. Abd Rabbuh also tells Hatim about his sexual relationship with his wife and how he does not consider her fatigue and sickness when he needs to satisfy his sexual call. Although Abd Rabbuh realizes that the Throne of the Lord shakes for the vice they commit, according to a Sheik he listened to in the Masjid, he still does not abstain and loses the battle of argument with the culture of *The Other*.

Educational Culture and its Relationship with Self-image:

Firstly, self-image is something that everyone knows about himself. He knows his own pros and cons, knows his emotions, motives and weak points. This was realized by Butheina, Hatim and Abd Rabbuh. Secondly, it is the social image that people know and that a person strives to be known as. This was also realized by the three characters. Thirdly, it is the ideal that a person wishes to be and strives to realize. This achievement is what distinguishes one person from another in social status. This was realized to a great extent by Botheina, moderately by Abd Rabbuh, and was missed by Hatim.

Based on the above, we state that the aspects of the examples presented contradict the vocabulary/components of the human natural instinct in general, and the Islamic ones in particular. It also demonstrates how the culture of *The Other* has been embedded in *I Myself's* culture, especially its ideological way of thinking and the attempt to plant itself slowly and in an unnoticeable manner. *I Myself's* culture will be highly altered by *The Other's* culture, if *I Myself* is weak and hollow. Hence, it is highly recommended to support and shape the culture of *I Myself* through the educational culture and, by circumference, the culture of *The Other* by objectively analyzing and criticizing it under the light of *I Myself's* culture so as to increase people's awareness of human societies and the universe.

Conclusion

In conclusion of this study and the theory on the relationship between culture and society, it has been proven that importing systematic educational systems is not feasible because they do not integrate with natives' culture, ambitions or plans for maintaining and developing their own society and culture. The same also applies to the media culture. We also conclude the relationship between the educational culture and how it would preserve and enhance society's culture. Finally, we discussed an example of the media culture, a film and how it is related to society, in addition to its cultural vocabulary presented through its characters to determine one type of relationship between the educational and media cultures. The most important results are as follows:

1. *I Myself* represents the society and its culture, as well as members of that society. *I Myself* seeks to preserve its heritage, stay alive, thrive and stay on course to achieve its ambitions in its systematic education, which reflects the society's culture, philosophy and goals. Systematic education also develops character, entity and members of society. Therefore, systematic education as a whole cannot be imported from other societies.

2. *The Other* is everything that is different from the society, including its cultural vocabulary, which is used in the systematic education system set by society and its official members who are in charge. As a result, systematic education must be produced locally by the *I Myself* society. As for the media culture, it is a public one and should not necessarily be produced locally.

3. It is only when the media culture realizes a society's goals and supports its cultural foundation, as well as reflects its philosophy and vision, that it will become a positive integration with the educational culture of the society, and vice versa.

4. Media culture, under the shade of cultural globalization, is considered *The Other's* since the conservative ones (Islamic societies) and the liberal ones (Western societies) will find *The Other's* culture offensive and, accordingly, will spare no effort in resisting it.

Recommendations:

It is necessary to follow up with the movie industry and review it with an objective discussion and constructive criticism, not only from an artistic point of view but also regarding its topic, content and values, and the sound human culture vocabulary presented by Islam.

Mechanism

This study suggests the forming of a committee including professionals from the fields of artistic criticism, jurisprudence, law, science and medicine. This committee would watch, discuss and analyse a film once it has been distributed to public theatres. The most important task for the committee would be to analyse the situations and characters in the light of the *I Myself* culture, and to present alternatives for those that are not in accordance with it, so that the members of society can be cultivated and tuned in to being ideal characters at both the personal and the social level.

References

Abd Ul-Ghany An-Noury & Abd Ul-Ghany Abboud: *Towards an Arab Philosophy on Education*, 2nd ed., Published by Al-Fikr Al-Araby, pp. 187-226.

Abd Ul-Munim Khafajy and Abd Ul-Aziz Sharaf (1992) *Arabic Eloquence amidst Imitation and Renovation*. Beirut: Al-Jeel House.

Abd Ur-Rahman Hassan Habnaka Al-Meidany (1985) *Invasion to the Core*, 2nd ed. Damascus: Al-Qalaml Print, publishing, & Distribution House.

Ahmed Kamel: *Contemporary Arab Media: Concepts, Messages, and Issues*. Abu Dhaby: Al-Maktaba Publishing.

Arabic Language (Assembly, 2005) *The Facilitating Dictionary*, pp. 68.

Emara Najeeb: *Media in the Light of Islam*. Al-ryad.

Fawziya Matar (2004) *Social System and Educational System*. Al-Aiyam, July 3rd, http://www.almenber.com/viewarticle Sayed Aj-Jayar: *Studies on Educational Notions in History*. Cairo: Gharib Bookstore.

Ibn Al-Manzoor: *Tongue of Arabs*. Cairo: Public Corporation for Authoring and Publications.

Ibrahim Imam (1969) *Media and Mass Communication*. Cairo: Al-anjlo Al-missrya.

Mohammed Ouda (1988) *Means of Communication and Social Variation*. Beirut: Arab Renaissance House.

Young People, Media Education and Civic Engagement in the Postcolonial World

Sanjay Asthana

This article will follow contemporary critical approaches to media education, youth, learning, and literacy by considering these as conceptual constellation that remains alert to the really existing social realties and life-worlds of young people and the communities.[1] The proposed paper shall identify several programs as case studies to explore how the praxis of media education is being carried out, especially among young adults in different regions of the world. Praxis may be understood "as a social or pedagogical process which enlists human efforts to understand the world more accurately in conjunction with a political will to transform social practices and relations" (Sholle and Denski, 1993). To this end, the paper will outline some major arguments about connecting theory and practice. It shall begin with a detailed historical review of literature on studies and writings pertaining to youth participation in the media and media literacy models. Further, it develops and builds literature on recent work in cultural and media theory, as well as scholarship in the humanities, social sciences, and philosophy to demonstrate the emergence of new models that seek to blend theory with praxis.

Media Education: Youth, Learning and Literacy

The paradigm of media education, as it is generally understood and applied in several contexts,[2] will be critiqued from a variety of theoretical and praxis-oriented angles. A considerable amount of scholarship has opened-up fresh perspectives on youth, learning, and literacy. This emerging work is more than a revision of the earlier paradigm. It is an attempt in redefining and reorienting categories and concepts to grasp the multiple ways of knowing in the world. For instance, as a social category, 'youth' has been trapped in a universalist definition drawn from western-based epistemology disregarding the multiple ways in which youth actually live in different regions of the world (Besley and Peters, 2005; Soto and Swadener 2002; UN World Youth Report, 2005). Along with this singular conceptualization, youth has been characterized as "persons-in-the-making," always in the state of "deficit,' plotted along a linear and stagist model. The critiques has also pointed out that this understanding of youth has been produced in social sciences research and numerous governmental and policy-related legislations that view 'youth as a problem' with an increased emphasis on "control within education and training." Further complicating this problem has been the persistent use of terms like "teenagers", "adolescent", "youth", that have been used interchangeably.

Contemporary discussions in critical media literacy (Buckingham, 2003: Feilitzen and Carlsson, 2002: Sefton-Green, 1998: Lankshear and McLaren, 1993) are grappling with what UNESCO had very aptly outlined over two decades ago through this following statement: "We must prepare young people for living in a world of powerful images, words, and sounds" (UNESCO, 1982). With the emergence of new paradigms and models, media literacy among the young adults has become a focus of several institutions and organizations. Recent scholarship on young adults have begun to question the developmental models that view young people as "persons in the making," thereby denying agency. The emerging new paradigms consider youth as protagonists who are capable of making decisions, exercising choices, and more important, as individuals who are active agents in promoting democratic processes and civic engagement. This is an innovative approach toward inculcating a critical stance among young people about the media world – a world where powerful images, words and sounds create reality. Here youngsters are provided opportunities to learn through their experience of visual images and words. This enables a critical reflection on the media discourse vis-à-vis their everyday lives.

Interestingly, most of these contemporary perspectives have looked back to earlier contributions of John Dewey and Paulo Freire – two original thinkers of education, democracy, and human development – to sketch models of learning and literacy. Dewey's theory of education, with its emphasis on interaction, reflection, and experience, and Freire's insights on dialogical education (Frymer, 2005) and developing consciousness has shaped contemporary discussions of media education, learning and literacy. Consequently, it becomes important to pursue this field as a broad rubric where principles and practices are interlinked in terms of a "constellation," that is dynamic and open-ended. A major influence that is driving the discussions is the impact of new information and communication technologies (ICTs) that are playing a significant role in enhancing youth participation and involvement in media. UNESCO's ongoing work, through a variety of programs and projects, points to the relevance of ICTs in education and youth development. Indeed, the role of ICTs and the notion of "media mixes" have been crucial in elaborating youth participation and involvement in the media that enable learning and education through fun and pleasure.

Methodology

The wide-ranging examples of youth participation in the media and the dialogical and experiential process of learning that this entails go beyond the instrumental acquisition of skills and techniques. The case studies, limited to developing, least developed, and under developed regions of the world, cover various media – newspapers, magazines, radio, television, and the new media – particularly the multiple uses of the Internet. A sample of forty media and youth programs, drawn after an exhaustive survey of a range of materials[3], were carefully studied to determine the best examples of innovative use and youth participation in the media. The rationale for selecting the programs as case studies was based on the following criteria: The focus was on programs that consider youth as active agents, rather than "persons in the making." The various youth produced programs are innovative in terms of content production, media deployment, and practices. The primary focus of the programs center on how young people understand and interpret their own life-worlds and the social world they inhabit. In analyzing the programs as case studies from different regions of the world, I shall identify similarities and differences in the various media and geographical regions as well as social and cultural factors specific to those regions. To explore and examine the range of youth involvement in media in the process of learning and literacy as well as the production of various media and internet-based materials – the following questions have been outlined: What are the various kinds of innovative uses and participation of youth in media? How does new media participation empower the youth? What role does technology play in youth participation in media?

The youth-led initiatives offer some good examples of young people's involvement in the media. This involvement is not a singular act: rather an active and collective process of learning. Within these social settings, young people create and develop their own perspectives and knowledge. Participation provides young people a context and community to explore imaginations and ideas. This process of learning, situating educational activity in the lived experience of young people, is dialogical and open ended. The various media become more than facilitators and instruments; they enable and mediate learning and literacy. They become "social networks" of learning.

Analysis

A. Young Journalists in Action

As one of the primary forms of communication, writing provides young people with a mode of self-expression that facilitates education and learning. Writing becomes more than an act or a craft of putting down ideas on paper: rather in and through writing youngsters create a sense of identity and being-in-the-world. This self-expression takes many forms – personal, public, social, and creative

– and engenders dialogue and participation. To young people the process of writing about their own self and the social world around them is the beginning of a life long journey of learning. The following sections sketch several examples of young people as writers and journalists, who as a community of learners demonstrate the range of possibilities in producing newspapers and magazines. In producing these print-based media, from inception to the finished products, the youngsters perform a wide variety of roles in making numerous micro and macro decisions regarding layout, design, graphics, reporting, editorial, advertising, marketing, etc. that gives them a sense of ownership and responsibility. The road to becoming journalists is a process that the youngsters are more than willing to become familiar with. In this regard, the two initiatives, *Trendsetters* from Zambia and *Timoun ak Medya*, Haiti serve as good examples of innovative media use by young people.

B. Learning Reporting Skills, Writing News Stories

Although writing and reporting are fundamental to journalism, broader skills and training are required to successfully produce and distribute a newspaper or a magazine. The youngsters are trained in the skills of writing, reporting, and editing through numerous seminars conducted by professional journalists. More importantly, the older youth, involved in producing a newspaper and magazine at the initiatives, serve as trainers to younger participants. From their older peers, the youngsters not only learn the day-to-day operations of running a newspaper and/or magazine, but also know to report, edit, and write news stories. An important development in print-based journalism, the increasing presence and use of new media – computers and the internet – have led to changes in how a newspaper and magazine is conceptualized and produced. This combination of different media commonly referred to as "mixed media" has generated excitement among youngsters at the various initiatives. Apart from simplifying the mundane procedures and tasks and enabling quicker learning of skills, the mixed media offers unique innovative possibilities for the youngsters as journalists. Studies have indicated that media mixes not only "nurture the innovative, adventurous and pleasurable ways in which participants can explore the possibilities of media,"[4] both in content creation as well as bringing together local and indigenous knowledge in dialogue with international and global ones. Some of the topics and themes explored by the young participants – health, environment, and children's rights – are good examples of this.

The young members of *Trendsetters* learn valuable journalism training from a variety of sources ranging from professional adult journalists from Zambia to UNICEF's regular training workshops. According to Mary Phiri-Tembo, one of the founding members of *Trendsetters*, young members acquire basic skills from in writing and reporting along with graphics and page layout from their peers while in the process of producing the newspaper. Young members consolidate what they learnt at workshops by doing it. *Trendsetters* follows professional guidelines and other journalistic code of ethics like other commercial or public service oriented media. The day-today operations of the newspaper and regular management and editorial meetings inculcate sense of involvement and participation among all members. Phiri-Tembo asserts that as a youth-led newspaper, *Trendsetters* provided a unique opportunity for young Zambians in becoming journalists. As a public forum for young members and a credible newspaper, *Trendsetters* soon began to get noticed by governmental officials and journalistic community in Zambia. With its particular focus on health, especially HIV/AIDS that ravaged Zambian society, *Trendsetters* gained respect from international community as well. For its journalistic reporting on HIV/AIDS, it was awarded the 1997 "best team reporting" Global Media Award from the Population Institute in the United States.

Although *Trendsetters* seeks to emulate other professional media organizations to maintain high standards, it distinguished itself from these adult-led and adult-run newspapers in terms of writing style and overall content creation. The writing and reporting is informal, vibrant and direct, frequently employing lively metaphors to connect with young people. According to Phiri-Tembo the adult-run newspapers, alienate youngsters with their didactic, top-down writing, and have boring and dull news reports. These newspapers, Phiri-Tembo opines, write and report on HIV/AIDS in terms of a 'youth problem,' and a scourge that needs to be eradicated. "This is all fine, but it is the tone that matters," Phiri-Tembo adds. Each issue of the newspaper has a couple of themes that are drawn from current popular discussions among the youth in Zambian society. To keep up and be relevant to the present day youngsters, new graphic styles are incorporated.

Timoun ak Medya from Haiti has been engaged in training children so as to build a network of child journalists who articulate basic children's rights to self-expression, education and equal participation. Two sponsors, Plan Haiti and the Panos Institute offer writing and reporting skills to children. These children, writing in Creole, English, French, and Spanish, produce comic books, posters, drawings, news stories, poetry, etc. It is important to note that UNICEF and UNESCO under the broader guidelines of United Nations have been promoting children's rights (that ought to be guaranteed as fundamental rights) by involving the world community, national governments, bureaucracies, non-governmental agencies, and other social actors.[5] The work being carried out at *Timoun ak Medya* represents a fine model of the kind of involvement UNICEF and UNESCO have been espousing. Here children do not just receive journalism training, but learn from each other as well. Jean-Claude Louis, Director of Panos Haiti says that children go on excursions to gain practical knowledge of reporting in terms of gathering information through interaction with various contacts and sources. The excursion trips also provide children opportunities in developing story ideas. For the past several years, Haiti has been going through civil unrest. The child journalists from *Timoun ak Medya* have written about the political issues in Haiti outlining their views on resolving the political impasse.

C. Health, Environment and Children's Rights

Young participants at *Trendsetters*, Zambia, Young Journalists Group, Vietnam, and *Timoun ak Medya*, Haiti dialogue, debate, and discuss news stories on health, environmental, and children's rights. Although topics covered seemed specific, the writing and reporting explored deeper underlying social and political causes and relations. For instance, at *Trendsetters* HIV/AIDS is discussed in terms of poverty as well as lack of knowledge about safe-sex practices. Children's rights are explored at *Timoun ak Medya* in relation to equal participation, media responsibility, and programming on children's issues.

At *Trendsetters*, some of the health related issues touch a deep chord in Zambian society. For example, abortion is a sensitive subject among the majority Christian population The *Trendsetters* newspaper pages directly discussed abortion in one of its issues that generated controversy in Zambia, but was beneficial to the sales of the newspaper. More importantly, it was the ability of the young writers to probe and examine a sensitive topic like abortion not only among the youngsters, but also among parents, church leaders, and governmental officials. Phiri-Tembo suggests that the gradual relaxation of abortion laws under growing pressure of public opinion has been a significant achievement. *Trendsetters* has also been able to discuss and demand a better reproductive health services for the Zambian youth. Through an interesting approach in conveying serious information via informal and fun-filled writing style, one with which young people directly connect, *Trendsetters* started a dialogue about sexually transmitted diseases, young women's sexual rights, sex education, in terms of safe sex, sexual abstinence, use of contraceptives, etc. Another interesting feature of *Trendsetters* is in bringing international HIV/ AIDS related ideas and information in dialogue with local and traditional knowledge about health. Thus, *Trendsetters* has been successful, in a large measure, to intervene in the debate in bringing about policy changes, not to mention the more crucial consciousness-raising among Zambian youth.

A particularly striking aspect about *Trendsetters*, apart from the fact that young members not only write stories, and are involved in the production, marketing, and distribution of the newspaper, are the discussions of HIV/AIDS, and sexual and reproductive health-related topics that are sketched in terms of their social contexts. While keeping the stories anchored to their underlying social issues, young members develop entertaining formats: combining serious news reportage with a human interest angle, and mixing a lively, entertaining style of presentation. Namonje Nakayika, involved with *Trendsetters* since its inception, displays maturity and sensitivity towards the social issues confronting children and youngsters from Zambia. She asserts that writing stories for the newspaper has been her passion, and points out that what youngsters like to read stories involving true-life experiences. "Every time we put the true-life experience on the front page, we get letters saying 'oh, that was so nice because I went through it too and my friend was going through a similar problem' something like that…

They don't want to hear HIV/AIDS if you give it to them straight, they won't listen," Nakayika asserts.[6]

Several other members of *Trendsetters*, like Nakayika, bring interesting backgrounds and a high level of commitment. Limpo Nicolette Chinika joined *Trendsetters* in 2001. In addition to writing news stories, she serves as an editorial assistant on the *Trendsetters* School edition of the newspaper. She explains that youngsters "have the right to express themselves in any way and they also have the right to information, and since I have the opportunity, I'd like to do that, I'd really like to take the message across if not through my writings then through the figure of speech".[7] Both Nakayika and Chinika offer a glimpse into *Trendsetters*' overall commitment to children's rights to free expression, and the role of journalism and media in education and learning.

Timoun ak Medya's overall strategy is to offer journalistic training and skills to its members with the writing and reporting process as a key aspect of the training. As written forms of expression that combine both creative and social dimensions, writing becomes the main avocation of these youngsters. Along with the elaboration of children's right to expression, and to media access, series of topics are covered. These topics emerge from the conversations between the young participants. The child journalists organize themselves in various groups – based on their mutual interests and the regions they belong to. These groups are then assigned to their respective local centers. Although adult supervision in terms of mentoring is needed, particular care is taken to involve the young members in deliberations and discussions. In order to generate co-participation and dialogue among the young members without any direct "intrusion" of the adults, a web site has been created that not only provides a "forum for the international exchange of ideas, experiences, comments and information among child journalists and interested children's group," but also numerous resources that might be needed. An important feature of this website has been the possibility of "collaboration and partnerships in story production among child journalists across borders" [within the various provinces of Haiti as well as other Caribbean islands]. The various local centers of *Timoun* have computers and the Internet access that young members can use.

Conclusion

The initiatives explored in this paper pointed out to several innovative features with regard to media content creation – from writing news stories with informality and seriousness to developing creative newspaper and magazine graphics design and layout. Although newspaper and magazine journalism offered the children and youngsters several opportunities and possibilities, it was the creative and transformative role played by these youngsters that is innovative and unique. An interesting point to note is that print and radio interventions

151

have been complementary. Children and young participants have drawn on the strengths of each media wherever necessary, and combined the two in producing some sort of a dialogue between the two. Newspaper and magazine articles have been taken-up for radio dialogue and discussions and vice versa. Further, conversations among the young newspaper reporters and radio broadcasters on community-related topics generated a greater sense of participation. In bringing media education and community development in dialogue and by providing concrete and innovative proposals for social change, the members of the group offer an interesting participatory development model not only for other children and youngsters, but also for the adult-world.

By combining several media forms into "media mixes" the young people utilized the opportunities provided by media technologies. This generated and sustained excitement among youngsters at the various initiatives. Through their engagement with the media the young members are bringing together local and indigenous knowledge in dialogue with international and global ones. This is visible in the topics and themes explored by the young participants – health, environment, and children's rights. The newspaper and magazine stories that were discussed above reveal some interesting facets of this cross-cultural dialogue. This is a unique instance of extending the notion of participation from their immediate surroundings to far-away places and regions.

Notes

1. The paper is drawn from my UNESCO book
2. The acquisition of technical, analytical and creative skills usually applied in classroom situations, curriculum development, and policy related legislations.
3. These include journals, books, and web resources. For instance, *What works in Youth Media* by Sheila Kinkade (2003), published by the International Youth Foundation, *A Closer Look*: Case Studies in Youth Media Production edited by Kathleen Tyner (2004), numerous media education-literacy websites like NORDICOM, MAGIC-UNICEF, Center for Media Literacy, etc.
4. ICT Innovations for Poverty Reduction, UNESCO, 2004, p. 12.
5. The UN Convention on the Rights of the Child in 1999 outlines in articles 12, 13, and 17 refer to Children's Right to free expression, Children's Right to the access of media, and protection against incriminating media materials that exploits children in various ways. Haiti signed the convention in 1990.
6. http://www.africaalive.org/interviews/interview3.htm
7. http://www.unicef.org/voy/explore/media/explore_899.html

Bibliography

Buckingham, David (2003) *Media Education: Literacy, Learning, and Contemporary Culture*. Cambridge, UK: Polity Press in association with Blackwell.

Dewey, J. (1966) *Democracy and Education: An Introduction to the Philosophy of Education*. New York: The free press.

Feilitzen, Cecilia von and Ulla Carlsson (2002) *Children, Young People and Media Globalization*. Göteborg: UNESCO International Clearinghouse on Children, Youth and Media, Nordicom, Göteborg University.

Freire, P. (1972) *Pedagogy of the Oppressed*. London: Penguin.

Greene, Maxine (2003) *Teaching Youth Media: A Critical Guide to Literacy, Video Production, and Social Change* (Series on School Reform, 36). Teacher's College Press.

Kinkade, Sheila and Christy Macy (2003) *What Works in Youth Media*. Baltimore,: International Youth Foundation.

Lankshear, Colin and Peter McLaren (Ed.) (1993) *Critical Literacy*: Politics, Praxis, and the Postmodern. Albany, NY: State University of New York Press.

Livingstone, Sonia (2001) *Children and their Changing Media Environment*: A European Comparative Study. Mahwah, N.J:L. Erlbaum Associates.

Sefton-Green, Julian (Ed.) (1998) *Digital Diversions*: Youth Culture in the Age of Multimedia. London: UCL Press.

Sholle, David and Stan Denski (1993) 'Reading and Writing the Media: Critical Media Literacy and Postmodernism' in Colin Lankshear and Peter McLaren, (Eds.) *Critical Literacy*.

Tyner, Kathleen (Ed.) (2004) *A Closer Look*: Case Studies in Youth Media Production. GPN.

UNESCO (2006) *Global Monitoring Report*.

United Nations (2005) *World Youth Report*: Young People Today, and in 2015.

153

Multidimensional and Multicultural Media Literacy
Social Challenges and Communicational Risks on the Edge between Cultural Heritage and Technological Development

Vítor Reia-Baptista

For quite some time, we have been "observing some of the new environments of media exposure"[1] and we may probably say, by now, that the multidimensional forms of media exposure that can be experienced daily through the use of different technologies and technological devic es are not always signs of corresponding multicultural media literacy phenomena. We also know, from earlier contexts and attempts to combine media, technology and literacy inside different cultural environments of different societies and public communication spheres, that the 'empowerment' effect that could be expected to arise from those exposure situations is not always a factor of cultural enrichment and, on the contrary, it assumes too many times the character of some alienation phenomenon or, at least, an alienator mode of media appropriation.

This statement seems to be rather actual for the different younger generations living all over the world among *New Environments of Media Exposure*, such as the internet, mobile phones, different 'pod' devices and mobile television, which have become a major and eventually the richest part of the youngsters' cultural daily way of life, i.e., their wider and multidimensional media cultures being built upon their daily media consumption and appropriations, representing, in fact, their main culture.

Still their entertaining, communicative and social lives also include older media, especially open signal and satellite television, video-games, personal hi-fi devices and films, among others. Nevertheless, their appropriations and usage patterns of these media technologies are in many ways rather specific, so one of the main risks, in a media literacy context, is the danger of generalisation about common patterns of appropriation. However, one general feature in our attitudes towards these media cultural effects has been taking them as they were often ambivalent: television is still seen both as educational and as a drug; mobile phones are perceived both as a nuisance and as a life-saver; computer games are viewed both as learning tools and as addictive timewasters and film

155

has been looked at since the very beginnings of the 7th art as a medium of great educational power as well as a medium with an enormous range of escapism dimensions. In fact, some results from different research projects[2] show that these new media environments and their appropriations imply, to a very high degree, multiple dimensions of different usage representing different added values of media culture and literacy. Furthermore, digital television and broad band connections open access to many more channels and multiple mobile devices allowing a much wider usage of music, images, games, communication patterns and on-line cultural migration across different platforms expanding enormously the range of contents – challenges and risks – available in every society, either they still preserve a strong cultural heritage or strive after patterns of fast technological development and adaptation. Within these, at first sight, 'old' and 'new' contexts, we must be prepared to explore the balance between challenge and risk, that follow along with the opportunities of this new global age, with an open mind, being prepared to learn alongside the youngsters that are already native users of multiple languages and technologies, but also being prepared to share with them our inherited multicultural multidimensional knowledge and literacies related to other general subjects like ethics and civic values.

Such an approach is absolutely necessary in order to achieve a more developed degree of a global stage of Media Literacy, which, in turn, may contribute to a better multicultural and multiethnic human understanding. In the context of global communication in which we all live today, such an adequate level of Media Literacy is, according to many of its most accepted definitions, in fact, rather difficult to achieve without a wide multicultural perspective, but, on the other side, Multiculturalism, how broad or narrow we may define it, is a concept that simply cannot exist today without a strong media component, including its most basic elements of media culture.

Transmitting Cultural Heritage
and Constructing Knowledge along with Media Culture

Probably, as I have said before[3], since mankind knows itself as mankind that such knowledge has been constructed and expressed through different narrative layers of mediated communication, structuring themselves upon another and giving origin to new patterns of narrative strategies along with new communication instruments and media devices such as new gestures, sounds, images, words, languages, discourses and all the new channels of communicative diffusion and exposure, from ancient theatre to modern film, or post-modern mobile audio and video deconstructed messages within computer processing networks, e.g. like 'You Tube', 'My Space', or 'Second Life', i.e. the media in general as we know them in their evolution until today. In fact, when we speak about new media, we are generally speaking about devices that have emerged in our daily life environments rather recently, but that managed rather quickly to reshape some of our ancestral habits of personal communication and our most common communicative patterns of different multicultural media usage. Many times, at a first glance, these new patterns of communication and media usage seem to be so complex that we feel tempted to claim that we are entering, with them and via them, into a new paradigm of personal and social communication. And it may well be so, that is why we must observe and study them from different perspectives and considering their different role within different cultural, social, artistic, industrial, economical and political contexts, but when we observe these new patterns a little closer, we can notice that although they are developing devices and postures upon new complex and differentiated channels and patterns of communication, those very same new environments of media exposure may not have developed, necessarily, so many new narrative functions that would differentiate them from older media. These narrative functions are, have been and will probably remain to be essential to the processes of collective memory preservation, cultural transmission and general knowledge construction, which represent, all of them, really important dimensions of global cognition processes for any society that aims to develop, along with its citizens, a deep sense of participation towards better and richer concepts of citizenship, either they may be eastern, western, northern or southern cultural related concepts.

So, let us then observe some significant cases of factual media literacy construction, from an historical and a multicultural point of view, to see if we can draw any relevant conclusions that may help us understand the media cultural processes, challenges and risks, that we may be facing in these new media environments of our daily mediated life.

The Case of Thomas Edison, the Cinema and the Educational Technology Paradigm

Since the very beginning of film history, film enthusiasts of all kinds, but specially industrialists and other film enterprisers, have been rather optimistic about the great possibilities of using films in educational environments. Thomas Edison, for example, is supposed to have said in the early twenties: "I believe that the motion picture is destined to revolutionize our educational system and that in a few years it will supplant largely, if not entirely, the use of textbooks."[4]

As we know today, it did not happen exactly that way. But, in spite of the failure of the prophecy, there are many other links and connections that have been established between motion pictures and education until our days, and I think that this process is faraway from being accomplished. These connections are not always clear enough, or so well known in the cinematographic and educational fields, whose agents are, generally and intuitively, aware of the existence of some links of mutual influence, but who do not act so often, at least consciously, in consequence of their presence and their implications as major factors of different processes of acquisition of media literacy.

It seems, then, that there is at least one good reason to do research within this field, or intersection of fields – cinema, media and pedagogy in a broad sense, which means to improve our knowledge about these patterns of influence. But I believe that there are a few other reasons too. Some of them presenting quite a number of really specific and almost palpable characteristics that assume great importance for the global communication processes, and therefore educational and cultural, going on in our modern societies, of which, cinema, television, video, books, pictures, texts, sounds, computers, records and other mediatic devices are integrated parts. To research and study this complex mediatic body is a task of great actual importance for a better definition of the field of media literacy as well as major factor for a wider understanding of the modern aspects of multiculturalism.

We do already know since a long time before, from the field of Educational Technology, that a film, when screened within a specific educational context, may assume some very peculiar pedagogical aspects according to its screening forms. We know, for example, that the same cinematographic sequence on a celluloid filmstrip and on a videotape require different screen situations and offer different pedagogical approaches. We also know, from the fields of Communication Sciences, that any film, as a mass communication medium, although screened within a non-specifically educational context, assumes always some general pedagogical aspects, which maybe called the pedagogical charge of film. These aspects are mainly of two different kinds: a supposed educational effect of a general ethic character and a real educational effect of a, mainly, semantic character. This means that films and television, probably, have been teaching us under the former century many different messages, interrelated with their content and form, that have been more or less good and more or less bad according to the existing predominant moral norms, but it means also that films and television have been teaching us, definitively and continuously, new and more complex reading ways to decode those messages. We have, in fact, learned under the years to understand more complex film texts and we have accomplished, at least in the western world, what we can call a developed 'film culture' in the sense that Béla Balázs gave to the term – a bunch of cultural codes that comprehend our reading skills of the 'form-language' and that condition our ways of understanding the filmic messages[5].

We can, then, ask ourselves what happens when films are screened in a completely new communication context – the multimedia one? Do the pedagogical dimensions of film remain as present and general as they have been untill now, or will it increase even more? Will the semantic aspects take over completely? Will the ethic aspects require new forms of classification of the filmic multimedia messages? Will our film culture change? And how? Will we need a new film educational approach? Or a new media literacy concept?

158

I think that we must observe how these questions have been raised before, under the development of our film cultures and observe how they are reflected now, in the new multimedia context, analysing and testing some examples that may help us infer some answers.

In fact, Edison was not the only one with rather optimistic visions for the development of a film pedagogy, and one could think that at least some of the more obvious structural connections would have been normally established between cinema and education. In fact, we cannot say, in a general way, that there were many stable institutional links between the different nations' cinematographic industries and their educational systems during the silent era, and although that early optimism has grown along with the development of the technologies and with the world wide promotional development of the cinema, in practice, it was only in the countries with a rather strong and early cinematographic industry, like U.S.A. and France, that a more durable connection between cinema and education could be established. In the US, for example, Larry Cuban tells us that there were published some early catalogues of educational films "listing over 1,000 film titles that could be rented by schools"[6] and that Thomas Edison, again, owned an early rental film library[7], while in France, Robert Lefranc informed us that there were installed 28 000 silent projectors of 9,5 mm in french schools at the end of the thirties[8]. An exception must be made, here, for the late Soviet Union, since its national cinematographic industry was deeply connected, in a formal way, to many instructional and cultural authorities and committees of the new country from the very beginning of the revolution, in fact, it became officially dependent from the ministery (people's comissariat) of education in 1919, as Jay Leyda tells us in his *History of the Russian and Soviet Film* [9], an example of those connections ca be observed, in the early thirties, in that unique experience of film pedagogy that was developed by Alexander Medvekin's among others, 'CINETRAIN'[10].

At this stage it may be advisable to establish some cultual differences between pedagogics and ethics, since this is, still today, a major topic of discussion between cultures and nations.

The Case of John Grierson,
Still the Cinema and the Ethics of Documentary

Ethics is an issue that has always been present in the general history of the cinema but especially in the history of Documentary. It is very much so today and in a much wider degree than we may imagine, from daily TV news to general documents and reports, implying a rather variable literacy approach in each context. This fact turns often the documentary film product into an axiom, i. e., the film document, like any other real document, is, or should be, a true document. The common presence of this axiom gave birth to some sort of a wide generalized but unwritten system of ethical principles, in other words, almost some sort of a global deontological code system for documentary films and filmmakers. In fact, the manipulation possibilities of such a system have always been many and quite different in nature, but they usually share a specific characteristic in common: the document's educational aim. And here, I am obviously not concerned with strictly didactic definitions of the documents' educational aims, but with a much wider and general definition which comprehends any intention to depict something in its real context for any specific purpose.

The strong pedagogic potential that is inherent to the former statement was profusely invoked in the work of John Grierson, both in films and writings, in ways that allude often and rather clearly to the different ethical aspects that are connected to the educational value of the cinema and establishing, necessarily, further connections between that value, or potential, and a much wider social, cultural and historical context.

Grierson thought that the Second World War happened, also, because education had failed to form the human mind to order human affairs of that time and gave us the idea that a new concept of education would be necessary for the modern times. As a matter of fact, he dedicated, while the world was still at war, an all part of his book *On Documentary* to the educational problem, part IV – 'Education: A New Concept'. He wrote in the beginning of the fisrt chapter of that part: "I suspect we have held on to concepts of education fit for the last century but no longer for this and have therefore failed to create the mental qualities and capacities our generation has needed."[11]

Then, he advances some perspectives, trying to define what kind of new educational concept he had in mind: "I merely mean that education is the key to the mobilization of men's minds to right ends or wrong ends, to order or chaos; and that is what education is. If men's minds have not been mobilized aright, the educational process has not been good enough. If, on the other hand, men's mind are in the future to be mobilized aright, it means an increase in the wisdom and power of the educational process. So, looking beyond the immediate, the greatest task of our time is not one for soldiers but one for educators and, because of the nature of the problem, it is certainly the hardest task they have ever been set."[12]

So, what we have here is a very powerful statement produced in the middle of the 20th century, with the world in a deep general crisis, by a major profile of documentary, aiming at very wide conclusions and establishing some very strong connections. First, Grierson states clearly that education is an ethical process that can choose between 'right ends and wrong ends'. Second, he states that the educational process has not been 'good enough' and needs to change, requiring more 'wisdom and power'. If Grierson lived today, I believe that he would replace the designation 'wisdom and power' with something more precise about information and a more efficient capacity of communication, or he would eventually name it just plain Media Literacy and Empowerment.

Such a statement implies indeed a main request for educators within different cultural contexts and we could say that many educators all over the world have produced similar statements not only in a specific context of education for peace, civic literacy, environmental awareness, cultural dignity or any other media literacy connected subjects, but even as the necessary educational guide lines towards the new nature of the increasing social and technological challenges of this new century. The media literacy novelty here is to assume that the role that Grierson played, namely that of an educator, was, in fact, the role of a film educator. Not anymore the cinematographer that can play some important educational role, but the cinematographer that is just and only an educator. And if there were any doubts about this assumption, Grierson specified it further: "The entire basis of comprehension and therefore of educational method may change: in fact it is now changing."..."No one, I hope, imagines that the new society with its wide horizons and complex perspectives can be taught in the old ways, and in fact we are discovering that the only methods which will convey the nature of the new society are dramatic methods. That is why the documentary film has achieved unique importance in the new world of education. It does not teach the new world by analysing it. Uniquely and for the first time it *communicates* the new world by showing it in its corporate and living nature."[13]

It is rather interesting to notice Grierson's emphazising of the word 'communicates' to characterize the functions of documentary film in the 'new world' while he states that the 'new society' needs, for its education 'dramatic methods'. We will see that this conjunction of functions and methods still are, today, some of the most effective pedagogical strategies that characterize the modern multimedia materials and their correspondent multimedia literacy, but also their request of multicultural contextualization in this 'brave new world' that we are living in, and its 'corporate and living nature', are, in fact, nothing else than the different cultural heritages that we try to mingle, many times through powerful media, but so many times also with rather little success.

The Case of New Multimedia,
Global Media Literacy and Multiculturalism

Travelling in time and technology, we can now turn our attention to other modern industrialists, or technology traders, and notice their beliefs, this time not only in cinema as a powerful pedagogical medium, but in multimedia, as a global phenomenon, in which cinema is taking a growing part.

John Sculley, one of the former chiefs of Apple Computer Inc, wrote in his foreword to *Interactive Multimedia*: "Imagine a classroom with a window on all the world's knowledge. Imagine a teacher with the capability to bring to life any image, any sound, any event. Imagine a student with the power to visit any place on earth at any time in history. Imagine a screen that can display in vivid colour the inner workings of a cell, the births and deaths of stars, the clashes of armies and the triumphs of art."... "I believe that all this will happen not simply

161

because people have the capability to make it happen, but also because people have a compelling need to make it happen."[14]

Once again, is very interesting to notice that the differences between the different cultural and historical beliefs in the pedagogical power of the media are almost not existing. However, that shows much more of how intensive and constant the industry's expectations to penetrate the educational market have been during all these years, than it reflects some really tested perspectives for the media, or its media literacy reflection within a pedagogical context. Nevertheless, we have to admit that these perspectives are much more realistic now, all over the world, than ever before because of the new technological media context in which they are drawn and which, in turn, makes that we cannot dismiss them anymore as a bunch of new/old prophecies based on the industry's best wishes. In fact, some of them are already happening every day and imply different effects upon our social and cultural structures. Thus, we must deal with them, trying to find what are the new facts that characterize these new media, their materials and their real implications, mainly pedagogical in fact, upon the communication processes that can be developed towards an audience, even if it consists of one only receiver, in a formal educational context, or any other context of implicit literacy usage of many multicultural faces and aspects.

The increasing development of daily life multimedia materials as new supporting vehicles of filmic languages, for example, and their educational use, have given rise to new questions and problems within cinema, communication and new contexts of usage and appropriation like satellite and digital television and its pedagogical implications. This fact, in turn, has lead many research works dealing with these problems into some new ways of approaching those very same mediatica vehicles, that is, the cinema, the films, the materials and the filmic languages in general, in their own mediatic context, trying to achieve a more accurate knowledge about the complex and multiple phenomena that characterize the different mediation processes within those contexts.

This kind of effort generally requires an interdisciplinary approach that covers the different fields in question and considers their historical, theoretical, technological, æsthetical, ethical and cultural characteristics as conditioning factors of the problems in scope, per se, or in mutual interaction. This means that most times it is rather difficult to delimit the fields of knowledge that have to be present in such analytical efforts towards a global understanding of the questions in study. To minimize this problem, it is absolutely necessary to define, as sharp as possible, the object of study and its specific fields of knowledge and that is not an easy task to undertake within any of the multicultural multimedia literacy contexts that we have to deal with.

This is, of course, a pretty old and very well-known problem for researchers of all subjects and matters, but, nevertheless, it develops some rather complex ramifications inside media studies as the research widens its perspective to comprehend a more global approach, like the multicultural perspective, and even when it sharpens its focus. Thus, it becomes more necessary to define with stringency the multimediatic and multicultural fields in study, than to try to exclude a priori, peripheral fields of knowledge that may seem irrelevant for the approach in sight at a first glance.

When I started this essay approaching examples that could illustrate a partial, but very problematic, vision of the fields of study, with some help from the more concrete intersection between cinema and education, I wanted to show, rather early, that any approach to the problem would need a wide perspective of analysis owing to the global pedagogical aspects of the communication processes in which the media literacy and the multicultural problems are really inserted.

The fields in question, here, are those that comprehend and shape the recent, but generally accepted designations – multimedia and multiculturalism, and although it possible to try to provide some more consistent and stringent definitions of the terms, it is necessary to introduce into the discussion their mediatic and cultural limits rather early, in order to open the discussion and the consequent global understanding of the problems within that discussion.

Multimedia and its multicultural equivalent may designate different information and communication processes that combine different mediatic and cultural limits and contexts and problems. One of the most important problems that have been often enunciated is, exactly, the one that questions the extent of the mediatic limits of the different vehicles supporting the original documents and works. For example, until which point are we still in the presence of a given film work, or of a given news sequence, when they are shown, no longer on the large screen of a movie theatre, projected from a celluloid reel – the original presentation form for which it was conceived – or on a relative small television screen, but beamed into a micro-mobile screen, controlled through sequences of alpha-numerical commands and, probably, shown to some very specific audiences, such as a class, a small working group, or a single, very special individual – the multimedia multicultural single receiver.

Another facet of the former problem is the one that questions how the language of the original work, generally assuming some literary shape and correspondent literacy understanding, may transmute its contents and forms into a new language system and eventually into a new work of different cultural implications.

These multiple aspects of the problem embody the main question of current media literacy, which is, in brief, to approach those problematic facets as they appear within a given film, tv or digital work, based on a literary or realistic original and assuming the shape of manipulative multimedia materials, requiring in general a global understanding of a much wider 'Pedagogy of Communication' – a designation that was coined by Raymond Ball in 1971 to describe the necessity of a new communicative educational approach at all cultural levels, at school, in the family, within the mass media and towards society, in order to gain new communication and literacy skills that were more adequate to our new global media societies.[15]

It is true that all these items and approach angles are not completely new. Some of them are already known from other contexts of media studies or media literacy and we can recognize some of their shapes and domains from former discussions about the differences between literature and theatre, handmade pictures and photographs, theatre and cinema, cinema and television, or, more recently, between cinema, video and computer-generated images and sounds. But the main question remains generally the same: different artistic and communicative languages based upon different mediatic devices require different analytical approaches to state different contextual and cultural implications. Nevertheless, there are some new aspects within the main questions that may confer a more pluridimensional character to the problem and these are those given by the necessary introduction of raising issues about global and local tolerance, global and local peace agreements and last but not least, global and local multiethnic understandings of the different mediatic and cultural heritages that surround us. All these are crucial aspects for any efficient media literacy and multicultural approach, so let us try not to forget them in our attempts to develop dialogue and communication over our multimediatic and multicultural barriers.

Notes

1. Reia-Baptista, 2006.
2. For example *MEDIAPPRO*, Reia-Baptista et alt, 2006.
3. Reia-Baptista, 2006.
4. As quoted by Cuban, 1986, p. 9.
5. Balázs, 1945, p. 34.
6. Cuban, op. cit., p. 12.
7. Ibidem.
8. Lefranc, 1981, p. 153.
9. Leyda, 1960, pp-121-126, p. 142.
10. Medvekin, 1973.
11. Grierson, 1946, p.122.
12. Ibid., p.123.
13. Ibid., p. 129.
14. In the forword to Ambron & Hooper, 1990, p. vii.
15. Ball, 1971.

Bibliography

Ambron, S. & Hooper, K. (1990) *Learning with Interactive Multimedia*. Washington: Microsoft Press/Apple Computer.

Balázs, Bela (1945) *Theory of the Film, Character and Growth of a New Art*. New York: Dover Publications (ed. 1970).

Ball, Raymond (1971) *Pedagogia da Comunicação*. Lisboa: Publ. Europa-América, (ed. 1981).

Cuban, Larry (1986) *Teachers and Machines*. New York: Teachers College Press.

Grierson, John (1946) *Grierson on Documentary*. London: Faber & Faber (ed. 1979).

Lefranc, Robert (1981) 'L'audiovisuel', in *Histoire Mondiale de LÉducation*, (ed. Mialaret, G.), Vol. 4, Paris: Presses Universitaires de France.

Medvekin, Alexander (1973) *El Cine como Propaganda Política – 294 dias sobre ruedas*. Madrid: Siglo Veintiuno Editores (ed. 1977).

Modood, Tariq (2007) *Multiculturalism*. Cambridge: Polity Press.

Reia-Baptista, V. (2006) 'New Environments of Media Exposure', in *Regulation, Awareness, Empowerment* (ed. Carlsson, U.) Göteborg: Nordicom, Göteborg University.

Reia-Baptista, V. et alt., (2006), *MEDIAPPRO – The Appropriation of New Media by Youth*, http://www.mediappro.org

V. Media Education in the Digital Age

Media Education
Crossing a Mental Rubicon*

Divina Frau-Meigs

When considering children and the use of media and technologies, two notions are often mentioned: *pleasure and power*, – pleasure in the games, power in the control of machines that leave parents behind. I would like to offer another set of notions, *risk and trust*. They seem to be the two mantras of the industry and the government alike. They underline the obstacles that media education has to overcome, including the concerns around harmful content and harmful behaviour. Beyond the tiresome feeling of stagnation, full media literacy implies that we all have to cross a mental Rubicon.

I. A Mental Rubicon

Outdated Patterns

Each new technology has emancipated a new constituency of people, who eventually become voters. Mass broadcasting coincided with women's active participation in civil life and access to vote, in many countries. The voting age also dropped drastically, from 25 to 18. Obviously, Internet holds the possibility of dropping the age limit even more, as young people are empowered. This may explain the tacit resistance of decision-makers, as it makes their chances for election or re-election less predictable.

Yet they are not the only ones to resist in their minds, if not in their words. Most business and civil society actors, and potential agents of change, still function on outdated, and sometimes contradictory, patterns about the child, the family, the media and ICT sector, and last but not least, the school system.

Outdated patterns about the child have it that young people are either powerless angels or powerful mavericks, when in fact research on media uses shows that they tend to be lazy and curious.

Outdated patterns about the family still consider it as a homogeneous unit, with both parents present, united and responsible, when in fact research shows that this "ideal" family has become a minority. The more likely family style tends to be a mix of mono-parental, divorced and recomposed groupings, where the child is often left alone with the media.

Outdated patterns about the media sector tend to "buy" the idea that media are transparent and responsible, when in fact they are rather opaque, tend to be both judge and party in self-regulation schemes and have a vested commercial interest in producing violence and other potentially harmful content. This content is not in demand by young people (whose tastes tend to go for action and interaction); it is not free (production and distribution costs matter); and it is not neutral as it thwarts the European strive for human rights and uses freedom of expression as a shield for commercial interests.

Outdated patterns about the school system present it as the last barrier against market forces, while it is prey to contradictory pedagogical stances, and to the violence of children who feel "ennui", the result of the double bind in which they are maintained, as the "highbrow" school culture denies their taste in the "lowbrow" media culture.

Misplaced Perceptions of Risk

These outdated patterns are mental and have a negative impact on our perception of risk, which is itself outdated, thus impairing the building of trust.

We are still acting against risk by a mix of regulation and self-regulation policies, with a whole range of self-censorship solutions for media accountability: the family hour, parental warnings, advisories, classification and technical filtering. The assumptions about these types of solutions are being belied by the reality of reception and use on the new media that encourage flux and immersion. They don't take into account children's agency and self-protection capabilities.

We are still acting on distorted definitions and perceptions of harmful content, violence and pornography. As a result, risk of trauma and psychological stress in news is not taken into account. Violence and pornography tend to migrate across borders and media (from TV shows to videogames, and back). Violence today can also be produced by young people who are not just victims but also perpetrators. We still haven't come to terms with conflicting theories of effects vs. uses and gratifications, when we should be dealing with the full impact of socialization via full-blown multi-media platforms.

We also have placed inordinate expectations on schools, in spite of the gaps and discrepancies in missions between schools and media. The former stands for hard work, evaluation, long-term investment, the latter for fun, play and short term entertainment. Also the teaching body has been expected to move along swiftly when school is a slow process of transmission that innovates only through appropriate tools (manuals, programs, training). The ICTs have often been construed as opposed to less new media when in fact they need to be placed in a continuum, when it comes to training and use at least. Children don't notice the difference of medium when they navigate on-line or use their portables in the street: it is all about interaction and power, for them. Other spaces than just schools are needed. These spaces exist but are underused: libraries, media centres, community workshops, not to mention the media themselves, especially portals and self-training tools and kits.

Nonetheless, all over Europe and the rest of the world, there is a relative consensus on the need to empower children, the need to balance rights of adult expression and commercial expression with children's rights, the preference for self-regulation and co-regulation rather than censorship or harsh government intervention. The other growing consensus is about media education, to prepare about risk and to foster trust, while keeping the balance of power and pleasure. This mental Rubicon of outdated patterns and lagging mental sets can be passed if we create a new covenant and a new social contract.

II. Media Education to Foster a New Social Contract

Empowering Tools

We are not starting from scratch. We can benefit from the existence of a number of documents that make a singular collection of powerful tools.

We have the European charter on media education, with clear principles, coming from researchers and teachers working in close collaboration. But we need to develop criteria for its implementation and indicators for its evaluation.

Beyond principles, we have the modular curriculum proposed in the kit for *Media Education. A guidebook for teachers, parents, professionals*, published by UNESCO in 2007, in English and French, with a contribution from the Council of Europe in the shape of its *Internet Literacy Handbook*. It works according to 4 key-concepts: production, languages, representations, publics. It offers the 3 C's of media education: Culture, Criticism, Creativity. It presents documents of easy use for teachers, for students, for parents and for professionals. The kit comes complete with a glossary, a FAQ and a list of resources, worldwide.

A series of policy recommendations have been issued, by the Council of Europe and other IGOs. The Council of Europe has proposed a recommendation "on empowering children in the new media and communications environment" that has been endorsed by the all the states (2006). The European Union is preparing a policy paper along the same lines (forthcoming, 2008), and the French national commission to UNESCO has been preparing the "Paris Agenda" with 12 recommendations for a change of scale in media education (2007).

We have a focus population, children, who will be becoming rarer and rarer in our societies and will be in charge of their future. They have been organized and self-organizing. The World Summit on Information Society has shown their capacity for making proposal and making their voices heard. Some of the recommendations of the Tunis Agenda (2005) foster the need to skill children to use all contents. They have also been relying more and more heavily on the resource persons of IGOs like UNICEF and UNESCO. Their rights have been spelled out, with the 3 P's of Protection, Provision and Participation. Reports like the "Monaco Report" from the Council of Europe (2005) shows that they still have to see their rights protected: the least protected rights are those related to sexual abuse, freedom of expression and opinion, respect for their image and their dignity.

From Principles to Action Lines

So, we have some guiding principles and a series of charters, tools, recommendations,...To cross the mental Rubicon and to reach a safe harbour, there remains to define action lines. These action lines are for scaling up all sorts of already existing initiatives and up-coming projects.

They imply to consider a certain amount of key issues:

- Media literacy and its definition;
- An integration of human rights awareness within media literacy;
- State and interstate dynamics;
- Strategies for transferability for "sustainable environments";
- A multi-stakeholder approach

III. Key Issues

An Encompassing Definition of Media Literacy as a "Journey to Empowerment"

The definition of media literacy needs to put internet in a continuum with other media. Each media has evolved over time with specific functions: the written press for agenda-setting, the audiovisual media for mass communication, etc. Internet provides an additional function, interactivity. These are all necessary for a media literate society and even though there is the promise of digital convergence, these functions will remain because they are necessary assets for employability, citizenship, etc. So media literacy needs to be seen as encompassing info-competence, visual literacy, etc.

The children's perspective shows some major trends among children's use of the internet: they prefer the IT free zone, they can move off-line, they wish for protection from "noise", they feel the need for individual control over time and space. The children look for peer relations and community, and connectedness is key to them. They have a sense of belonging on the virtual networks that feel "real" to them. They need materials designed for their everyday life. They perceive literacy as a way of empowering themselves, and of empowering adults. Factors of self-esteem are important. They need time and space for their issues. The issue of well-being as contrasted to addiction is a concern to them, with the distinction between strong and weak children. They don't have the same perception of harm as the adults, as they fear harassment and hazing more than extreme violence or pornography...

The involvement of children and young people in the production of teaching material and peer mentoring is real and associated with the need to identify the key skills necessary for a media literacy core, to be integrated either as a subject per se or to already existing subjects. This core should incorporate both communication skills and information retrieving and producing skills. It should be accompanied with guidelines for developing media literacy in schools and homes and for combining low tech/high tech materials, as a means of keeping up with technological and content innovations. It must be supported by research, to take into account the context of use and exchange, the teaching methods and the profile of the various learners.

The responsibility of media professionals in the production of teaching materials and filtering tools tends to be recognized by the profession itself. But this cannot be assumed alone, as the private sector has no such legitimacy for undertaking alone the development of criteria for white/black listing and pedagogical skills and content progression and evaluation. Parents, educators, librarians should cooperate together with children to foster greater degrees of responsibility among all actors implicated and ensure that everybody, children and adults alike, can regulate their own access, use and appropriation of the internet.

These research trends taken into consideration, the definition of empowerment can be added to a definition of education: it is a process, related to lifelong learning, a "journey to empowerment" but that cannot morally be put on the sole responsibility of the adult or the child as many structural and economical parameters escapes the individual. Empowerment is associated to the need of developing self-empowering tools on the Internet, like the game "decode the web", developed by internet providers, or The *internet literacy manual*, recently published by the Council of Europe. Empowerment is also related to well-being on the internet, and to actions of protection, preparation and participation. Children's practices such as testing, previewing, browsing need to be built on; they relate to experience goods and relational goods, as intangible assets that rest on enduring interpersonal relationships and provide both intrinsic and instrumental benefits. They take into account time spent on the networks and personal relationships, which includes emotions, involvement and responsiveness.

This analysis provides the rationale for some action lines about media education:

- *Introduce a mechanism, preferably as a clearinghouse or a portal, to collect and report on, as well as facilitate the transfer of, best practices regarding information and media literacy.* This should allow the pooling of existing information; it should facilitate the emergence of a core media literacy package, with requirements for skills, competences and evaluations, to be used all across Europe and the rest of the world.

- *Encourage national surveys regarding children's usage of the Internet, in particular with reference to their motivations and conduct at different developmental ages.* This should help every country to evaluate the state of media competence if not literacy among young people and to use their already acquired know-how and hands-on approach to speed up skilling and tooling.

- *Develop a full research program on media literacy.* This program should aim at producing indicators via research. These indicators need to be refined beyond access and use. Appropriation and indirect appropriation measurements are needed, to evaluate the real efficacy of info-competence. Considering media as relational and experience goods could be key.

- *Encourage a media education day or a media education award to reward media education best practice.* This should send a positive signal that media education is not just about negative criticism but also participates in the industrial and cultural development of a country.

An Integration of Human Rights Awareness within Media Literacy as "Stages of Connectedness"

Education for democratic citizenship refers not only to information for critical thinking and active participation but also about rights. This could be accompanied by a taxonomy of "harmful content" and "Risk of Harm", as expressed in a recent report to the Council of Europe. This notion of rights has to come out of a renewed view of the child as active producer of content and not just passive recipient. As a result, a renewed vision of on-line/off-line activities and relations children have developed also needs to be taken into account. The real added-value of Internet and its interactivity takes here its full meaning to capture the scope of children's activities (content production, dissemination and appropriation). This has implications for the protection of their human rights, and their own awareness of the responsibilities it entails for them too.

Exploring, measuring and calibrating risk of harm from online activities and behaviours also requires research and criteria of evaluation. The difficulties in dealing with this issue always appear with regard to violence in video games. The concerns of adults are often mitigated by the children's stance on their perception of the difference between reality and fiction. The examples of campaigns against cyber-stalking based on humour or suspense bring to the fore the need of finding alternative solutions to censorship, preferably via media education and awareness-raising. Regulation and regulatory pressures appear increasingly as a necessary solution a posteriori, when solutions coming out of self-regulation and co-regulation have failed. Calling on other actors' responsibilities as well relies on a holistic perception of children, taking into account their capacity for self-protection and self-help, their capacity to draw on peer networks. Adults should come as a resource nonetheless and children themselves call on the authority of adults to "filter" adult attitudes meant to harm children. Social networking criteria, around relational and experience goods, again come to the fore; social connectedness appears as essential to the child's well-being and his/her emotional development.

This entails some precautionary tales about the balance between freedom of expression, privacy and children's rights (protection, provision, participation), – that tend to be easily forgotten, especially the last one. Stages of connectedness are called for, for the children to be more aware of their rights but also to be more aware of their infringements on the rights of adults. Conversely adults should be more aware of children's right to participation at early stages and implementation stages of media education, in schools and in informal settings (including via on-line tools). This is related to concerns over the role of the state in regulation and its potential for censorship, particularly in emerging post-socialist or post-authoritarian countries where democratic tools are still fragile and at the stage of early implementation. A positive example can be seen in *Compas*, a manual for human rights education, and also in the Safer internet project that is run all over Europe. The Swedish media council has created a slogan suggesting that parents should not ask children "how was your day at school?" but "how was your day on-line"!

This analysis provides the rationale for action lines about human rights education via media education:

- *Sensitise, raise awareness, and facilitate discussion on the human rights roles and responsibilities of state and non-state actors (as well of children and young people) who impact on children and young people's use of, and well-being regarding, Internet and mobile phone services and technologies (i.e. private sector and media).* This should improve understanding of these rights, and allow for a better consensus on the balance to be found between freedom of expression, privacy and rights of minors.

- *Integrate human rights media education into every discipline of children's education and training.* Media education if it includes issues of access, respect of others, anonymity, copyright, etc. should be able to address human rights concerns and help spread a concrete knowledge of their existence, for children who often have a very abstract and disconnected knowledge of them. Media ethics and human rights are thus intermeshed.

- *Update human rights literacy and educational materials with regard to Internet and mobile phone technologies and services.* Interactivity and virtuality are not disconnected from reality and real-life interactions. So human rights should be transferred to the new technologies rapidly, without lagging behind innovation.

- *Encourage human rights training and awareness of those young webmasters who monitor social networking sites.* This is in connection to role-modelling and peer-to-peer interaction in the networks, where children tend to rely on the authority of their peers rather than on the one of adults. Workshops for youth leaders, as potential agents of change, were also proposed, as part of digital inclusion.

- *Insist on human rights proofed software and hardware.* Social responsibility of ISPs should be called upon, to think of human rights at the level of design rather than implementation of their products and services.

- *Encourage human rights hotlines as a means of informing and empowering users to fully and properly exercise their rights and freedoms online.* Hotlines should be different when directed to adults or to children. They should be designed to be "age sensitive" and also to be language sensitive. They should act like instruments of navigation, literally to "orient" the users in making sense of the risks and advantages of the media.

State and Interstate Dynamics as a Means of "Rebooting Life"

There is a general consensus by all, including children, that the state remains the ultimate guarantor of human rights protection. The government's role is seen as key in minimizing risk to citizens. Media literacy, especially in relation to safe use of ICTs and promotion of human rights, appears to be intimately linked with state responsibilities. It should be incorporated in the national school curriculum; it should also empower parents and adults, via lifelong training literacy courses for them, starting with teachers. Teachers are seen as an obstacle to quality education if they are not themselves properly trained. The production of a tool kit could also be part of the initial and continuous training of teachers.

States are also seen as having a responsibility in changing the training methods of teachers. Technology is seen as less of a problem as pedagogy. More dialogue with the schools and the state, with the schools and the local community, is called for. So updated training and continuous training for teachers is seen as a key to success. To complement teachers, the major role to be played by librarians, especially those in the schools and in communities, needs to be stressed. They are often the interface of children and information in schools and they understand the status of the materials at hand and have a long-time experience of how to integrate them and make them accessible to children.

The core curriculum could be developed with professionals and young people, so that creative software for young people could be produced, with the design of materials connected with their everyday lives. These materials should integrate new content on media education and human rights, as a criterion for quality. The idea of sustainable development is attached to such an integration, as a paradigm in which citizenship, consumer rights and media literacy are key notions to take into account. The role of the state is seen as one of "rebooting" life for people, finding the right scale of interaction and of connectedness for parents and children alike

The state should also foster self-regulatory solutions. Filters, white and black lists, and hotlines for parents and children are to be considered, as well as better collaboration between governments, especially for checking on the ethics of international companies and businesses. However the state should stimulate collaboration with the other actors, industry and civil society. They should work together in providing those back-up services for scaling up. States are seen as the major promoters of tools and skilling opportunities, especially in non-formal settings for the education of children and adults. Reaching out to adults, via awareness campaigns, but also via courses and seminars is seen as essential. Reaching out to children can be done through games; game portals should be targeted for providing tips on how to behave on the internet. For both age groups, the methods suggested are participatory and based on experiential learning.

This analysis provided the rationale for action lines on state and interstate dynamics:

- *Translate Recommendation (2006) 12 on empowering children and young people in new information and communications environment into the languages of the 46 Council of Europe member states. Extend its interest to other countries worldwide.* The development of core curricula for human rights and media education should be an outcome of this translation. The elaboration of standards for web content developed for children should be another outcome of this general effort.

- *Insist on national, regional and local discussion regarding media education.* Appropriation and implementation of the various documents, charters, kits, recommendations in existence can stimulate interstate dynamics and provide regional and local solutions and applications.

- *Provide access and in the meantime, encourage "low-tech" means, such as electronic media and the written press, to empower those who do not have or who have limited access to the Internet.* The responsibility of the state is to maintain as much equity as possible in access to all regions. But the lack of access should not be an alibi not to provide media literacy and info-competence as low tech tools can provide very basic entry points to the main issues of risk of harm and human rights. Besides, they can correspond better to local learning styles (cinema tradition in some Eastern countries, written press tradition in others…).

Strategies for Transferability for "Sustainable Environments"

Sustainability can also be seen as a commitment to localization of media education, especially in teacher training, as "no size fits all". Transferability is considered as one of the best ways for such scaling up. Best practices can be identified through existing media literacy programmes of education delivered in various European countries as well as media awareness campaigns worldwide. They were provided by NGOs, often in conjunction with the state or with IGOs like UNESCO. Nobody's children is an example of a small NGO having launched a campaign on child abuse in Slovenia. In Bulgaria, the state agency on protection of children created a successful "teenager club" offering computer games without violence, like a driving circuit to teach how to drive. Poland developed a striking television campaign on "You never know who stands on the other side", to warn of on-line abuse risks.

Transferability can be examined under different angles: from one media to other media; from one country to other countries; from one language to other languages. The use of other media remains important as they are other sources of information for parents and children alike. Interesting examples of campaigns in Slovenia led on television and in the press exemplify the notion that low tech can conveniently complement high tech, traditional media complement new media.

The same possibilities for transfer appear for teaching materials: they can be on paper, as some basic practices and modules can be prepared without highly sophisticated technical support. The issue of direct access can thus be by-passed, until a country can progressively be equipped. What is needed is transferability of methodologies and know-how for passing on good practices efficiently, beyond their mere translation to another country's language. It may imply strategies for "commutation", for instance asking young people and creative producers to imagine together how the meaning of a media text or an information website would change if one of its elements were modified. What would happen if the producers used a different person/star, another iconography, another language? Such a stance stresses the importance to map the professions at the interface between content and local users.

This analysis provides the rationale for action lines about transferability:

- *Develop strategies to localise the transfer of information and media literacy initiatives and best practices.* It is important to repatriate or to revive existing practices at the local level to preserve linguistic diversity, digital heritage and creativity.

- *Share methodologies for sustainable development and for transferability.* Translation is not enough, there has to be some kind of "commutation process", for transfer methods, so that they become lived-in by the users. Modifications of this kind require valuing the professions that do creative work in transfer.

- *Develop strategies for peer-to-peer coaching of children and young people.*
  Children can be active in translating and transferring practices that they
  like. On-line, they tend to look at the performance of sites, games, portals
  and they trust the reputation that other peers have built.

The Multi-stakeholder Approach Revisited and Enlarged
as a Means of "Scaling Up"

The multistakeholder approach recommended by the World Summit on Information Society and its Tunis Agenda needs to be both enlarged and refined: enlarged
to other actors, refined in the complementarities to be expected.

The dynamics around childhood show necessary changes in the image of
the children and their role in the culture needs to be reassessed. Young people
need to be seen as relatively competent and curious beings, and as a legitimate
actor to be introduced in multi-stakeholder platforms for media literacy. Such
introduction should not go without preparation. The importance of making sure
that young people's voices are heard and are not expressed just in "emotional",
"hot" terms, that undermines their credibility is imperative as the only way for
them to match the level of preparation of adult experts. Preparatory work can
be done and media education can be one of the best places to do so. They
need to be part of the implementation process at the design stage, and have full
participation in the creation of standards and regulations for them

Private-public partnerships need to integrate the civic dimension. They should
be expressed as public-private-civic partnerships. Civil society around media
education is very mixed: parents, librarians, teachers, activists, … The complementarity of expertise and strategies is quite apparent. These multiple partnerships nonetheless should not erase the fact that everyone needs to remain in its
role and its major functions.

Another actor has emerged: International Governmental Organizations (IGOs),
like the Council of Europe, UNICEF and UNESCO. IGOs are the fourth partner in
the tripartite agreement of departure. Their relation to NGOs needs to be refined,
as they seem to be a means of interstate dynamics and of successful European
and even global governance. There is co-dependence between them. IGOs are
emanations of the nation-states and their authority, and they can instrumentalize
NGOs but conversely, IGOs can be partly instrumentalized by NGOs, as they
need them for their expertise and their facilitating culture on the local level.
They are in many ways indispensable for their own functioning. So a dynamics
becomes possible, that may allow some normative outputs on issues like human rights, freedom of expression and media education, among many others.
In this co-evolution with IGOs, civil society can exert some leverage on national
powers, circuitously, by dint of careful monitoring, reporting and incubating of
ideas and practices. The notion of governance via co-regulation meets here the
threshold of state sovereignty…

179

So to conclude:

The Internet is part of the real world and the technologies and services which it carries form part of the continuum of media. Information competence is part of media literacy.

These technologies and services are positive tools which should not be feared (especially by adult educators such as teachers and parents) but rather critically embraced as a means of exercising rights and freedoms.

Media literacy and training are essential in order for children and young people to participate fully and responsibly in the Information Society and in full respect for, and the exercise of, their rights and freedoms online.

The provision of media literacy should target those without or who have limited access to the Internet.

Plans of action are necessary to provide a common shared vision and to prioritize needs and implementation strategies.

Media literacy has to be seen as the First Amendment in a possible "Information Society Bill of Rights": without it, all the other rights (dignity, provision, privacy, sustainability, employability,…) are not possible, as they cannot be expressed, broadcast, criticized and adopted.

References

Buckingham David (2007) *Media Education: Literacy, Learning and Contemporary Culture*. Boston: MIT.

Frau-Meigs, Divina (2004) 'Media Regulation, Self-regulation and Education: Debunking Some Myths and Retooling Some Working Paradigms', in U. Carlsson and C. von Feilitzen (eds) *Promote or Protect? Perspectives on Media Literacy and Media Regulations*. Göteborg: The International Clearinghouse on Children, Youth and Media, Nordicom, Göteborg University, 23-39.

Frau-Meigs, Divina (2006) 'Public Service on Digital Media: Letting Young People's Situation Determine the Timing and Format?', in U. Carlsson and C. von Felitzen (eds) *In the Service of Young People. Studies and Reflections on Media in the Digital Age*. Göteborg: The International Clearinghouse on Children, Youth and Media, Nordicom, Göteborg University, 13-26.

Gonnet, Jacques (2003) *Les médias et la curiosité du monde* (2003) Paris: PUF.

Jacquinot, Geneviève (ed.) (2002) *Les jeunes et les médias. Perspectives de recherche dans le monde*. Paris: L'Harmattan.

Livingstone, Sonia (2002) *Young People and New Media. Childhood and the Changing Media Environment*. London: Sage.

Potter, W. James (2006) *Media Literacy*. London: Sage.

UNESCO (2006) *Media Education. A Kit for Teachers, Parents and Professionals*. Divina Frau-Meigs (ed.). Paris: Unesco (in French and English).

---

* This article is an updated version of a report produced as an outcome of a two-day international conference held by the Council of Europe, jointly with UNESCO and UNICEF in Yerevan, Armenia (October 2006). The report, entitled 'Council of Europe Pan-European Forum in Human Rights in the Information Society: Empowering Children and Young people', can be found at www.coe.int/t/e/human_rights/media/Links/Events/Forum2006YEREVAN_en. Copyright: Council of Europe.

The Role of School Media Education

Muhammed El-Khateeb

Media education has an important effect on producing desired changes in educational vision, perceptions and school practices. Few schools have been attentive to providing media education services, despite their vital importance in forming or reshaping them. Today there are many cultural elements whose pace, integration and spread are major factors of influence. However, media education can help educators gain control over these factors so that they can be further utilized in attaining goals.

One of the contemporary issues addressed by media education is teaching youth the methods of understanding and appreciating matters, coexistence with others, the requirements of the modern age and mechanisms of interaction with globalization. It also attends to preparing youth for both expected and unforeseen events, and empowers them to survive rather than surrender or seek isolation, rejection or justification or to blame others. Media education is also concerned with helping students understand their rights and duties, appreciate the values of consultation, sincerity, patriotism, true belonging, respect for others, just freedom, facing rumours and misleading ideas, and fighting ideological deviance through appropriate means. Media education provides opportunities for dealing with psychological, cultural and social problems students suffer from at school. These include cultural, technological and political ignorance, the need to manage tensions resulting from communication with others, lack of harmony, bias and a focus on what is local and native.

Media education plays an important role in helping students acquire sound social, critical, problem-solving and association skills, synthesis, speaking, reading and writing skills, in addition to social and cultural skills that help them communicate effectively. These skills would clearly allow them to comprehend cultural specifics when it comes to different variables of civilization and related generalizations.

In addition, media education helps to create a good role model among students since it develops their presentation skills, recognition of achievement, endurance, patience and consolidation of important social and health concept skills. Media education can be offered in many different ways using various channels such as teachers, school curriculum, school journalism, radio broadcast, extracurricular activities, school exhibitions, festivals, art activities and other school events held regularly, quarterly or annually. The ultimate goal is to prepare the student to be an effective member of his community with a positive attitude towards others, work and various aspects of life, who participates effectively in dealing with problems related to his environment and society, and is capable of achieving the conditions of sound citizenship through his actions and behaviour.

Background

Most societies today witness hidden or exposed competition between the media and educational systems. This competition has led to dangerous contradictions in the minds individuals and their ways of thinking. The educational system is based on the values of the system, represented in the disciplined scholastic content, and the values of the competition in learning and achievement, represented in the self-learning process and the individuality of education. The media system is based on mass communication, which cares for what is new without contemplating its content and is concerned with the various topics without concentrating on a specified specialty. Moreover, presented are entertainment programs, which are easily understood irrespective of the weakness of their style or the naivety of their linguistic terminologies. This exposes the contradiction between educational and media systems.

This contradiction has resulted in a kind of collision in the relation between the media and educational institutions. Moreover, there is a clear distinction between the school culture, which depends on knowledge of the academic pedagogic type and the media culture, which depends on the mass media of the propagandistic type, based on propaganda and interest. Although there is a cultural contrast, presented by the media and educational institutions, and even though there is a contrast in their objectives, aims, media and methods, there are fields of harmony and similarity between media and educational institutions. Both involve a process of communication and contribute to the social upbringing of the individual who spends a great part of his life surrounded by and learning through media, as well as through educational system

The problem of education does not exist only in the influence of media on a generation, but also in the way the generation deals with what is introduced by the mass media. At this point, the role of media education enables students to acquire the ability to select and criticize, in addition to the skill of selecting the best, which leads to an integrated and balanced growth of their personalities.

Thus, the first international conference on media education (awareness and skilful selection) is considered a first step in building a huge structure, praised by the educational and media institutions as providing a critical media education for coming generations.

The General Framework of the Article

The Obscure Relation between Education and Media

Arguments concerning the relation between media and education are not new. Previous studies and symposiums have shown that there are many similarities and differences between them. The technological development has imposed an important aspect of integration between media and education, whereby media has become one of the axes of the educational process. Media education has been included in the educational specialties becoming common at educational institutions.

With the spread of mass communication in the outside media realm, and with the competition and conflict among different types of national and foreign cultures, it is obvious that papers, magazines, childrens books, adventure films, TV programs and Internet sites have influenced behaviour, concepts, values traditions and cultural identity. Thus, the problem on which this article concentrates is crystallized in the following main question: *"What is the role that school may play in the media education?"* This article tries to answer this question through several sub-questions:

1. What is the function of the media in contemporary society?

2. What is the function of education in contemporary society?

3. What are the objectives of media education and its fields and merits?

4. What is the function of schools in media education?

This article gains its importance from the relation between the media and education, and from the development of modern techniques of communication and media systems. The role of media is not less important than that of schools or the family in social upbringing; on the contrary, it may be more important as its elements are exciting and renewing. It is hoped that this article can present some recommendations through which it will be possible to guide schools in playing an effective role in media education.

This article uses the documentary approach, one of the descriptive approaches, to induct previous studies in addition to conferences, books and scientific articles to answer the questions the article has posed and to reach its objectives.

The Role of the Media and Educational Institutions in Contemporary Society

The Function of the Media

Media in contemporary society play a great role in the upbringing of individuals with the help of belittling time and place in addition to its fast and easy response to modern technologies and sciences, as well as the mutuality of the human experience. Media also introduce various cultural experiences, behavioural modes and ways of life from a variety of individuals inside the community. Media are able to treat economic and political issues (which resulted in making these issues) have great influence in forming public opinion and comprise an important method of continuous education.

Media have managed to invade homes, streets and schools and to create a great change in social values. If an organized educational process is not able to cope with this tremendous development or does not face it, this will lead to randomness and confusion in the educational process. Gradually, developed countries have managed to control the international mass media, whereas developing countries have broken away from the restraints of interaction with media.

Because of the influence of the media's role on opinions, values, behaviour and emotions, it is necessary for educators and media actors to exert joint efforts in reinforcing the process of media education and in developing its role in contemporary society.

The Function of Education in Contemporary Society

Education is a human process, connected with the existence of man on earth. This process is continuous, a lifelong event. It is also a social process, bearing the culture of society and its objectives. Moreover, education is concerned with all educational and cultural influences, with frequent individual encounters through specialized and unspecialized educational institutions, regular or irregular, intended or unintended. Education influences the social upbringing along a path that brings prosperity to for man, his community and society (all human beings) through his interaction with different life situations, in addition to deepening his comprehension of his social roles. As a result, the coordination and cooperation among the educational media form the supreme objective; society wants to achieve an integrated upbringing within a generation and accomplish a positive co-existence with international society.

Similarities and Differences between the Roles
of Media and Education in Contemporary Society

Education is made up of integrated specialties that have close relations to other human sciences. It is possible to distinguish between the role of education and that of media in contemporary society as follows:

1. Mass media are distinguished by their rapid response to modern sciences and technologies; this does not take place in education.

2. The media are a mere reflection of the general culture of society as well as of the sub-cultures of different social groups, whereas school culture is confined to the school curriculum, which has as its foundation the cultural heritage of society.

3. Media provide users with vast opportunities for enjoyment and entertainment, while education does not offer such opportunities to its students.

4. Media spread rapidly and have an influence in reforming the minds of spectators through direct and indirect methods of convincing as well as effective arguments, not to mention the good quality of sound and kinetic effects as well as the variety and flexibility of programs. All these are difficult to achieve with educational aids.

5. Education has an impact on the balanced development of mankind from a physical, mental, moral, ritual, social and cultural perspective so that ones character is developed to the best attainable level. The mass media, in their turn, do not play such a role as they are considered an indirect educational aid and cannot follow or amend behaviour.

6   Media present the news, which aims at enlightening and convincing adaptation and joint understanding among individuals. Education is concerned with transferring the intellectual and cultural heritage, after purifying it, to coming generations in addition to developing their mental skills and abilities.

Media Education

Media education is a process of the ideal employment of mass media for the achievement of educational goals set by the governments education and information policy.

The Objectives of Media Education

Media education strives to accomplish the following objectives:

1. To participate in infusing the Islamic creed and spreading it, in addition to supplying recipients with the values and instructions of Islam.

2. To maintain the Islamic educational heritage and spread it, in addition to identifying scientific and educational efforts.

3. To develop intellectual attitudes contributing to reinforcing social cohesion and accomplishing the formulation of consciousness, which face the individuals behaviour in life and reinforce the social control of students.

4. To participate in spreading educational awareness to all levels of the different educational sectors.

5. To objectively cover the different processes of education and learning and the documentation of their activities.

6. To find media channels to address continued learning, remote learning and learning disabilities.

7. To introduce new and modern developments in the realm of educational thinking as well as educational and informational techniques, and to encourage research in the field of media education.

The Base of Media Education and Its Approaches are as Follows

1. To be committed to Islam in all points of view about the universe, mankind and life.

2. To be tightly connected to the Islamic nations heritage, its history and civilization, and to benefit from its great ancestors and its historical monuments.

3. To deepen the sense of loyalty at home.

4. To concentrate on the pillars of the educational process in the media message (school curriculum science student and parents).

5. To assert that the Arabic language is the vessel of Islam and the store of its culture, and should thus be considered the approved language of media education.

6. To actively interact with universal intellectual developments in the fields of science, culture and the arts.

Means of Media

Media education includes mass communication: Internet, TV, radio, press, exhibitions, museums, symposiums, theatre, libraries, social activities and lectures. In the following, the roles of some of these media players in media education are discussed.

Internet

The most important characteristic of the Internet is the ability to browse websites. Its function is not limited to being a huge library of easily accessible documents; it also offers other network services such as electronic mail and the transfer of files, as well as displaying multimedia through sound and pictures.

Television

Television is considered one of the most effective media of information and has an influence on its viewers as it presents programs aimed at educating the individual and providing knowledge. New experiences are screened in the frame of interesting shows, coping with the psychological principles of the process of learning. Television has much potential, causing it to be widely used in learning aspects as it uses all audible and visual means like films, models and samples, as well as cultural and natural sources of environment such as exhibitions, maps, drawings and scientific explanations.

Many researchers do not see a problem in the influence of television in educating the child, as much as in the way this generation has dealt with what television presents on programs and materials. From this point of view, the role of the school is to educate new generations in acquiring the ability to choose, criticize and make decisions.

Press

Because the press plays a great educational role in raising new generations, interest in the school press has been increased, whether it is a general school magazine, wall boards or school group bulletins that lead to developing students talents and press readiness. This takes place alongside training in honesty, impartiality and objectivity, as well as the coverage of all the press realms. Educational institutions have directed their efforts at encouraging free reading and discussion of press topics to train students in differentiating between creditable and unreliable content.

Radio

Radio has a great and important influence due to its dangerous role in formulating peoples minds using the direct and indirect methods of

convincing through conversation, recitation and sound effects, especially as its programs satisfy most tastes and different cultural levels.
The school radio has become a complementary educational activity for students,
and has been used directly in the educational process of learning, in addition to
specific educational programs coping with school curriculum. It presents various
educational experiences.

Scholastic Media Education

The Objectives of Scholastic Media Education

Scholastic media education accomplishes many educational objectives, represented in many fields.

The Increase of the Effectiveness of School Educational Work

School media education plays an important role in developing and increasing
the effectiveness of school educational work through the following practices:

A establishing a relation between the school and life

B accomplishing social cohesion

C understanding the different universal visions

D reinforcing students consultative concepts

E realizing the concepts of social justice and social coherence

F understanding the indications of career education

Coping with Civilization Challenges

The vast spread of globalization has led to different cultural challenges. The task
of scholastic media education is now to help students cope with these cultural
and civilization challenges, such as

a reinforcing the Islamic identity and confronting value change

b coping with cultural interaction challenges and

c existing tensions between local and global issues, modernity and traditions,
   as well as spiritual and material issues.

Promoting Students' School Life

Scholastic media education touches a large number of fields related to a students school life, such as

A   helping schools develop a real educational environment in which understanding, straightforwardness and discussions are at their most advanced

B   reinforcing the schools considerable position as a value-acquiring institution

C   helping students reconsider negative concepts of objects, issues and persons

D   helping schools and students cross narrow boundaries to more comprehensive, spacious and unconfined domains

E   enabling schools to conduct self-evaluation

F   preparing students for courageous learning adventures

G   enhancing leadership qualities in students

Fields of Scholastic Media Education

The following are the most important fields of scholastic media education.
   School Games
   School Arts
   School Radio Stations and Journalism
   Other Media: There are other several sources of scholastic media education that play a great role in developing cultural and social consciousness inside the school community. Examples of these are the school library, joint teacher-student meetings, administrator-student meetings, parent meetings and general school lectures involving participants from the school or visitors. Educational films are shown at school, excursions are organized to places near or far as well as to clubs and summer camps within the country or abroad; schools are also connected to information networks.

Merits of Scholastic Media Education

Scholastic media education provides students with many important characteristics, such as:

1.   coexistence with technological, political, economic, cultural and social changes that have resulted from rapid developments in thoughts, values, visions and techniques

2. a number of requirements in the frame of social mobilization

3. help in realizing their positions

4. help in understanding their rights and duties and the rights and duties of others

5. help in understanding the significance of globalization, what it means and ways to deal with it

6. encouragement in using and enjoying the school library and its books, and enhancement of their reading habits as a means of education, entertainment and treatment

7. enhancement of their skilful selection of cultural, educational and recreational programs

8. protection from intellectual and cultural influences harmful to their values and beliefs

9. training in scientific thinking through searching for information and then classifying, organizing, analyzing and drawing conclusions

10. participation with them in planning different activities as well as media programs, either individually or collectively

Obstacles to School Media Education

1. the value and importance of scholastic activities are not understood

2. an inability of teachers to organize school activities

3. a lack of sufficient time for activities

4. an unavailability of efficient teachers who can employ information technology for educational purposes

5. a strong contrast between the schools culture and the culture advocated by the mass media

Recommendations

To promote scholastic media education, some recommendations are offered below to activate the schools role in media education:

1. invite educational institutions to make the best use of the media institutions capabilities and the mass media for the benefit of the educational process

2. call for better coordination between the education and media sectors for better planning of the educational content offered to students

3. call for media institutions to periodically evaluate media materials targeting students in the light of the media, psychological and educational criteria

4. call for teachers to help their students acquire behavioural types that concentrate on developing critical thinking and social values that enable them to adapt to changing lifestyles and give them the required skills to look at things from an objective point of view

Media Education and School Curriculum

Susanne Krucsay

Media rule our private sphere as much as they do our working life. The technical facilities for multiplication, transfer and networking are gaining an ever greater influence on the "natural" environment of pupils and students; they are part of their reality, their world. Education should accompany and encourage children and adolescents in their relationships to the world/reality.

The share that the media have in our experience of the world/reality is constantly growing – a new dimension of reality has been created by the emergence of highly developed technologies. Considering that a reflective encounter and discourse with realities is a fundamental part of the science of education, the conclusion is that media pedagogy should become a much more integrated part of pedagogy. Pedagogy must double as media pedagogy.

What is "Media"?

First I would like to point out that the term 'media' is used in a comprehensive sense: Media education concerns all communication media and their combinations, made possible by the so-called New Media. These communication media are constituent parts of all texts, regardless of the technology: printed and spoken word, graphics, sound, still and moving pictures. The New Media (including the Internet), being developments and combinations of the above-mentioned modules, are essentially *technologies* that serve their distribution and have an effect on several social dimensions. Critical reflection on their possible effects is also included in media education.

It is particularly in the use of the New Media that issues of individual and social relevance emerge in a media-education context, ranging beyond the mere use of the media in a specific field.

Examples: What does the sheer volume of information mean for the human capacity to process information? What processes of selection, structuring and professionalisation need to be established? How can the credibility and reliability of information be safeguarded? What are the implications of media convergence? What does content convergence, i.e. the mixture of games and movies, objective information and emotive elements, etc., mean for processing? What is the reference frame we use for computer simulation? What are the consequences of blurring the borderlines and blending the contents of the terms "real" "virtual" and "fictional"?

What is Education?

Going as far back as Humboldt, one of the founders of educational theory in the 18th century, we find that human beings are endowed with a competence to become educated (Bildsamkeit). We have the firm intention to strengthen and elevate the powers of our nature, to create something. But in the same way that the sheer power to create needs an object to practice upon and pure thought needs material to live on, we also need a world outside ourselves. This can only be resolved through associating our ego with the world (Humboldt, cited in Benner p.133).

Appropriating the world, creating a close connection with it, developing and maturing through a close interaction with it is, based on man's inherent characteristic of being willing to be educated (formed) as seen in this short passage of Humboldt, a workable definition of education.

What is Media Education?

According to Ferguson, "Media education is an endless enquiry into the way we make sense of the world and the way others make sense of the world for us" (Ferguson, p. 20). Looking at the two definitions, by Humboldt on the one hand and Ferguson on the other, superficially, one cannot help detecting some similarity between them, the two main agents being "we" and the "world". On second thought, however, there is a marked difference: Whereas Humboldt's world is a fixed entity, not to be questioned, Ferguson does not refer to a defined world as such, but rather to the ways and methods the agents use to create relations with the world, trying to make sense of it. This approach also addresses the "we" as autonomous beings whose constructions of the world vary according to our own selves.

Still, the relationship between the two definitions is closer than the present position and significance of media education in our educational systems imply.

Status Quo

In present educational theories, as bases for official school programmes or curricula, media education is treated on sidetracks. It is, at best, an important accessory.

Media appear in schools in two ways:

- Either they are used as educational tools, vehicles to transport subject-specific contents and aims (media as objects of reflection – media didactics), or

- they are treated as subject matter in its own right, i.e. media as subjects of reflection, which, in a rigid sense, is media education.

Integrative Media Education

Experiences in Austrian schools indicate that whereas the first of these two ways is a common practice, there are still uncertainties concerning the integration of the second. Thus, these two directions rarely merge. Social reality is not, or is at best seldom, reflected in school practice. Pedagogy is called on to respond to the changing conditions with adequate answers.

Considering that the topics discussed in the media touch upon all fields of understanding and action, media education is not limited to individual subjects or age groups. Rather, each teacher is obliged to consider them as an educational principle in all subjects with due regard to the relevant subject, as is provided for in the curricula.

For this, project-oriented teaching methods are recommended.

In doing so, integrating the mass media into teaching must not be seen as simply using the media as an impulse for teaching a specific subject or as an illustration for the presentation of a subject. Rather, in using and examining the media, awareness should be raised regarding how they influence our view of the world and how this impacts social and political decision-making.

It is especially because the media appear to depict the world so spontaneously and naturally that the following should always be included in our thoughts:

Media are never neutral vessels of information. The images, which we think are depictions of reality, are actually shaped, professionally constructed – and this is why their decoding requires a high potential of media competence.

Similarly, in the natural sciences – which are assigned a high degree of objectiveness in the traditional discourse – the key questions (*who* informs *whom* of *what*, and with *what intention?*) we use to dissect media texts are of eminent importance – and should be applied exactly the same as in media texts, which are clearly and obviously "made".

Critical media analysis does not obstruct – as is often feared by practitioners of didactics – the subject-specific information content of the media. Quite on the contrary: dealing with the interfaces between the subject-specific content and the mediation share contributed by a medium adds significantly to the degree of media competence as well as to the subject-specific knowledge yield. The insight that even those audio-visual media that are specially designed for teaching cannot be objective shakes the belief in the rightness and truth of other media (such as school textbooks). Thinking of concepts like truth or rightness will lead to the questioning of the seemingly naturalness and obviousness of many images that suggest an authentic truth.

Intersections of Subject-Specific and Media-Specific Contents

A. Across the Curriculum

Curricula are still a constitutive element of teaching. The main structural feature of curricula is the division into the specific subject. A feasible way to achieve a closer and more organic integration of the media aspect is the identification of the intersections between subject-related and media-related contents and the aims of the curricula. This approach is a productive way to examine curricula and stimulate teachers' creative potential to detect interrelations between media and their subject in passages where the media are not explicitly mentioned.

A systematic compilation and complementation of the subject-specific points of integration for media education is still missing. A number of *key questions* can help to determine and clearly mark the overlapping areas:

1a. Constitutive element - What are the consequences of the development of media on the self-image of the subject?

1b. To what degree and in what ways is the subject involved in the development of the media?

2. Intertextuality – To what extent is the content of the subject present in the media? To what extent do they bring about a change of the traditional range of the subject?

3. How can the double function of the media, i.e. as subject as well as educational tool, be adequately used?

At this point, a few words about Item 1:

How do I determine the nature, the essence of what is the constitutive character of my particular discipline?

Dealing with these questions can promote a rational use of curricular combinations. Integrative media education contributes to discovering and emphasizing contexts that are constitutive elements of both the subject and media, whereas curricula in general rather aim at a differentiation.

First, let us identify the *constitutive element* of the subject:

- e.g., languages –the *text* (written/spoken, and in combination with various sign systems)

- e.g., biology – *nature – proximity to nature*

- e.g., geography – *space, landscape*

- e.g., civics – *power, socialisation*

These elements transport value judgments, which in turn facilitate the integration of media into teaching or, often, make it difficult. This is why these elements should be made accessible to a rational discourse, as they are part and parcel of the specific culture of the discipline.

These few examples should demonstrate that the question regarding the specific relation of the discipline and media opens up a vast field of cross-curricular, or rather transdisciplinary, questions covering and identifying media as an important part of the cultural, social and technological development.

As a second step, we can now proceed towards defining how the constitutive element relates to media:

- A text stands for itself as a medium in its own right.

- Nature with all its phenomena has been described rather than depicted

- The concept of space, landscape has traditionally been transported by visual media.

This means that in one case the proximity to the media can be traced back rather far, and in the other cases the traditional distance to media representations must be overcome.

B. Media Education as Part of Native Language Teaching

Media studies should be an integrative part of the native language curricula. In our tradition, language has been the main carrier of information and has been studied as the principal means of communication. German as a subject in school has the aim to, for example, enable students to take part in communication in society (Boeckmann, p.6) Language literacy on the sender's and the recipient's sides has therefore justly been the ultimate goal in the teaching of native language. Language and language literacy have formed the basic pillar of the subject thus far. Both address spoken and written linear text. It is only logical in a time when other forms of symbolic meaning are gaining importance that increasingly more young people are reluctant to engage in traditional forms of text. So the subject, be it German, English or French (possibly with the addition of the words 'communication'), should be open to accepting and dealing with other sign systems as well. Moreover, this opening could bring with itself a fresh breeze by directing more attention to semiotics and Cultural Studies. Especially taking the stream of Cultural Studies into account would be a productive approach towards turning more to the lives of children and young people. The ever-increasing chasm between the 'high literature' taught and fostered in schools and the texts (in the above-mentioned all-inclusive manner) used in children's and young people's private lives could thus be narrowed.

Conclusion: Media Education as an Agent of Change and Sustainability

UNESCO has proclaimed the decade 2005-2015 the decade of sustainability: ten years during which special emphasis should be placed on awakening and raising the awareness of children and young people of how important it is to consider the significance of particular fields of problems that affect our lives and sometimes also the lives of our descendants. These fields are usually associated with environment, climate and energy resources, areas that are essential to the survival of mankind and should definitely be integrated into education. What I mean in this context is a change of the paradigm of education, of pedagogy in the epistemological sense.

Media education across the curriculum is not a cross-curricular practice; it is, rather, a transcurricular approach that transcends and dissolves the borders between the disciplines in school. In the same way, it is a link between school and the life worlds of children and young people outside school – we all know there is a divide between the two that we should attempt to bridge. Media are, or rather should be, as the name implies, mediators and call for a number of competences/abilities that prove useful and productive for lifelong learning:

We need the *ability to deal with a multitude of diverging standpoints*, which in turn requires the skill to *deconstruct and reconstruct the standpoints of others*. In this way *problem-solving capacities* are trained, just as at the same time *students* can experience themselves *as active constructors in a social context*.

Understanding is not merely reproducing content, but is also *critical questioning of conditions and motivations* as a basis for *acquiring knowledge autonomously*.

We increasingly need methods such as *dialogue, cooperation*, considering *creative affective elements* as equal partners alongside the cognitive aspects.

Sustainability in education means providing our students with skills and abilities that not only make them fit for professional life but enrich them both individually and socially. Equipped with these tools, they are prepared for lifelong learning, a goal that the Romans put down 2000 years ago as a maxim for teaching: *"Non scholae, sed vitae discimus."*

References

Beck, Ulrich (1986) *Risikogesellschaft. Auf dem Weg in eine andere Moderne*. Frankfurt.

Benner, Dietrich (1987) *Allgemeine Pädagogik. Grundlagentexte Pädagogik*. Juventa. Weinheim und München.

Bock Irmgard (1978) *Kommunikation und Erziehung. Grundzüge ihrer Beziehungen*. Darmstadt. Wissenschaftliche Buchgesellschaft.

Boeckmann, Klaus (1996) Medienpädagogik und Deutschunterricht: Eine mögliche Zukunft, *Medienimpulse* 17, Sept.1996, pp. 4-7.

Freire, Paolo (1973) *Pädagogik der Unterdrückten*. Hamburg: Reinbek.

Ferguson, Robert (1991) What is Media Education for? In: Prinsloo/Criticos (eds.) *Media Matters in South Africa*. Media Resource Centre. Durban 1991, pp.19-24.

Giesecke, Hermann (1985) *Das Ende der Erziehung*. Stuttgart.

Hurrelmann, Bettina (1994) Kinder und Medien. In: Merten, Klaus, Schmidt Siegried J., Weischenberg, Siegfried (eds.) *Die Wirklichkeit der Medien. Eine Einführung in die Kommunikationswissenschaft*. Opladen 1994, p.377 ff.

Moser, Heinz (1995) *Einführung in die Medienpädagogik*. Leske+Budrich: Opladen.

Petzold, Hilarion: G./SIEPER, Johanna: Quellen und Konzepte Integrativer Agogik. In: Petzold Brown (eds.): *Gestalt-Pädagogik, Konzepte der Integrativen Erziehung*. München, Pfeiffer, pp.14-36.

Wermke, Jutta 1996) Medienpädagogik und Fachdidaktik, Teil 1: Integration als Prozeß. In: *Deutschunterricht, Berlin 49* (1996), pp.440-450.

Introducing Multimedia in the Classroom

Pier Cesare Rivoltella

An Epistemological Premise: Multimedia as a "Soft" Idea

The Italian philosopher Gianni Vattimo (1994, 3), discussing Hermeneutics and its cultural affirmation in the '80s, argues that this meant a loss of meaning. According to him, after a pioneering period (in the '60s and '70s) during which it had to be brought to the attention of the cultural arena, Hermeneutics became "a sort of koiné, of common idiom, within the western culture not only form the philosophical point of view". So, today it is very difficult to find a social scientist who does not admit to referring to Hermeneutics in his personal work, with the result that if everything is Hermeneutics we have no more criteria for distinguishing this point of view from the others.

Here we can recognize the two main phases of the social affirmation of an idea: first, it must be brought to the attention of the scientific (and the wider social) community; second, it becomes "cool", thus forcing everyone to start using it.

There is a paradox in this process: the social diffusion of an idea is often (always?) indirectly proportional to the defence of its original meaning. When an idea imposes itself, the reason is that it is epistemologically "soft"; this means that it can be "pulled" in every direction and fit every different object perfectly (Neveu, 1994), explaining everything. The fact that it is soft, even granting it social success, does not reveal the strength of the idea but instead its progressive weakness: the more it gains success, the more it fits in different fields of knowledge, and the more it loses its definition and clarity. As Popper noted, when a scientific hypothesis is too explicative, we need to be diffident: it is probably false!

The case of multimedia in education can be easily compared to that of Hermeneutics.

The first phase of the affirmation of multimedia was in the '80s. Supported by its defenders' prophetic tones, it has gradually won over school scepticism;

first through its familiarization (the best way to overcome fears and doubts) and later proposing itself as a therapeutic chance to refresh school or, even, guide its transition to a new state. This act of cultural suasion contributed not only to forging teachers' sensibility (and a sort of messianic wait) regarding multimedia, but also to obtaining strong investments in tools and machines.

Schools gradually entered the second phase (the actual one), when multimedia gradually imposed itself as "koiné", as a "common idiom" for didactics, as a new institutional paradigm. The consequence is a form of "multimedia ecumenism" tending to solve the whole didactic experience in certain leading activities, such as hypermedia production and on-line activities (from e-learning to social networking).

The risk here is the same that Vattimo argued about Hermeneutics; that is, the risk of losing the original meaning of multimedia, making of it a didactic *passpartout*. This risk implies three other critical situations.

Firstly, there is a risk of the temptation to use multimedia to answer every educational or didactic need even when we can count on other cheaper and more effective solutions.

A second risk, as Papert revealed, is that computers do not support innovation or guide school change, but only represent the tool used by schools to reinforce old teaching methods, as the example of Computer Assisted Teaching shows.

This idea brings about the last risk, the fact that multimedia could become "institutional", losing its push for innovation and becoming a routine.

In this way the vital circle of the idea seems to be accomplished: from the starting "rush" epoch, to the affirmation as the new didactic standard, to the large diffusion as common practice. As Benjamin argued, the avant-guard is always destined to turn into tradition.

Multimedia and Knowledge Logic

This premise forces us to question the meaning of "making multimedia" in today's school system, to look for its deep reasons, its "original" meaning, besides superficial enthusiasm and generalizations. The answer can be found in the fact that multimedia identifies the technical materializing form of some of the most recent research acquisitions referred to the psycho-cognitive, cultural and didactic perspectives.

1. One of the most discussed themes within the psychology of learning is the need to extend the concept of intelligence beyond the limits of logic and linguistic knowledge, on which we have built approximately two thousand years of education practices in Western countries.

Howard Gardner, referring to human intelligence as a *multiple intelligence* including more than these two fundamental dimensions, argues that someone lacking in logical and linguistic attitudes can possess musical intelligence, being able to move across the space with a perfect mastering of his body (*spatial and cinestesic intelligence*), communicating well with people (*personal intelligence*). This certainly does not imply a crisis of logical rationality or a loss of the importance of reflective thinking on which it is based: the ability to make inferences starting from previously stored knowledge still represents an essential cognitive state in the human being (Norman, 1998). But it is not the only one. It finds a fundamental complement in other, more experiential, knowledge forms. Every form of intelligence can be found in every single person according to different schemes and mixes: "while everyone has these intelligences, we cannot find any individual with the same combination of intelligences. Someone of us is stronger in linguistic intelligence, someone in the spatial one. Even the way we combine them or not combine them is different from person to person" (Gardner, 1997).

In this psycho-cognitive presupposition, the concept of multimedia finds a first basic reason for its didactic integration. As it is semiotically built on the combination of a multiplicity of codes and languages (written and oral words, sounds, images), it can easily be adapted to individuals needing *diversified* and *personalized* didactic paths: "we can treat people as they were identical, supporting just a common form of intelligence, or we can try to understand children's intelligences and personalize, individualize education. (...) Here comes out the role played by technology, in the process of individualization of curriculum, of materials, of subjects for students, and in offering them different possibilities to master materials" (Gardner, 1997).

2. This polycentric and multimodal structure of intelligence also demonstrates a deep change in the relationship of our society to culture and knowledge. According to Pierre Levy (1997), the critical node of this change can be found in the Age of Illumination, particularly in the project of the *Encyclopedie* promoted by Diderot and D'Alembert. This historical moment, according to the French philosopher, is the last attempt by Western man to completely master knowledge: from this moment on, it will be increasingly clear that "knowledge has definetively passed into the sphere of what cannot be mastered". We can explain what this means in three remarks:

First, today *knowledge* is becoming a *flux*, signed by the quick aging of competencies. The speed of information transmission has its main consequence in the fact that an individual's "initial" knowledge at the beginning of his professional career appears inadequate even after a few months: thus, the difference between the time for training and that for social and professional experience is disappearing.

We can also think of *knowledge as exchange*. Working in the Information Society means creating and sharing knowledge, and this requires open structures supporting self-learning processes: "With the same material resources and economical connections, the winners are the group that are able to work with pleasure, that learn fast, keeping faith to their own engagements, recognizing themselves as individuals, making territories open rather than protecting them" (Levy, 1994).

Last, following McLuhan's idea, we can evoke the idea of *knowledge as prosthesis*, as an extension of our cognitive functions. In this way, databases and repositories extend our memory, virtual worlds (like *Second Life*) extend our imagination, tele-presence (like in *MSN Messenger* or *Skype*) extends our communication chances and perceptions.

Multimedia acts in this context as *cognitive artefact*, as an instrument through which individuals can order their knowledge, thus ordering the world. This means recognizing behind technology a deep cultural meaning and considering that multimedia has a real value: a distributed and non-totalizing rationality (flux-knowledge), building knowledge through interactivity (exchange-knowledge) and proposing itself as a frame for our cognitive abilities (prosthesis-knowledge).

3. A last set of reflections can originate from the idea of knowledge value of practice, connected to some recent psychopedagogic research perspectives (Pellerey, 1997) offering us at least three basic indications:

The first comes from the hermeneutic culture, particularly from Rorty (1982; 1989) and his hypothesis, according to which acting ability does not depend on the application of abstract frames but on the elaboration of action patterns fixed in previous experiences.

This new role of experience as form of knowledge is confirmed by the central role recognized to operative intelligence by cognitive psychology. Overcoming the simple idea that praxis is only the applicative moment of theoretical thinking, a new conceptualization can be affirmed, identifying in praxis a complex process similar to the theoretical intelligence. We talk about meta-components, components of service and knowledge acquisition components. "Meta-components refer to the processes used to plan, control and evaluate the operative activities of problem solving. Components of service are processes used to translate into practice the instruction indicated by the meta-components. While knowledge acquisition competences are the one implied to learn and solve problems" (Pellerey, 1997; 1135).

The natural space within which this kind of operative intelligence is acting is comprised of communities, demonstrated by research on the social dimension in moral habitus construction (McIntyre, 1984) and in learning development (Bruner, 1996).

On this level as well, the matching of multimedia and research is perfect. The consideration of praxis as form of knowledge, the possibility to refer to a real "operative intelligence", the perspective of collaborative learning, can be seen as principles on which multimedia didactics are based.

Multimedia at School: From Social Needs to Methodological Recommendations

Today, (Multi) Media Education must meet three strong social needs:

- *alphabetization* – creating a "familiar" space for technologies at school, teaching how to read and write using multimedia, preparing youth to "exit" into a society that is structurally built on technologies (*Knowledge Society*) and demands of people a radical change in their own profile in the completion of their productive performances (*knowledge workers*);

- *cultural reflection* – dealing with the "philosophical" dimension of technologies (Maragliano, 1998), questioning how knowledge and competencies can be re-thought within this new context. This issue is directly linked to the others concerning how to find maps to surf non-hierarchical knowledge (the "mosaic culture" education sociologists refer to), or how to find new criteria to evaluate and check information sources (how to distinguish, on the Internet, pertinent from superficial information). Multimedia, apart form being a set of technologies, must be referred to as a cognitive condition of educators;

- *education* – passing from a school system in which media are a "window", to a new school system in which they comprise the real environment of education. This idea of multimedia at school as environment must be translated into: 1) a systemic action, involving the whole organization; 2) a multi-level action (coordinating, teaching, educating, tutoring); 3) a link between school, extra school and the territory.

According to the previous considerations the answer to these needs could be materialized in some methodological indications about the introduction of multimedia in schools: in this case technology, more than a set of practices or abilities, must be considered culture, moving from a *productive* idea to a *cognitive* one. Here, we can fix some nodes that could help define a new (Multi) Media Education.

1. First, we have to integrate multimedia within an educational approach centred on languages and processes of communication (*social-centred*) more than on the mastery of single tools (*media-centred*). The frame of this kind of integration is an idea of *(Multi) Media Education* sensitive to media cultures (Caron & Caronia, 2005; Pasquier, 2005), attentive to their effects on learning processes (Rivoltella, 2007) and, above all, is not imagined as a set of specialized competencies of some teachers, but as the *working style* of every teacher as educator (Jacquinot, 2007) — even if this idea does not have to lead to didactic spontaneity, but conceives of thematical areas and unavoidable attention points that cannot be neglected by teachers.

2. Traditional didactics is usually built on a model normally called *unidirectional/transmissive*: "'Unidirectional', as the route of information is on a one way direction, from a source (school, teachers, media) to a receiver (student, audience, reader); "transmissive", in terms of what Paulo Freire named 'banking education', where the one who knows is the one who has a set of knowledge and the one who does not know is lacking those knowledges" (Pinto & Pereira, 1998; 7). We need a paradigmatic change toward a new *relational/cooperative* didactic model: relational, as information travels in every direction and every single element of the system (medium, student, teacher) can act as source or receiver; cooperative, as there is not knowledge to transmit, but to build together in terms of negotiation.

3. The traditional "critical reading" approach (Masterman, 1985), based on literary analysis and textual criticism, has already been upgraded by *Audience Studies* through more explicit attention to the role of reception contexts. Clearly, it appears inadequate when we approach specific forms of text – as multimedia, SMS, CMC tools, blogs – with non-linear structures, complex architectures, interactive nature, continuous updating. On the one hand, we have to search for tools that are able to answer the new needs expressed by these new forms of communication, and on the other hand we need to enforce the work on contexts and reception.

In this way, the essential priorities are based on those already expressed in Media Education, but need a new methodological framework. Just think of the Internet, representing an open place with no filters for anyone. We can find everything there: insanity, fiction and lurking, as well as information and exchange possibilities that represent a real learning resource. What is the meaning of an education as regards responsible access to Internet? What criteria can be suggested for avoiding risks in an unprotected territory, that is so accessible to anyone, where pornography is not only something to see but transforms into a possibility to communicate on-line or meet face to face, within a game where image crosses the border into real life?

But if we consider that every technology user, besides being a potential receiver, can easily transform into a communication producer (and this is particularly true today, with the diffusion of author-generated content via mobile phones and digital cameras), we need to pay attention not only to the education of a critical reader but also to the education of a responsible actor: the old recipe "To help communicators be responsible means to educate users" is in this case an overcome motto as everyone can simultaneously be critical as user and responsible as producer. In both cases, ethical and civil issues are strongly imposing: it will be necessary to help researchers and professionals reflect on this level.

Multimedia and the Curriculum

To understand how (Multi) Media Education has to be managed so that it finds a place in the curriculum, we need to take into account some variables useful to the teacher in planning activities and to the policymakers for imagining how to lead the change.

The first is the presence of main **intellectual traditions** that must be reconsidered not as exclusive teaching paradigms, but as co-existing dimensions of a unique cultural approach:

- sociological research on the relationship between media and human behaviour (*Media Effects*);

- the application of semiotic tools to support the critical analysis of media messages (*Literary Criticism*);

- the approach to images closed to forms, lines, design (*Aesthetics*).

The practices of Media and Education in the classrooms are based not only on intellectual traditions, but also on **methodological choices**. Here we have two more perspectives that are important to develop:

- strategies for *reading and listening* to (multi) Media texts (text analysis);

- strategies for *writing and speaking* about (multi) Media products (video making, multimedia production).

These practices always include a **conceptualization** of the media we can define as *linguistic-instrumental*, to which teachers and schools mainly refer today. According to this, media are both languages (students must be able to read and write them) and tools (students need to know how they work and how to use them properly).

This basic conceptualization can be spread according to three preferential attentions:

- *expressive attention* (art, music, language), particularly clear in one's native language. This attention makes it possible in many educative experiences for multimedia to be the real frame into which to develop cross-disciplinary competences that can be useful in other subjects (social studies, literature and so on);

- *technical attention* (technology), according to which media are compared to other materials and technological tools used by human beings over time;

- *textual attention*. This reference is evident in art. Media products, considered as images (as the images of art), can be a natural focus of analysis activities aimed to the construction of a critical reader.

Finally, we can refer to the **logic** that organizes the presence of (Multi) Media Education in the curriculum. It can be explained from mainly two perspectives: a *disciplinary* perspective, thematical, which orients (Multi) Media Education as a subject, developed by a specialized teacher for a fixed amount of lesson hours per week; and a *cross-curricular* perspective, basically *non-thematical*, whereby media "meet" the different school disciplines.

Table 1. Curricular Integration of ME: Main Description Topics

Idea of media	Method/attentions	Paradigms	Theories on media
Linguistic	Analysis, Textual attention	Inoculatory, Critical Reading, Social Studies	Literary Criticism, Cultural Studies, Media Effects
Instrumental	Production, Technical and Expressive Attention	Popular Arts, Social Studies	Cultural Studies, Aesthetics

Conclusion

School is permeated today by a process of over-responsibilization. In this direction, we can quote both the crisis experienced today by the family as institution, running the risk of passing the whole task of education to the school, and the growing complexity of the social system. The multi-ethnical and multi-cultural society seems to give the school a new charge connected to intercultural education; the society of technologies and chemistry demands an environmental education; the society of abundance, drugs and eating disease demands a health education. Media and ICT risk adding a new profile to this society (the Information Society, the Communication Society) and claiming a new education, that is (Multi, New, Digital) Media Education.

It is clear that this solution, creating specific areas for every aspect within education, does not appear as sustainable as it would imply; it imposes on one hand a need to increase school time over its natural limits, and on the other hand a set of difficulties in receiving a proper combination and connection with disciplinary knowledge belonging to school tradition. Otherwise, it is impossible to disagree with the fact that every pupil and teacher feels the ineludible need to handle media in a context, like the one we are examining, whereby only few experiences happen without the mediation of these technologies.

Here we see the need for reflection involving policy makers, even before education agencies, a reflection we have hardly seen but that we undoubtedly must demand. An agenda for this discussion could include four main problems:

- change must be promoted, primarily on an *organizational level*. This means: a clear choice made by school management, the idea that media (and of

Media Education) is a quality indicator of a school, the ability to interpret new school scenarios related to flexibility and curriculum;

- there is a second important level, the *logistic* one. We move from the organization to the policy on technology, which involves some definitely relevant issues linked to didactics: where and how can we locate our technological resources, select different functions normally related to the use of technology, design activities in favour of a diffused technological culture and conduct projects on a mid- to long-term basis;

- on the *didactic* level, modular structure must be discussed (it is difficult to locate transversal media curriculum in a modular frame), as must cooperative work (Media Education needs a group dimension), meaningful learning (media curriculum helps the idea of finding the essential – Gardner, 1999), culture of documentation and evaluation, meta-cognition;

- the last level on which change must be addressed is *training*. Some indication can be suggested: to invest in a mid- to long-term period, overcoming the logic of intensive but episodic training; to properly connect activities to main goals, thinking training and working as a continuous process; to provide a place for tutoring, listening to teachers' needs to not be abandoned after the initial training but to be followed during the evaluation process as well, within didactic praxis of what is learned.

References

Bruner, J. (1996) *Culture of Education.* Harvard (Ma): Harvard University Press.

Caron, A., Caronia, L. (2005) *Cultures Mobiles.* Montreal: Presses dell'Université de Montreal.

Gardner, H. (1997) *Multiple Intelligence and New Technologies.* Interview with "Mediamente", Turin, 10 April. Available in Internet, URL: http//www.rai.it/mediamente.

Id., Education Without Dogma. *Dissent* 36, 2.

Id. (1997) *La cyberculture et l'éducation.* Paper presented at the International Conference *Scuola in rete: educare alla comunicazione,* Venice, Italy.

Id. (1999) *The Disciplined Mind.* New York: Simon & Schuster.

Jacquinot, G. (2007) Dall'educazione ai media alle "mediaculture": ci vogliono sempre degli inventori!. In: M. Morcellini, P.C. Rivoltella (a cura di). *La sapienza di comunicare. Dieci anni di Media Education in Italia e in Europa.* Trento: Erickson, pp. 131-141.

Levy, P. (1994). *L'intelligènce collective.* Paris: La Decouvèrte.

MacIntyre, A. (1984) *After Virtue. Essays in Moral Philosophy.* Notre Dame (In): University of Notre Dame Press.

Maragliano, R. (1998) *Tre ipertesti su multimedialità e formazione.* Roma-Bari: Laterza.

Masterman, L. (1985) *Teaching the media.* London: Routledge.

Neveu, E. (1994) *Une Société de communication?* Paris: Montchrestien.

Norman, D.A. (1998) *The Invisibile Computer.* Cambridge (Ma): MIT Press.

Pasquier, D. (2005) *Cultures lycéennes, la tirannie de la majorité.* Paris: Autrement.

Pellerey, M. (1997) Modernità, postmodernità e educazione. La rinascita del valore conoscitivo della pratica. *Orientamenti pedagogici,* 264, XLIV, 6, pp.1131-1149.

Pinto, M., Pereira, S. (1998) *L'éducation aux médias et la formation des enseignants*. Actes du Forum *Les jeunes et le medias, demain*. Paris: GRREM, p.7.

Rivoltella, P.C. (2008) (ed.) *Digital Literacy. Tools and Methodologies for the Information Society*. Hershey (Pa): IGI.

Rorty, R. (1982) Hermeneutics, General Studies, and Teaching. *Synergos* 2, pp.1-15.

Vattimo, G. (1994). *Oltre l'interpretazione*. Bari-Roma: Laterza.

Developing Skills of Interaction with the Screen in Saudi Families

Hanan Ashi

In the 21st century, Saudi families are facing huge challenges with the rapid development of visual media technology. Hence, children who lack media education skills will be left behind on the information globe. This is because media education empowers children in interacting consciously and cognitively with the rocketing developments in visual technology and also enhances their independent character, giving them more control over their present and future. Consequently, this will not only reflect positively on the development of Saudi society in general but will also help families deal with the negative cultural and moral effects of the visual media tsunami. Although both schools and Saudi civil society play an important role they cannot replace the Saudi family, which is the foundation for what skills children acquire in media education.

Interacting with the screen is a necessity but is also a known source of immense social risk. All forms of screens are accused of inculcating values, norms and moral standards that are untrustworthy and equivocal models, as well as destroying of the native Arabic language. An example of a degrading situation is some educational programmes being presented by belly-dancers or famous actors, to teach young viewers values and ethics. Moreover, images of virtuous men and women are often depicted by the media as boring and dull. Thus, to be a modern woman or a successful man, there is pressure on one to adopt a (socially objectionable) character from the screen as a role model. Alcoholism, smoking, extravagance and fashionable, lavish clothing with bizarre haircuts, or even imitations of vulgar and naughty characters in walking and talking, have become the skills that youth aspire to learn. At the same time, lying, deception and conniving are considered intelligence, cleverness and ingenuity (Nasif, 2006, Al-Yahya, 1991). Addiction to the screen, therefore, is no less harmful than addiction to narcotics.

Furthermore, the screen usually distorts the concept of progressiveness by misrepresenting it. It socializes young people and children based on the false conception of modernity and civilization. The visual media glorify superficiality and artificiality, and praise novelty for its own sake while degrading conventionality for its merit. Old cars and clothes are regarded as strange, to be ridiculed and exchanged for something up-to-date and fashionable; otherwise, a person will be considered backward or out-of-date. Also, the visual media glorify dancers, actors, football players and politicians as more important than scientists, engineers, teachers and doctors. Here, the media tend to have an anaesthetic effect on young viewers, which prevents them from perceiving reality, pushing them into an unhealthy illusive world that promotes the social evils of violence, hate, revenge and blackmail. While visual media aim at entertainment, they often demand that life on the screen continue in real life. However, such a call is unachievable in reality, which often leads viewers to frustration and nervous breakdowns due to the pressures of living up to what they consider ideal (Mander, 1978, Muhamed, 1999). Added to this is the negative impact of the media on family members due to late nights, laziness and problems with vision. Also, the screen seems to have replaced other social activities and relationships, causing family members to withdraw from or become strangers to each other (Al-Sherbini & Sadik, 2000, Hindi, 1998).

Saudi families are considered to be a source of strong protection and an unyielding shield for their members against the harmful effects of the screen. However, the reality seems to be different. Saudi families who bounce between strictness and leniency can be generally distinguished according to their styles of interaction with the screen. On one extreme is the socio-oriented family and on the other is the laissez-faire family.

The Socio-Oriented Protective Family Model in Saudi Arabia

Figure 1. The Saudi Socio-oriented Protective Family and the Screen

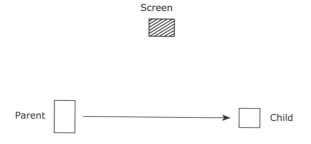

In the first type, the protective socio-oriented family, parents avoid arguments with their children and do not accept any kind of rebellion against rules they have

established. The family imposes a restrictive style of socialization that involves inflicting strict regulations of exposure of the family, especially children, to the screen. For example, the parents control the time children spend in front of the screen and the type of materials they view. Little impetus is provided to develop a broad-minded, thoughtful outlook on the world (Al-Gareeb, 2001). Children are regarded by their families as unselective, uncritical and unsophisticated viewers, lacking the skills required to make sense of television and use it in responsible and sensible ways. The socio-oriented parents vociferously accuse television of being responsible for all the vices and anxieties among children. It is considered the root and the fruit of every social ill, from violence, sex and brainwashing to consumerism, illiteracy and even more. The Saudi socio-oriented family seems to approve of Mander's *Four Arguments for the Elimination of Television*, which states that "if television hypnotises, brainwashes, controls the mind, makes people stupid and turns everyone into 'zombies', then in fact, someone should call the police." (Mander (1978, 160).

Thus, no other medium has caused anxiety for the Saudi socio-oriented protective family as much as the screen has in its influence on children. Moreover, with the influx of hundreds of TV channels and Internet sites, along with the introduction of Bluetooth in mobile phones, their anxiety has accelerated to its peak as children can gain uncontrolled access to adult-oriented material much more than ever before. Consequently, for a socio-oriented protective family, children's access to previously forbidden adult information expels them from the garden of childhood and innocence.

Therefore, as a protective family, the socio-oriented family's attitude towards the screen is aggressive. Surprisingly, however, the socio-oriented parents tend to be heavy viewers themselves, watching television out of habit (Gunter & McAleer, 1997). Unselective viewing, or inactive passive viewing, is the habituated use of television for diversion or to pass time or relax and is regarded as non-purposeful, unintentional and ritualistic viewing (Ashi, 2003). Consequently, children in such families also tend to be unselective whenever there is an opportunity. Such children are quick to point out contradictions between what parents say and what they actually do (Al-Gareeb, 2001). Hence, if adults are enticed by visual media when they tune in, children will learn to do likewise.

The Laissez-Faire Family Model in Saudi Arabia

At the other extreme in Saudi society is the laissez-faire family. In this type of family, there is little parent-child communication, and the child is influenced more by peer groups outside the home. This family uses the unfocused style of socialization, whereby parents do not have clear rules or regulations regarding the family's exposure to the screen. Members of the family may view visual media materials alone or in the company of others. However, their gathering is not

Figure 2. The Saudi Laissez-Faire Family and the Screen

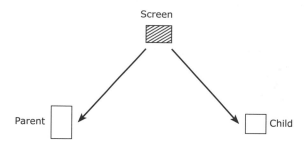

for the purpose of analyzing and assessing the type of materials viewed, but for entertainment and diversion (Ashi, 2003). Parenthood in the laissez-faire family often becomes an exercise in disaster avoidance and damage control, because the parents' influence does not seem to have any effect (Zafer, 1991).

All societies (and Saudi society is no exception), modern as well as ancient, consist of those who – from either ignorance, lack of means or sheer carelessness – neglect children and allow them to be exposed to all types of materials. Social pressures (important or unimportant) keep us busy, and economic pressures (real or perceived) keep us working. Time passes and the children grow up without us, spending more time on their own or in the company of their peers of a television set, merely because the moral representatives of society do not fill the vacuum, which the television and the street readily do (Al-Sherbini & Sadik, 2000, Ashi, 2003). In general, and in Saudi society in particular, a laissez-faire family lets strangers on television dictate what their children will learn and do.

Commenting on the socialization practices and their relationship to the screen among families in Saudi Arabia, Al-Gareeb (2001) found in his study, entitled "Identity Problems between Televised Media and Family Socialization of Arab Child", that when elders in a family watch programmes that are contradictory to what they advise, their children often tend to become hypocrites and liars. This is especially apparent when there is an absence of freedom of expression or the ability to debate opinions within the family. Consequently, such children fail to absorb values that help establish a progressive cultural identity or prevent it from being distorted. In fact, the main causes of incorrect socialization are what allow the screen to occupy the weak spaces and cracks in family relationships. This, in turn, intensifies the distance between children and parents, leading them to adopt behaviours that are contradictory to the values of their society, which are replaced by the values of the screen (Al-Gareeb, 2001).

In his research, Zafer (1991) identifies the following incorrect types of socialization:

- Overprotection

- The establishment of rigid rules that are restrictive to behaviour

- Severe punishment as the only way to enforce respectable behaviour and train children in obedience and discipline

- A child feeling rejected by parents

- Spoiling

- Channels of communication being closed between family members

- Unrealistic expectations of the parents from the child

- Favouring one child over others

- Corrupt role modelling

These inappropriate forms of socialization at an early stage of childhood makes a child unsettled as he/she falls short of compassion, care and the gratification of psychological and social needs, along with receiving inadequate guidance and irresponsible role modelling. Therefore, such a child grows up without a healthy reference to help him/her face the ideological floods and alluring consumerism. The absence of such a point of reference forces the child to establish a substitute reference inspired by the screen (Zafer, 1991), making the Saudi child vulnerable to the penetration of unconventional visual media.

The Concept-Oriented Family Model in Saudi Arabia

Figure 3. The Ideal Saudi Concept-Oriented Family and the Screen

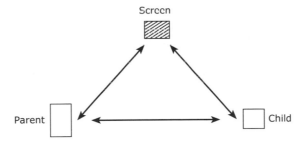

A new model of socializing children with the screen in the Saudi family is needed in order to reform the unhealthy relationship within the family triangle – of parents, children and visual media. A viable and suitable model in the context of Saudi Arabia would be through concept orientation, which relies on critical thinking and analytical assessment. A concept-oriented Saudi family would be a desired alternative to the socio-oriented and laissez-faire families and their approaches to interaction with the screen. In this model, the family would encourage their children to explore and experience, and to express their ideas and feelings, even though they may be controversial or challenging to the conventional beliefs and traditions of the society. This is implemented through an evaluative style during discussions about programmes with family members in order to help them analyze and assess the messages presented on the screen (Gunter & McAleer 1997). For example, the family will enhance the child's understanding of implicit messages as well as the values of visual media and advertising by pointing out the negative aspects presented by the characters. In addition, the concept-oriented family will examine the content of the programmes and explain the difference between reality and fantasy and the detachment of the characters of the screen from the real world (Al-Ofy, 1994). Children in this type of family do not absorb passively like a sponge, but instead 'engage' and 'talk back' to the television set by questioning and challenging the reality and objectivity of what they watch; they are media-literate. The Saudi family that adopts this model will be selective in their viewing, switching on only for particular material rather than out of habit, which in turn influences the child's responses to the medium and results in a higher level of critical awareness (Al-Ofy, 1994, Gunner & McAleer, 1997). Unlike the socio-oriented family, the concept-oriented family viewing is instrumental, goal-directed, purposeful, intentional and selective. In fact, for the concept-oriented family, "parent-child communication patterns are among the most persuasive influences in child socialisation and development. It is not simply the existence of certain rules within the home that matter; the way in which they are applied is equally important" (Gunter & McAleer 1997, 186). Therefore, the sooner the Saudi child learns to select and critically view the screen the better, and this is augmented if the family guidelines for television viewing are in place so that the child will have no problem maintaining them as he/she grows.

A child becomes a discriminating viewer around the age of six months, when he/she develops the cognitive abilities of 'size constancy,' 'shape constancy' and 'object constancy'. Understanding what is seen on television requires all these skills. Therefore, for the concept-oriented family, children of all ages can learn to comprehend and think critically about the way the screen portrays people and their behaviour (Axelrod, 1997). Building on this argument, the concept-oriented family contradicts Piaget's theory of cognitive development, which has remained more tied to the idea of a universal individual who must develop all the way through particular stages before reaching adult maturity (Gauntlett 1998). On the contrary, the concept-oriented family agrees with many experts in child development who state that infants and toddlers learn more than we think they do. They are simply waiting until they have the language skills to let us know. From the concept-oriented family point of view all children are not considered average; they are not even above average. In fact, they are considered geniuses. These children are not born geniuses; their early years were instead characterised by a nurturing family environment in which their parents emphasised intellectual curiosity, hard work and responsibility with a stress on enjoyment of learning.

Therefore, when television comes into the picture, the concept-oriented family uses a clinical eye to place the medium under the magnifying glass to explain the messages of advertising, as well as the subtle – and not so subtle – themes in children's and adults' programmes, which is called critical viewing or media literacy. Actually, the phrase "critical viewing" does not mean condemnation but stands for the diagnosis, analysis, explanation and understanding of information consciously instead of simply receiving or absorbing it. It is only through the skills of critical thinking (which is highly cognitive) that children will become less easily influenced or harmed by the messages they receive from television (Convigton 2004, Kavoori 2004, Buckingham, 2003, Axelrod, 1997). Therefore, the regulation of television by critical viewing begins at home in a concept-oriented family environment.

Critical viewing also refers to the viewer's ability to break the codes involved in the screenplay industry and understand everything that revolves around it in this device. This is not limited to understanding the imbedded content but could exceed it to include understanding the technical secrets of the screen, which means understanding moves and shots associated with the camera and the technology of light, makeup and montage, as well as good comprehension of production and directing. This knowledge does not necessarily mean that the person is scientifically well-informed about these technologies, but he/she possesses fair knowledge of their meaning, performance and significance concerning the work on the screen. Thus, every Saudi family has the ability to be in control as long as it comprehends some of these simple guidelines when dealing with the screen. There are various skills that Saudi parents could acquire to help their children and spare them the negative influences associated with the screen, making the best use of it to enrich their linguistic, behavioural, mental and cognitive skills (Al-Ofy, 1994).

Some of these important skills are:

First: There should be enough awareness of the use of the screen, avoiding it as a method of reward or punishment so as not to give it great significance (Hendi, 1998).

Second: Saudi parents should start with themselves, by acting as role models in terms of limited, selective viewing, as they are the ideal example to whom their children look up. Children of constant, addicted TV and video viewers become addicted themselves, as they learn through imitation and simulation (Al-Gareeb, 2001). The screen is tempting and can easily be controlling, and is the easiest form of activity a child can indulge in. Therefore, it is the Saudi parents' great responsibility to teach their children the significance of causal viewing, and the child should ask him/herself all the time: Why am I viewing this material? What are the advantages I gain from it? What is it trying to tell me? (Al-Ofy, 1994).

217

A good, successful method would be minimizing exposure time through the use of a favourites list from the Internet, or a VCR or DVD to record the intended TV programs, or by referring to printed TV program guides for different channels to specify the times intended programs are aired, thereby committing to viewing only during these times, thereby avoiding the random navigation between channels and websites (Axelrod, 1997).

Spare time should be occupied by significant activities, be they social (like visiting relatives or volunteering in charitable institutes), cultural (like reading or learning to use the computer), artistic (like drawing, painting or handcrafts), athletic (including all kinds of sports) or religious (like getting children into the habit of Islamic manners) (Al-Sherbini & Sadik, 2000).

Third: It is important that Saudi parents speak with their children about the screen and its use. Parents should speak freely with their children about reality and fiction in TV, video games and the Internet, pointing out how different it is from reality. Parents should also be aware of the different kinds of programs such as cartoons, documentaries, fiction and comedy and their respective screen technologies, to provide a realistic assessment. Parents should explain to children the different forms of shooting technologies like different angles, the effects of lighting, character personifying, sound and visual effects and the psychological influences of all these elements together. It is important that parents help children understand the Western origins of the scenes depicted and the purpose behind them.

Take a football game, for example. Many shots are taken of the ball from different angles, as a goal is being scored and the ball hits the net, all to glorify this moment. Another example can be illustrated when the camera shows a person or an object as very small in size, or in a position of weakness from an upper angle view compared to showing a person or an object large in size or in a position of focus and strength from a lower , or when the camera takes a balanced view and the shot is a direct angle right from the front of that person or object.

In addition, children should learn that the camera shows events through different ways in which the viewer is drawn near or taken further away from the character or event shown, according to the distance of the camera:

- There is the *extreme close-up*, in which the focus is on the details of the face or things to highlight or emphasize an idea, a conflict or a condition of nervousness, such as a look of fear.

- There is also the *close-up*, which focuses on one part of the object or one body part of the human being (head/arm/leg), serving the purpose of directing the viewer's attention to this part and creating a situation of sympathy or a bond with the character or object.

- The *medium shot* is usually done inside the studio, and is usually from the head to the waist, which indicates an image of seriousness and significance as well as conveying an objective character (such as for news reporters).

- The *long shot*, which is used to tie the person into the surrounding environment to either attach him/her to the surrounding people or clarify his/her relationship to the place (Hansen et al, 1998, Downes & Miller 1998).

Thus, it is crucial that parents discuss with their children the director's intentions. He may highlight a person's emotional state (e.g., embarrassment) by showing a close-up conveying a negative image of the person, who may in actual life have an honest and stable personality. The camera could also work to show the opposite, showing a hypocritical, cunning character as an honest one by taking distant shots of him while he is talking about embarrassing or disturbing matters, and zooming in on his face when he is asked simple questions that are irrelevant to the difficult situation (Al-Ofy, 1994).

There are some TV formats that do not have an actual counterpart in the real world, and are used to symbolize a transformation in time, place or content, such as zoom in & out, dissolves, fades, and slow & fast motion, which must be explained by parents. There is also the constant change of topics, characters, sounds, scenes and special visual effects associated with shooting tricks and visual illusions, such as fusing two scenes together to become one using chromakey, whereby a green or blue background is replaced by another colour or background. For example, in a scene where Superman is shown in space, the shooting is done with the actor in front of a green background, using chromakey. The green background is then replaced with an image of the sky, so that the actor appears to be flying. This technology is more eye-catching than other known visual effects, such as zoom in and cut, vertical and horizontal moves of the camera, and various sound effects (Axlerod, 1997, Al-Ofy, 1994).

Parents should also explain the impact of the light and colours used to give certain impressions about the characters and objects being shot; these impressions could be either positive or negative. Red, for example, reflects warmth, liveliness and freedom. On the other hand, blue reflects a state of coldness, loneliness and isolation. Likewise, sharp light emphasizes a state of nervousness and anxiety whereas soft light emphasizes a state of relaxation, comfort and quiet (Downes & Miller, 1998).

In addition to the importance of explaining shooting technologies to children, parents should explain the systems in which measures, values and thinking patterns fall and which highlight media messages and the characters presented, and how this influences the viewer. Take, for example, how the villain or terrorist is never an American or European, but is usually dark-skinned – mostly an Arab, Latin American, or a foreigner from a poorer class. Interviewing a group of American students (before Sept. 11), Axelrod found that they viewed "all Arabs as terrorists who don't know any thing about civilization" (Axelrod 1997, 91).

The American screen stresses a strong tie between the lower, non-American classes of human beings and the absence of beauty and lack of morality in them. Thus, the villain or terrorist is a person who does not apply Western capitalism or does not comply with it at all (Al-Ofy, 1994). There is also the concept that poorness is always a synonym for murder and violence, whereas wealth and money are necessarily equivalent to happiness and success (Axelrod, 1997).

On the other hand, the hero could be from a severely poor family, fighting members of the controlling wealthy class and using all possible means to reach his goal by stealing and murdering (Al-Ofy, 1994). This is depicted from the point of view that as long as the purpose is a noble the "needs justify the means" (Axelrod, 1997). Parents should also speak to their children to inculcate an awareness of how the culture of pleasure is encouraged through scenes of illegal, immoral relationships, which the screen promotes without any mention of their negative consequences. There should also be an awareness of the disadvantages of the consumer culture that is encouraged through advertising in clear or hidden messages, conveyed through tricks and psychological deception merely for financial gain (Mander, 1978). Parents should discuss shallow characters constantly personified on the screen, which are usually given larger dimensions than they actually deserve in a manner that makes them decision-makers simply because they are actors, singers or football players, regardless of their actual contribution to their societies (Nasif, 2006, Al-Yahya, 1991).

If such meanings and implications are not explained to the child, he/she will grow up with foreign concepts in his/her mind about beauty, taste, morals and lifestyles taken from formulas and TV codes transmitting the cultural and social patterns from which they originate. Children in general, and Saudi children in particular, are vulnerable to receiving these patterns and images unconsciously (Al-Ofy, 1994), which could lead to a sense of inferiority or false, shallow and destructive values.

Therefore, it is the duty of parents to create awareness in their children by discussing the harmful effects of the culture of pleasure (through illegitimate and immoral relationships) that neglects to mention its negative consequences.

Saudi parents could benefit from the model developed by Thoman & Jolls (2005) in their kit entitled *Literacy for the 21st Century* to start a dialogue with their children about the screen. This is achieved by asking detailed questions regarding any visual media message presented on the screen to create an awareness about its content, form, aims and effects. These questions will help decode the symbol system of the messages that relate to our existing views, experience and conceptions of reality and have a varied effect on the interpretation by different viewers.

1. What makes this message seem real or unreal?

2. How is this message compatible with your lived experience of the world?

3. How are different social groups represented?

4. What social messages are a part of the message's implication?

5. What types of behaviours and consequences are portrayed?

6.   What type of person is the viewer invited to associate with?

7.   What is deleted from the message?

8.   Whose views are represented?

9.   What is the message genre?

10. What techniques are utilized to catch my attention?

11. What conventions of storytelling are used in this message?

12. What sort of visual symbolism is used to form the message?

13. What types of persuasive or emotional allures are used in this message?

14. What technologies were utilized to create this message?

15. How is this message similar to and different from others with related content?

16. Who constructed this message?

17. What is the producer's objective?

18. Who is the target viewer?

19. Who have economic decisions affected the construction of this message?

20. What motives might an individual have for being attracted to this message?

21. How do different people respond psychologically to this message?

22. How might various people interpret this message differently?

Conclusions and Recommendations

Thus, contrary to children in the socio-oriented protective and the laissez-faire families, Saudi children whose parents train them for critical viewing through media education will be more capable of understanding what is on the screen and predicting the time sequence of events. Also, they will be more capable of gaining new cognitive skills from the visual media structure, such as such as using the technique of zooming in and out on a problem situation, decomposing difficult situations into small segments and learning to connect the parts with the whole using the cut-and-paste technique. This is in addition to understanding the process of production as well as understanding the superficial and suspicious values and standards of the screen messages. Furthermore, children in these enlightened types of Saudi families will acquire new vocabulary and knowledge, which will help them to further their scientific and cognitive achievements and develop a constructive personality. Consequently, this will have a clearly positive effect on the healthy development of the society.

Despite the importance of the role of the Saudi family in the socialization of the children for visual media education, it does not reduce the accountability of Saudi society, leaders and policy-makers to prevent and immunize the society against the cultural viruses and detrimental attacks of visual media materials. Saudi society must share with the family the great responsibility of the child's media and cultural socialization. Therefore, we recommend and demand the establishment of media education in the kingdom of Saudi Arabia through:

- Introducing media education as a major at colleges and universities

- Teaching media education at an early stage in school

- Encouraging children to participate in all forms of media production

- Encouraging parents to participate in workshops and courses in media education

- Establishing local, national and international conferences and symposia periodically and enriching research in this field

References

Al-Ofy, A. (1994) TV and Child: What is the Medium and How to Read it?, *King Saud University Journal*, Vol. 6, (2), pp. 617-427.

Al-Gareeb, A. (2001) Identity Problems between Televised Media and Family Socialisation of Arab Child, *Childhood & Development Magazine*, (2): 192-147.

Al-Sherbini, Z. & Sadik, .Y (2000) *Socialisation of Child*. Cairo: Dar Al-Fiker Al-Arabi.

Al-Yahya, T. (1991) *Fingerprints on My Child*. Riyadh: Dar Al-Watan for publication.

Ashi, H. (2003) *Saudi Children's Viewing Interests in the Age of Globalisation: A Case Study in Jeddah*. Unpublished PhD Thesis, Leicester: University of Leicester.

Axelrod, L. (1997) *TV-proof Your Kids*. New Jersey: Carol Publishing Group.

Buckingham, D. (2003) *Media Education: Literacy, Learning and Contemporary Culture*. London: Polity Press.

Convigton Jr., W. (2004) Creativity in Teaching Media Literacy, *International Journal of Instructional Media*, 2004, Vol. 31 (2), pp. 119-124.

Downes, B. & Miller, S. (1998) *Teach Yourself Media Studies*. London: Hodder & Stoughton.

Gauntlett, D. (1998) 10 Things Wrong with the Effect Model, in R. Dickinson, R. Harindranath & O. Linné (Eds.) *Approaches to Audiences: A Reader*. London: Arnold.

Gunter, B. & McAleer, J. (1997) *Children & Television*. London: Routledge.

Hansen, A. et al (1998) *Mass Communication Research Methods*. London: Macmillan Press Ltd.

Hindi, S (1998) *Impact of Mass Media on Child*. Amman: Dar Al-Fiker for Printing, Publication and Distribution.

Kavoori, A. (2004) Critical Media Pedagogy: Lessons from the Thinking Television Projects, *Howard Journal of Communications*, Apr-Jun 2004, Vol. 15 (2), pp. 99-114.

Mander, J. (1978) *Four Arguments for the Elimination of Television*. New York: William Marrow & Company, Inc.

Muhamed, I (1999) *Cultural Invasion in the Media of the Muslim Child Culture: Types and Effects*. Almansura: Dar Al-kalima for publication and Distribution

Nasif, F. (2006) *Muslim Family in the Age of Globalisation*. Jeddah: Dar Al-Adalus Al-Khadra.

Thoman, E. & Jolls, T. (2005) *Literacy for the 21st Century: An Overview & Orientation Guide to Media Literacy Education*. USA: Center for Media Literacy (www.medialit.org)

Zafer, Ahmed (1991) *Some Incorrect Types of Upbringing: Compilation about Juvenile Delinquency*. Tripoli: Al-Adal Publications.

Role of the Family in Forming the Rational Interaction with Mass Media
A Case Study of a Saudi Family

Fathia Al Qurashy

The family is one of the most important educational organizations helping to maintain a society's identity and continuity. There are also other organizations and groups that help to achieve stability and balance in society. At the same time, some kind of non-integration or contradiction among these organizations may emerge. Some contradiction may also emerge between what the family tries to do through the socialization process and what these organizations do.

Mass media of communication play an important role in educating individuals and helping to unify a society and overcome differences between the sub-cultures in it. They may also help to provide a common culture, which helps to control individuals' behaviour and direct them in order to achieve the social and economic developmental goals of the society.

Mass media have come to be one of society's educational organizations. At the same time, it is difficult to control the content of these media. Some try to achieve the commercial objectives of individuals and institutions, which may not take into account a society's ethical criteria and values. Though mass media are expected to form a cultural focus around which individuals gather, to achieve the society's goals, some may present certain content that contradicts its culture and values. In turn this may lead to, and help in encouraging, conflict and non-integration. Even some ideas advocated by mass media may oppose the values of human society as a whole. Therefore, we should admit that mass media may have both positive and negative effects on society (Al Hadeef, 1998: 30-45). These may include:

a. Change of attitudes: this is not only limited to individuals and issues but also includes certain values and behaviour patterns. Hence, the attitude may change from friendly to aggressive and from opposition to acceptance or appreciation.

b. Cognitive change: This is more serious than only changing attitudes. Here, the nature of an individual's perception of life may change. This change may also suggest different tools for success which may vary from reality and common concepts.

c. Socialization: most mass media try to remove certain values and replace them with others. This happens through what the media present in terms of models that may contradict the needs of social and economic life that the family tries to adapt their children to.

d. Emotional excitement: mass media may try to raise unhappy or hateful feelings by concentrating on violence and the irritation of instincts in order to easily lead individuals.

e. Social control: this happens when media try to form unified public opinions and attitudes so that these new opinions and attitudes will become part of societal culture.

f. Forming reality: mass media may intend to portray some aspects of reality and hide others. At the same time, mass media play an important role in forming images and stereotypes of people, situations and other things. The images portrayed by mass media may not be correct, and this leads to a distortion of reality.

g. Change of reality through the appreciation and specific personalities, situations or ideas.

The findings of many studies and analyses have indicated that the mass media have many effects on society, leading behaviour and changing perceptions. Some of these studies may ignore the role of the social surroundings in which the mass media operate. Psycho-sociological theory indicates that individuals' behaviours are not merely reactions, but the result of their capacities for perceiving meaning, symbols and interpretations of realities or situations (Abraham, 1980: 209-210). Most studies do not show the active interaction between individuals and mass media. This rational and active interaction may be availed through the family, which is an important transmitting mediator between the individual and his social and cultural environment (Goode, 1964: 2).

Review of Literature

On the following pages, a review of some relevant studies will be presented.

In a study entitled "Role of Mass Media in Changing Habits and Values in Saudi Society", a sample of (248) persons from a village called Khalees was surveyed. The findings of the survey show that the Saudi radio has, to a great extent, played a role in changing people's attitudes. Radio has linked people with social development and growth, and has also had certain religious, social and educational effects. It was also shown that religious and Islamic programmes presented on Saudi radio represent a suitable frame for changing bad and negative habits and reinforcing good and positive one (Karim, 1985).

In a study on the role of television in changing value structures, a sample of foreign and local children's programmes were analyzed and (200) students were interviewed. The study showed that television has a positive influence in the sense that it develops a child's personality and increases his feeling of citizenship. It also teaches children how to talk and discuss, as well as enlarging their imagination and providing them with useful information. The study results also showed that television also has certain negative influences, such as decreasing children's reading habits and teaching them violence and aggression (Al Kahtany, 1996).

The role of television in socialization was examined in a study relying on content analysis and a survey of a sample of parents in Riyadh. The results show that 78.6% of fathers, 87.4% of mothers and 88.4% of children spend most of their spare time watching television. Entertainment programmes were the most preferred among all family members (Al Shehry, 1986).

Another study was carried out by Al Shamsi (1988) to examine the situation of the child between family values and mass media values. The study concluded that mass media are very dangerous and threaten the society's values. Mass media content also tries to present to the child alternative values to replace his own family's and society's values. These new media values, according to the study findings, are also supported by some of those in charge of media in the Arabic and Islamic worlds (Al Shamsi, 1999).

It was concluded that most of the above studies as well as others on the effect of mass media have ignored two important issues:

- The interaction between children and mass media usually occurs at two levels, quantitative and qualitative. This interaction also happens in social contexts, which also has a great effect in determining the quality of this interaction.

- The family is the most important socialization organization, in its role as a transmitting mediator of the social and cultural effects children are exposed to.

Although the family has lost many of its functions in Saudi society, but it still has a great effect on functions that remain in its domain, e.g. socialization and emotional support for children. The role of the family in these two interconnected functions is very strong. It stems from the family's role as a transmitting mediator of the social and cultural effects its members are exposed to. Therefore, the family's role here is substantial in deciding the kinds of effects its members are exposed to, as well as the nature of interaction between its members and these effects, and their perceptions of these effects. In this respect, there are two kinds of interaction:

227

1. Negative interaction, which occurs between children and mass media. Here, mass media have the upper hand and are more influential.

2. Active interaction, whereby the influence is mutual between the mass media and the individuals. This is a healthy kind of interaction and helps to achieve benefits for the two parties, and consequently achieve its required benefit.

The change in structure of the family's role and busy parents may lead to limited time shared with children. This also affects the role of the family in advising their children and its role in the socialization process in general. This has led to mass media being more influential to children. In other words, the family cannot compete with the mass media here.

Psychological and social theories stress the importance of awareness and perception, stressing that these are our tools for interpreting all we face in our environment. This interpretation of the environment determines how we are influenced by it and our responses to it. These theories assume that the individual is capable of logical interpretation of mattes, which leads to satisfying his benefits. However, the determinants of action may vary from one person to another and from one group to another. Therefore, we expect that the nature of families' perceptions and interpretations of what they receive from mass media varies.

The result is two types of families:

1. Those that not care about the values, habits and traditions of their society. Consequently, these families do not care about perfecting their roles in transferring and maintaining values. They also do not care about what may affect their children's socialization. These families also allow their children to be exposed to all types of effects in their environment, or even effects from outside their own environment, without any observation/control.

2. Those that place a great deal of importance on traditions and social values, and are keen to transfer them to children. These families do their best to remove any obstacles that may obstruct this transferring process. They may also exaggerate this attempt by isolating their children from their social and cultural environment outside the family borders. This may be successful a regards matters and personalities children may interact with, but it is impossible in the case of mass media because they are widespread and have various channels; also, children are exposed to mass media content even at educational institutions, or indirectly through their friends who may tell them about the media content in a more exciting and interesting manner than their family does.

Actual Saudi Models for
Rational Family Interaction with Mass Media

A study was conducted on a purposive sample of Saudi families from Jeddah, the Western province of Saudi Arabia, to learn about the way they deal with mass media and the roles they play. These families were interviewed, and four models were constructed with respect to dealing with mass media. They all include a rational and active interaction between the families and mass media.

These models will be presented with special attention to the characteristics of the family; i.e. socio-economic status, relationship between the parents, relationship with the children. The mothers were also given the chance to describe how they managed to protect their children from the negative influences of mass media.

First Model

The first family contains eight members, and all children perform well at school. They are also religious and pray at the prescribed times. The family's income is average, and both parents have good jobs. The relationship between the parents is stable; they may have their differences but always give priority to their children and do their best to show them a good example. The parents also use different methods in raising their children, but all according to the society's culture and values.

The mother in this family mentioned that television and Internet are only available in the family's common living room. She also controls what the children can watch, by blocking channels that air content that contradicts their culture. At the same time, the children have access to the remote control to use the television, and watch only the channels that match their culture.

When certain programmes or scenes contradict their culture, the mother usually comments and talks to the children about the danger of this kind of content. The mother opposed the introduction of some of the foreign television channels that may be dangerous to the children, from a cultural viewpoint. However, the father may allow some of these channels in response to the children's insistence. Hence, the mother is stricter with regard to the social criteria and values. She always reminds the children about rules, ethics and values, and advises them to pray regularly. The parents in this family have not provided their children with Internet access, so that their time will be used for studies and homework. Internet is allowed only when the children have started at university.

Second Model

The second family has seven members, with parents who were raised in a conservative environment. All children do well in their studies and pray at the appropriate times. The income of the family is average and the parents have average jobs. The relationship between the parents is stable and they agree on many issues and methods with respect to bringing up their children.

The mother indicated that television is available only in the living room. Though it is on all the time during the evening, the parents control what is watched. Channels opposing the culture of their society have been blocked. When some "culturally unaccepted scenes" appear on the screen, the channel is changed immediately. The parents also tend to watch religious programmes and have a common dialogue. The children also take part in housework, as the mother does not like to have a maid help her. The parents have established a bedtime and a time for watching television for the children. Internet is allowed only when the children have started at university. They are also allowed to leave their brothers and sisters during entertainment and fun time to spend time with friends. The family members usually spend the weekends with relatives with whom they share values and a conservative lifestyle.

Third Model

The third family, with five members and a higher socio-economic status, has lived for a long time in Western society. The children do well in their studies and pray at the appropriate times, and in mosques. The parents usually set specific times for watching television, and the children are left on their own one day a week to watch whatever they want. The television is in the living room only. The parents care about their children's welfare and have frequent talks with them. The only television channels allowed are those that do not air any programmes that may contradict their culture and social norms. The children are not allowed to play games that involve gambling, or to play videogames. The parents are serious with regard to their children reading and memorizing the Holy Koran. The children are also not allowed to socialize with other children from outside their immediate family and other relatives.

The internet was allowed at home early, but the children must use it in the open and are not allowed to keep their passwords secret from their parents. The mother is also against the idea of making many mass media available to children.

Fourth Model

The fourth family consists of eight members and is very conservative, and the father is unemployed. The family is supported by income from the oldest daughter, who works. The children are all doing well in their studies and pray at the appropriate times. The parents use a wide range of good educational methods in bringing up their children such as encouraging, giving examples, telling stories and giving direct instructions. The family has only local television channels with no DS TV, and they have a video-game console for. The children help with housework, have access to the Internet only for educational purposes, and are not allowed to go out.

Though the above number of models for rationally dealing with mass media was limited, they reflect the fact that there is a great deal of concern for children's dealing with mass media. A family's protection of its children from mass media content varies from one situation to another, but in all models various educational methods were used. Parents were also in agreement that they should control their children's exposure to mass media. The families also placed restrictions on their children's socializing with others besides their relatives and immediate family. Mothers were stricter than fathers with respect to their commitment to social, religious and cultural norms and values. This led to more protective roles of mothers than fathers for the well being of the family and the sake of the children. It also seems that preventing children from going out with their friends outside school is another protective role that families play.

From the models presented above, one may also conclude that the mothers are more attached to their culture than the fathers are. This may be due to the way women are socialized in Saudi society. Girls are not allowed to do what most boys are, due to the cultural restrictions, especially regarding outdoor activities. As a consequence, mothers try to apply the same rules they lived by, or were socialized to, on their children.

Discussion and Conclusion

According to the concept of interaction, and in the light of having a number of studies, we saw that some families interact with mass media very rationally and are therefore not affected by the negative content of mass media. It was also noted that these kinds of families usually have children who do well in school. This high achievement at school also contributes to the rational and active interaction with mass media.

Here we must be clear about the active and rational interaction with mass media. Certain dimensions indicate the rational and active interaction of families and children with mass media. These indicators act together, completing each other, and will be discussed in the following lines.

1. It must be acknowledged that there are both negative and positive aspects of the exposure to mass media. Some families see that mass media have some negative content that have negative effects on those who are exposed to it. In this respect they refer to televised violence. This also leads to the waste of children's time, which could be otherwise used in a better manner. There is also no doubt that mass media may play a vital role in teaching children and educating them about good value. Mass media also, through their wide spread, can present children

with good examples in life. Parents' awareness of the effects of mass media may also help them educate their children on how to deal with mass media and use their content in the light of social and cultural norms in society.

2. It is important to realize that it is impossible to completely isolate children from the exposure to mass media. Mass media have become numerous and various. It is not possible to imagine any house without mass media, which has become very important even for work and education. Mass media also use many exciting methods that make them more interesting and appealing than other methods. They have thus become, as some say, "harm which is necessary" (Al Askary, 2002: 153-199). This requires a dialogue between parents and their children, and the development of critical thinking to resist what children may face in negative mass media content. At the same time, there is a need to watch and observe what children see in mass media (Al Sherbeeny, 2003: 152).

3. It is also vital to realize the importance of using necessary and complementary educational methods to avoid negative effects of mass media on children. Mass media's sharing role with families in directing and educating children may cause problems for the family's role in the socialization process, especially if there is a contradiction between what the family and the mass media say. This is sometimes a tough competition, as the mass media have many methods and ways of persuasion at their disposal while families may ignore some of the important indirect educational methods (Ramadan, 1995: 34) such as giving examples, telling stories, allowing for fun and entertainment, and showing religious responsibilities and advice for using the mind and thinking (Al Halawany, 1983: 18). These indirect educational methods are as important as direct methods, such as punishment. In other words, families must use all the different methods to direct and guide their children. Without a combination of methods, the family cannot cultivate values in their children (Al Samalouty, 1980: 137-151).

4. There must be an agreement between parents on their view of mass media and how to deal with them. The stability of the family enables it to carry out its functions in a favourable and supportive environment. Different views are one of the main sources of problems inside families, especially problems related to the raising of children and the techniques used. Continuity is one important characteristic of the family that distinguishes it from mass media. However, differences in opinion between parents about the mass media and different channels to allow children to watch, as well as how to deal with mass media, may lead to a vague situation. Conversely, parents' agreement on matters related to mass media helps them to guide their children and to engage the children more in the social and cultural norms and values of society. This also leads to a situation in which children exercise some kind of self-censorship without any interference from their parents and therefore will not be affected by negative content in mass media (Meky, 2007: 138-142).

At the same time, parents' awareness and appreciation of the negative and positive effects of mass media and the impossibility of avoiding it reinforce their dealing with it. There is also no doubt that their use of different and various educational techniques in bringing up their children unifies their attitude towards these media. It also leads to a rational and active interaction with mass media, which helps to reinforce the family's techniques in socialization and achieve its goals. At the same time, it helps to avoid what may contradict the values and goals of the family and society as a whole (Basem, 1989: 117-139).

5. It is important to provide children with sufficient emotional support to complement the socialization process. The family remains the source that is expected to provide all emotional support, and consequently the care for different psychological, cognitive and physical needs of the family members. Many studies about the exposure to mass media have shown that audiences seek mass media to gratify certain declared or undeclared desires such as information seeking, entertainment, social interaction and identity determination (Al Hadeef, 1998: 26-27). Gratification of these kinds of needs require that the family recognize their children's needs. It is also important to consider the individual differences among children, and to note that a family's lifestyle also mediates the influences of mass media on children. Mass media may make use of social and economic circumstances to present the solution to specific problems and give people what they are lacking, therefore increasing their influence on children (Al Hadeef, 1998, 52-53).

As the protection of children and ensuring their safety comprises one vital role of the family, it must protect children from any fears or dangers they may experience from the exposure to mass media. The family may also prevent children from watching certain programmes that may have negative effects on them.

6. All content that may oppose the religious and social values and human ethical rules, whether in local or international media, should be resisted. Each society has its own main culture as well as sub-cultures. Human societies have been distinguished from all other communities by the existence of cultural rules that control and guide behaviour to achieve the continuity, stability and development of these societies. Because of differences among families with respect to their abilities to minimize the threatening influences of mass media, it is possible that the mass media content will have some direct or indirect influence on individuals and societies.

When the content of mass media conflict with the culture and the religion of a society, they are threatening and negative. Three important issues must be well protected, in Saudi society as well as in other Arab and Islamic societies, i.e. self, money and dignity. Any mass media materials that are in conflict with the above three items are negative and must be avoided. Therefore, it is important to have some kind of rational and active interaction with mass media. It is also important to be selective in dealing with media content.

To conclude, it is recommended that mass media content should not violate a society's cultural and religious rules and values. The Saudi society has its own particularities, with religion playing an important role. Therefore, any media content that does not match the religious rules is considered unwelcome by many, especially the socialization agents in society. At the same time, there is a need to encourage individuals and families to take part in the production of messages transmitted through the mass media, as socialization and education are to some extent a joint responsibility between mass media and the family. The family must also be aware of its responsibility and be a well informed mediator that mediates the effects and influences of mass media, so that it can carry out its functions together with all other socializing organizations in the society.

References

Abraham, Francis M. (1980) *Modern Sociological Theory: An Introduction*. Delhi: Oxford Press.

Basem, S. (1989) Role of Perception in Determining Societal Problems, *Magazine of Social Sciences*, Vol. 17, No. 1, pp. 117-138.

Goode, W. (1964) *The Family*. New Jersey: Prentice-Hall, Inc., Englewood Cliffs.

Karyim, Badur Ahmed (1985) *The Role of Radio In Changing Habits and Values in Saudi Society*, A Dissertation Submitted to Sociology Department, as part of the requirement for the Master degree, in King Abdul Azeez University, Jeddah (293).

Al Askary, S. (2002) *Values and Mass Media*. Beirut: Dar El Jeel.

Al Hadeef, M.A. (1998) *How Mass Media Affect: A Study on Theories and Techniques*. Riyadh: EL Obikan Print House.

Al Halawany, F. (1983) *A critical Study for the Recent Educational Techniques within Islam*. Jeddah: Tehama.

Al Qahtany, Fawzyah (1996) *Television and the Change of Values Structure: A Study of the Mental Image Making of the Social Visions for Children and its Social Implications*, Dissertation Submitted to Sociology Department, as part of the requirement for the Master degree, King Abdul Azeez University.

AL Samalouty, N.M. (1980) *The Islamic Approach to the Study of Society*. Jeddah: Dar El Shrouk.

Al Shamsi, Ibraheem Ahmed (1999) *The Child between family Values and Media Values*, unpublished paper presented in Al Sharja university, United Arab Emirates, April, 1999, http://www.shomooos.com.

AL Sherbeeny, Z. & Yusriayh Sadek (2003) *Socialization of the Child and Role of Parents in Solving Problems*. Cairo: Dar El Fekr El Araby.

Ramadan, K. (1995) *Common Types of Socialization in the Arab World*. Qatar: Faculty of Education.

Al Shehry, H.S. (1986) *Television and Family Socialization*. Unpublished MA Thesis, Riyadh: King Saoud University.

Meky, A.M. (2007) *Dynamic of the Family in the Age of Globalization*. Beirut: Arabi Association for Publishing and Distribution.

Media Education
International Strategies

Cary Bazalgette

I have worked in the field of media education for over thirty years, most of it in both national and international contexts, so probably the most useful contribution I can make to this discussion is to share some of the insights I've gained over that time.

My salary at the British Film Institute was always paid by the British taxpayer, so the main focus of my work was on how to develop media education in a national context. That's been a long struggle and it still continues, although there have been some gains: about 6 per cent of our 14-19 age group take optional courses in media or film studies, and increasing numbers of schools and local education authorities are making a commitment to media education as part of literacy for the 5-14 age group.

In the international context, my first experience of discussing media education in was in Lausanne in 1988. Since then, I've spoken at about 36 conferences in 20 countries on five continents. I've also helped to organise two international conferences on media education – together with other colleagues, some of whom are also here. The Toulouse conference in 1990, New Directions in Media Education, was a global conference – it was attended by 145 delegates from 45 countries, including Egypt and Jordan – and it was supported by UNESCO and the Council of Europe. In 2004, the Belfast conference on Media Education in Europe was supported by the European Commission and welcomed 105 delegates from 23 countries.

All in all, that constitutes a pretty disgraceful contribution to global warming, so what can I offer to justify it all? What's driven all this work has been the idea that media education ought to be an entitlement for everyone, from the earliest years of schooling. I've been particularly interested throughout my professional life in children's access to media education – and by "children" I don't mean legal definitions, but simply people who are prepared to think of themselves as children – that is, people younger than about 12. But of course media education should also continue throughout life. That idea of general entitlement paraphrases declarations made by UNESCO in January 1982 and by the Council of Europe Standing Conference of Ministers of Education in October 1989. What it actually means is another issue that I'll come to later. So I would like to offer six "test questions" for application to any proposals for an international strategy, which could help to test its likely effectiveness in securing a general entitlement to media education for all learners.

To start with, I want to issue a sort of "health warning" in relation to anything we discuss today. It is this: any strategies for media education, national or international, need to be subject to one essential reality check from the outset, which is, *"who benefits?"* There is one right answer to that question, and a lot of wrong ones. The right answer is, "learners". If a project does not in the end benefit learners, then it needs some serious reconsideration. And although benefits can very often be indirect, and the learner may be an "end-user" several stops down the line, there has to be a demonstrable benefit in terms of real learning outcomes, from any project, proposal or initiative. One example of a strategy that couldn't do this is the idea that I've seen floated in the UK and also at European level, that media education should aim to maximise audiences for media products. That's not a legitimate aim for an education strategy, because the beneficiaries are media producers, not learners.

Secondly – and I know this is just stating the obvious but it probably needs reiterating nevertheless – media education is the responsibility of national governments, not international bodies. It is not like international trade or warfare or environmental damage: it takes place inside cultures and societies, and is subject to national needs and expectations. At an international level we can make all the declarations we like, but national governments don't have to take any notice of them and on the whole they don't. What governments do take notice of in the international sphere are things like the PISA survey which provides comparative evidence from different countries about the achievements of 15-year-olds: this is useful to governments because it provides something beyond what they can do at a national level. So for example credible evidence about the specific benefits of media education in an international study of learning outcomes probably would be of interest to at least some national education ministries. So I think the second test question we have to apply to any international strategy is "what does it offer that can't be provided at national level?" This is often expressed as *"what's the added value?"*

One of the things I discovered as an organiser of international conferences is how easy it is to get academics to attend and how difficult it is to get anyone else to attend. University staff are expected to participate in international networks and gatherings, to read papers at conferences and to publish articles and books about their work. The academic industry is built on these expectations, and career development depends upon it. Therefore, international projects and conferences in any area of education – and media education is no exception – are inevitably dominated by academics. Of course, it is very important and

236

useful for academic researchers in this field to exchange their knowledge and theories, and to provide evidence to educators and to policy-makers about the value of media education and what best practice looks like.

But I would also argue that, as an international strategy for the development of media education, academic networking is not enough. We have to find ways of extending the international dialogue to the people who are closer to the everyday experience of teaching and learning, and that means classroom teachers and students. Too often, it's teachers rather than learners who are regarded as the "end-users" in international education projects: people who need to be told what to do and to wake up to the realities of the media age. It's true that teacher training is an important factor in the development of media education and I'll come back to that later. But let's not forget that we have a huge amount to learn from schoolteachers and from learners – they can and should be on the platform at our conferences.

Most of my thinking on the topic has been developed in collaboration with teachers – and best of all, with teachers in classrooms with children, as well as being able to reflect on that experience with them. This is particularly important in media education because it is still so new for most teachers and children, and because the media themselves are changing so rapidly. We should not be making simple assumptions about what children know, what their responses are to specific aspects of the media, and what their media skills are: we need constantly to review this. So my third test question is, *"who's involved?"* I don't believe that purely top-down or single-sector initiatives work as well as those which encourage education professionals to think outside the box, move outside their comfort zones, and work together with people in other sectors. I think maybe I'm particularly aware of this because I've always found myself trying to work across two, three or even four different sectors – academic, bureaucratic, education and media – and I've seen how difficult and frustrating it can be, but also how productive it can be as well.

There are enormous pressures on all of us who are struggling for large-scale change, to keep our ideas simple. It's much more attractive, particularly to funders, to be able to offer a single clear idea: a website, a teaching resource (such as a textbook, a DVD, a curriculum outline), or a training programme. But the uncomfortable truth is that single-strand initiatives aren't very effective. It feels satisfying to produce a teaching resource: it looks impressive, it weighs satisfactorily heavy in the hand or sparkles beautifully on the computer screen – but what happens to it? My original role at the BFI was to develop teaching resources, and I've learned this the hard way: teaching resources by themselves achieve very little. They have to be supported by training programmes – and there has to be some kind of structured incentive for teachers to attend such programmes.

Another simple goal that people imagine as very important – I know I did for quite a while – is getting media education inscribed into the curriculum. On the other hand, training programmes by themselves likewise don't achieve very much unless they are supported by resources. And none of these things has much credibility unless the initiative includes objective, independent evaluation of the learning outcomes achieved. Lots of national curricula all over the world have requirements for media education written into them – but unless these are supported by resources, training and assessment, the only people who take any notice of them are isolated enthusiasts. The Canadians made much of the fact that they had substantial media education requirements written into the curricula of several provinces – but no thinking had gone into the provision of initial teacher training, the allocation of school budgets, or the assessment of outcomes. So very little work actually took place in the schools – and it was easy for new political regimes to take the requirements out again. The basic problem with simple initiatives like these is that they are not strategic: strategies are essentially multi-stranded. The development of new initiatives in education is a complex process, and strategies have to address that complexity. So my fourth test question is, *"is it strategic?"* At the very least, and attempt at direct intervention in teaching and learning has to combine the three strands of resources, training and evaluation – any one of these on its own will fail.

One of the commonest – and most obnoxious – tendencies in media education these days is the high-profile creative project. Lots of money is constantly being poured into initiatives that enable groups of children and youth to make media products, usually films. They get their hands on some wonderful equipment; often they get important media professionals to show them how to do it; the film gets shown in festivals and wildly applauded by everyone from friends and family to celebrities who are delighted to be seen endorsing such obviously worthwhile activity. And then what? Let's consider what those children have actually learned. If – as is usually the case – this is their first experience of filmmaking, a great deal of what they have done has been done without a very clear sense – on the children's part – of what the outcome will be. It's hard for children making a storyboard or creating models for animation, to understand quite how this contributes to the finished product. And in a very large number of cases, the children get excluded from the most creative part of the process, which is editing the film (this is usually on the basis that it is too boring for them, although the real reason is that it is too hard or too expensive for the organisers to manage). So it is only when the final product is actually seen, that the children involved really understand what it is that they have done. So they are then ready to start real filmmaking, that is, embarking on a project where they know in advance what the process involves and where the creative decisions are made. But by then it's too late! The project is over, the funding has all been used up, and the circus has left town – but the children's real long term interests as learners have been ignored.

Of course it is very tempting to get drawn into these kinds of project, because it's usually one of the easiest things to get funded, and it's a quick way to get a high profile for media education. But if we apply our first test question about the real benefits to learners, we have to recognise that these are pretty limited.

So my fifth test question is, *"is it sustainable?"* Are we talking about a project or an initiative that will enable learners to go on learning? Is there a legacy, in the form of trained people, investment in equipment, evaluative evidence, and policy commitment, that will enable learners to revisit their media education experiences and take them further? If not, is it worth bothering with?

Now I come to my last test question. This conference has demonstrated that there are not one but many different versions of media education being debated. This is confusing and annoying to policy-makers: they need a clear message on which to act. However, in an international context we cannot expect to have a single definition that prescribes educational content, because our cultural contexts differ widely and our ideas about appropriateness and moral standards differ as well. What we can do is agree more generic standards that can apply to educational provision in different cultural contexts, and that go beyond the unrealistic idea that media education can be simply about "protecting children from bad media".

Let me suggest that media education – whatever its content – should always include three integrated strands of learning. Two have been discussed here:

* The acquisition of *critical* tools for analysis of the media, and

* The development of *creative* skills in making media.

But there is a third strand, without which the first two cannot be effective. This is the need for learners to broaden their *cultural* experiences of the media. In our eagerness to accuse the media of bad influences, we forget that they also offer us fantastic opportunities to recognise and enhance our common humanity. Let us not forget this! We must make sure that our children have the chance to see media that they may not find in the mainstream channels – but that do exist and can be found. In a worldwide context there are films, TV programmes, blogs and websites that offer us amazing possibilities for intercultural understanding, for profound moral insights, for brave journalism and for democratic participation. We have to ensure that children get access to these and that they grow up with high expectations of what the media ought to be able to achieve, not with suspicion and cynicism.

As these three strands – in English anyway – all start with a "C", we can call them the "three C's" and ask of any international strategy whether it would embrace and enable learning *by engaging with all three C's.*

So there we have our six test questions for any strategic international initiative or intervention:

* *who benefits?*

* *what's the added value?*

* *who's involved?*

* *is it strategic?*

- *is it sustainable?*

- *does it engage with the 'three C's'?*

These questions are not culturally specific. They would be just as pertinent in Islamic cultures as in any other, because they are grounded in the universal practicalities of managing change and developing good educational provision.

As a kind of coda to these questions, I would like to offer the Charter for Media Literacy as a strategy that might offer some help towards the evolution of international activity that is more joined up and is more sensitive to these six questions.

The Charter evolved out of many earlier attempts to set up a European network for media educators, all of which foundered on the impossibility of growing such a network within the limited time span of most funding provision, and the expense of creating a bureaucracy that could support a membership organization. You can find out more about the evolution of the Charter on its website, www.euromedialiteracy.eu, and in two forthcoming articles which are cited below. Essentially, the Charter offers a definition of media literacy as a set of outcomes, not as content or pedagogy, and thus inherently more likely to win agreement. It also stipulates the "three Cs" as essential strands of education for media literacy.

I am not going to make any extravagant claims for the Charter. The aim of the group who set it up is simply to try and provide a focal point for consensus around an agreed definition, and to demonstrate that consensus in concrete terms by providing a website to collect Charter signatories. What we hope for in the longer term is that this website can start to function as a networking service: but this can only happen if Charter signatories decide that it is useful and worthwhile for them to publish their media education plans on the site and to enter into dialogue with others. Will this happen? I don't know – we have to wait and see!

References

Bachmair, B and Bazalgette, C. (2007) 'The European Charter for Media Literacy: meaning and potential' in *Research in Comparative and International Education* (RCIE) at www.wwwords. co.uk/RCIE (forthcoming).

Bazalgette, C., Bevort, E. and Savino, J. (Eds.) (1992) *New Directions: Media Education Worldwide*, London: BFI and Paris: CLEMI: papers emerging from the first global conference on media education held in Toulouse, France, July 1990, with support from UNESCO.

Bazalgette, Cary (2007) 'The European Charter for Media Literacy', *Revista Comunicar* no 24 (forthcoming)

Council of Europe: the 16th session of the Standing Conference of European Ministers of Education, Istanbul, 11-12 October 1989, in its "Resolution on the Information Society: A Challenge for Education Policies?" clause 5, declared that "media education should begin as early as possible and continue throughout schooling" see http://www.coe.int/t/e/cultural_co-operation/education/standing_conferences/j.26thsessionistanbul1989.asp#TopOfPage.

European Charter for Media Literacy: see www.euromedialiteracy.eu.

Media-educ (2004) *Media Education in Europe* (CD ROM report of the international conference, Belfast, 13-14-15 May 2004)

PISA: OECD Programme for International Student Assessment which surveys 15-year-olds in the principal industrialised countries on a three-year rolling programme – see http://www.pisa.oecd.org/pages/0,2987,en_32252351_32235731_1_1_1_1_1,00.htm

UNESCO Declaration on Media Education – issued unanimously by the representatives of 19 nations at UNESCO's International Symposium of Media Education at Grünwald, Federal Republic of Germany, 22nd January 1982. see Len Masterman (1985) *Teaching the Media,* London: Comedia, Appendix C, pp 340-341.

VI. Media Literacy in Practice

Transforming Literacy

Cary Bazalgette

Literacy is more than the ability to read and write. It is the repertoire of knowledge, understanding and skills that enables us all to participate in social, cultural and political life. Obviously this repertoire now has to include the ability to "read" and "write" in media other than print: in moving images and audio, and in the hypertext structures of the digital world.

Since 1999 the British Film Institute has been pioneering a new approach to literacy, using short but powerful films as "texts" for classroom study. This approach has been taken up by 60 of the 147 local authorities in England, and forms the basis of important developmental projects in Scotland and Northern Ireland. Over 1000 teachers have so far been trained to teach about film as part of literacy, many of them through the BFI's "lead practitioner" scheme, which has helped local authorities to establish programmes for the development of moving image media literacy in their schools.

This initiative has met with huge enthusiasm in schools. Literacy consultants and advisers believe that it is having a significant impact on literacy standards and children's overall achievement and motivation, as well as providing children with enjoyable and important new cultural experiences. The time has come for this activity to be "scaled up" as a substantial project with rigorous evaluation. This would establish robust evidence about the distinctive learning outcomes associated with film-based work, and build confidence at national policy level about the ways in which such work can raise standards in schools.

Film and Print – What's the Link?

Four- and five-year-old children arrive in school with a lot of experience of moving image media. Many have TV sets and DVD players in their bedrooms, and their own collections of their favourite films and programmes. Through this experience, they have gained some understanding of concepts like narrative, genre, character, setting and time, even if they can't express them very clearly.

Teachers are usually wary of children's enthusiasm for film and TV. They assume it discourages children from learning to read, and limits their spoken language. But research shows that film and TV viewing can actually help children learn to read, by developing skills like inference and prediction, which are essential to comprehension.[1] This is why it makes sense to integrate the viewing and discussion of films into literacy learning, so that young children can be helped to articulate what they already know about "texts" (whether audio-visual or verbal) and understand how this knowledge underpins the world of print media as well.

"Not Just any Film"

What sort of films can be viewed and discussed in the short time-scale of classroom sessions? 90-minute feature films are obviously too long, and using short clips defeats the object of the exercise, which is to understand how complete narrative structures work, or how characters develop over the course of a whole story. The obvious answer is to use short films.

Good short films are more like poems than novels: intense, densely textured, and often open to many levels of interpretation. Because short films have limited appeal in the commercial marketplace and are funded from diverse sources, they often have little or no dialogue so that they can be easily sold to different countries. They can therefore offer intensely "filmic" experiences, using images and movement, sequence and duration, sound and music to tell their stories.

It is part of the BFI's job to encourage people to see films other than the commercial mainstream. Film is a distinctive medium in its own right, with its own multimodal language that people from all cultures can understand, and a rich history stretching back more than 100 years. So when the National Literacy Strategy[2] approached the BFI in 1999 to help them consider the relationship between print and moving image media, this seemed an opportunity to produce resources for schools that would not only support literacy learning, but would provide children with completely new film viewing experiences. It is not however easy to find short films suitable for children that are rich enough to reward repeated viewing and close analysis: a huge amount of research, previewing and discussion with teachers went on to produce each resource.

The "Shorts" Resources

The BFI first "shorts" resource was *Story Shorts*, published in 2002 for Key Stage 2 children (aged 7-11). It includes five short films (four animated, one live action) and a substantial teachers' book, developed in collaboration with teachers and pupils in 35 schools. This was followed by *Starting Stories* for Early Years and

Key Stage 1 (aged 3-7), and then by *Screening Shorts* for Key Stage 3 (ages 11-14). *Moving Shorts* and *Real Shorts* for KS 3 and 4 (ages 14-16), *Starting Stories 2* and *Story Shorts 2* are all being published during 2006-07.[3]

The National Literacy Strategy was excited by the first two resources and bought copies for all local authorities in England. In-service training was provided to teachers across the UK, and interest started to grow. The publication of the United Kingdom Literacy Association report, *Raising Achievement in Boys' Writing,* endorsed the use of film, and this was a starting-point for many of the teachers using the resources.[4]

More than Just a Stimulus

In the first two years of the "shorts" initiative, take-up was slow, despite ecstatic reviews and enthusiastic promotion by the National Strategies. Some big barriers stand in the way of teachers using film in literacy teaching. First of all, film has lower status than books in British culture. The predominant perception of film in the UK is the Hollywood blockbuster: glamorous, entertaining, industrially produced, predictable and easy to understand – nothing to do with the kinds of learning that are supposed to go on in school. The idea that film has a distinctive "language" that has its own rules and complexities and can be learned about, is surprising or daunting to most teachers. But because children like films, teachers are happy to recognise their potential as a stimulus in the classroom: a starting point for the "proper work" of reading and writing.

Teachers find it very hard to get beyond this into a deeper understanding of how film and print texts actually share key features, and how literacy teaching can be enhanced and extended through a direct study of films as texts in their own right. Most teachers have very little access to non-mainstream films and so have no expectation that films could be offering a powerful challenge and a stimulus to children's analytical skills, rather than just to their emotions.

The BFI Lead Practitioner Scheme

In 2004 the BFI embarked on a new initiative to establish film more securely within literacy teaching. Encouraged by the National Strategies, they decided to try and develop a nationwide Lead Practitioner scheme that would build a stronger, infrastructural basis for the development of film study within literacy, using Local Authorities' own finance. They offered all Local Authorities (LAs) the chance to nominate advisers, consultants or leading literacy teachers working in Early Years and Key Stages 1-3, to receive training from the BFI and to lead the realisation of local action plans for moving image media education. 77 (ie more than half) of the LAs in England expressed interest in the scheme, and 60 have so far agreed to pay for between two and six places each on one of the five three day residential training workshops that the BFI provided through 2005-06. These workshops provided an intensive experience in both film analysis and in creative work with moving images – using computers and editing software, not cameras.

Key Insights

Teachers working with the BFI resources have discovered two important new insights into children's capacity to learn about texts:

- Children's pre-school encounters with audiovisual media mean that by school age their ability to analyse and talk about moving image media is much more sophisticated than their ability to analyse and talk about written texts.

- As a consequence, they are capable of engaging with moving image texts that are much more complex and challenging than the books they are beginning to read.

In other words, children are being patronised and under-stimulated by much of the moving image material they encounter in everyday viewing and film-going. Their responses to the films in the BFI resources have been extraordinary: excitement, fascination, increased concentration and motivation are constantly reported by teachers, together with demands to see the films again and again. Teachers also claim that pupils gain increased vocabulary, confidence and ability to both speak and write much more extensively.

Many teachers also became excited about the possibilities for creative work with moving images, using a range of software including animation and PowerPoint packages, and drawing on techniques from drama and music. From this work emerged the realisation that creative activity in moving images is greatly enhanced if children also have opportunities to see and discuss films. There are thus three key dimensions of moving image media learning:

- Cultural: the opportunity to see and discuss a wider range of films

- Critical: the acquisition of analytical techniques

- Creative: the chance to play and experiment with moving images as a way of expressing ideas and stories.

Next Steps

The BFI Lead Practitioners have returned to their local authorities fired with enthusiasm for training others, for creating and circulating schemes of work, and for integrating film with other new approaches to literacy. Many LAs have built film work into their forward planning: over £750,000 in total has been committed by the LAs involved. The BFI Shorts Initiative is being evaluated by

Dr Jackie Marsh of the University of Sheffield and Dr Eve Bearne of the United Kingdom Literacy Association. Their report will appear later in 2007. But their interim report already states that

> The BFI should seek funding from the Department for Education and Skills (DfES) for an extension of this scheme. Given its early successes, despite limited funding, it is clear that the properly-funded extension of the scheme would have a significant impact on moving image education from Foundation Stage to Key Stage 3 in England. (Interim recommendations, page 6)

The problem now faced by the BFI is that, as a relatively small and poorly-funded organisation, it cannot continue to provide the staffing resource to meet the heavy demand generated by the success of this scheme. So it has to find an exit strategy that will enable the scheme to continue developing, probably by bringing in other partners. Given that the BFI is already in receipt of Government funding, a bid for further finance on the lines suggested by Marsh and Bearne could be more effective if it came from an independent consortium.

Wider Implications

The key lesson of this initiative for media educators is that media education initiatives can be more successful if they are based on positive gains for children in terms of their cultural experiences and their competence as communicators. The initiative also constructs media education as an integral part of literacy, rather than as an additional, separate "literacy". The "fit" with traditional literacy is enhanced by the project's belief in the cultural value of film, rather than presenting the media as a potential danger or threat. The BFI believes that "protectionist" approaches to media are a poor educational strategy because of their implied negative view of the media. Media education ought to inculcate high expectations of what the media can achieve, rather than suspicions about what they might inflict. With this as a starting-point, children can go on to develop critical skills in media analysis and identify problems such as stereotyping and bias, but can also imagine possibilities for change.

Notes

1. See Paul W. van den Broek (2001) "The Role of Television Viewing in the development of Reading Comprehension" at http://www.ciera.org/library/archive/2001-02/04OCT99-58-MSarchive. html and Paul W. van den Broek et al (2005) "Assessment of Comprehension Abilities in Young Children" in S. Paris and S. Stahl (eds) *New Directions in Assessment of Reading Comprehension* (pp 107-130) Mahwah: Erlbaum (in press).
2. The National Literacy Strategy has now evolved into part of the Primary National Strategy; for the new framework for primary literacy, see http://www.standards.dfes.gov.uk/primaryframeworks.

3. For details of the BFI resources go to www.bfi.org.uk/education/resources.
4. UKLA Research Papers (2005) "Raising Achievement in Boys' Writing" can be ordered online from http://www.ukla.org/journals_publications/buy_books_online.php?ProdID=0000093.

Teaching about Media
Media Education, Learning, and Literacy:
Sketching a Dialogic Process

Sanjay Asthana

The following two initiatives from India, organised in terms of specific media, through a series of sketches and vignettes, explore how young people learn and develop innovative uses of media in diverse socio-cultural settings. In the Cybermohalla project, youngsters work with a range of digital media and produce experimental digital works, computer animation, write texts using graphics publish wall magazines, edit books, etc. The main aim is to give a forum where the youngsters not only explore their creativity, but also comment on the social and moral topics that impact their lives. *Mapping the Neighbourhood* is conceptualized as an alternative learning experience through the use of ICT and community maps in the learning process and is based on participatory learning and collection of relevant information of the locality. Throughout this exploration a fine balance has been attempted between theory and practice as young people's voices – dialogue and deliberations – are articulated. Young people gain access to tools of media production in a variety of ways; from training and imparting basic to advanced technical skills, using production facilities and equipment to learning about script writing, story boarding, lighting, set design, page design, layout, digital graphics, and computers. The acquisition of media-making, knowledge and skills, embedded in the lived experience of young people, offers unique perspectives, a vision and a voice that need to be examined to understand youth participation in media. More importantly, these are instances of teaching and learning about the media.

New Media Explorations

That increasing technological convergence and innovations are reshaping the media in content creation and distribution is a point that we need not belabor. Indeed, this publication itself is an outcome of some of the developments in images graphics and book design. Print, electronic and digital forms overlap and become simultaneously available, thereby providing an interesting mélange of older information and communication technologies (ICTs) with the newer ones. The emergence of computers, Internet, the World Wide Web, and various mobile communication devices has raised optimism among developmental agencies and media education practitioners. There are two responses: one celebratory and euphoric and the other cautious, but optimistic. UNESCO has been engaged in developing policies and programmes that are cautious and optimistic. Consequently, questions are asked and discussions carried-out on the transformative potential of these emergent ICTs for children and young people. In this context, it is appropriate to ask whether these technologies could enable enhanced participation and help overcome barriers to education. In what ways, if at all, children and young people interact with these technologies? In the following chapter, I looked at two initiatives from India where children and young people are exploring new media technologies for informal learning and personal development.

ICTs and the Learning Experience

Cybermohalla (Cyber-Neighbourhood) is an experimental project designed to enable democratic access to information and communication technologies among poor young women and men in Delhi, India. These young participants (ages of 15 and 23), mostly school dropouts visit the Compughar (literally, a house of computers, in Hindi), a media lab with several low-cost desktop computers and free software, to freely express their ideas and imaginations from the mundane to the serious. Working at the media lab these participants write, draw and sketch a range of interesting verbal and visual narratives and texts published as books, diaries, magazines, and wallpaper that become available in print as well as digitized formats. The following account describes the philosophy of the project:

One can approach the Cybermohalla project from many directions. One can begin with a critique of the technological imagination and the excessive universe of the dominant mediascape, and then go on to map a counter strategy which grounds itself on access, sharing and democratic extensibility. One can see it as an experiment to engage with media technologies and software 'tactically', and create multiple local media contexts emerging within the larger media network that the Internet seems to engender. Still one can see it as an engagement with local history, experiences, modes of expressions and creativity (http://www.sarai. net/community/saraicomm.htm).

From this description, it is clear that Cybermohalla is about adopting alternative strategies to explore and engage the ICTs so as to provide young people opportunities for learning and education. The Hindi-Urdu words that are combined with English to produce terms like "Cybermohalla" and "Compughar," capture the evocative and open-ended features of new media technologies. These technologies are not rooted in a singular space and place, but as de-territorialised forms offer unique possibilities for informal learning that can be actualized in non-linear ways. For instance, reflections of young participants on the everyday life in the city are sprinkled with personal experiences, creative self-expressions, and commentaries that offer some concrete suggestions on social and political issues. The ICTs also open up "spaces of dialogue" for the young participants: conversations and discussions lead to collective participation in a variety of multimedia experimental works. "What binds them together is their experimentation and play with diverse media forms (photography, animation, sound recording, text, etc.) to improvise and create cross-media works – texts, collages, posters, print publications, videos, installations." These multimedia projects – involving new ICTs and "media mixes" – not only generate excitement among the youngsters, but also overcome the deficiencies of the older and traditional models of education and learning, particularly in the formal systems of education.

One example where ICTs are being incorporated into the formal school learning settings is the Mapping the Neighbourhood Project in India. The project, conceptualized and developed by the Centre for Spatial Database Management and Solution (CSDMS), an independent organisation with support from the Department of Science and Technology of Government of India, involves school children from the rural and urban regions of Almora and Nainital of Uttaranchal province of North India. The basic approach to community mapping has been to visually construct a "map" of the places and spaces in the community. It has been widely used as a tool for planning and development of various projects. The Mapping the Neighbourhood project extends the concept by involving school children in the process. The main purpose of the project is to provide school children opportunities to learn about their regional geography and landscape and share this with other members of the community. The school children learn about global information system through workshops organised at their respective schools. The students work with personal digital assistants (PDAs) and global positioning systems (GPS) technologies to map their neighbourhoods. Another goal is to bring students in dialogue with local and rural communities about the integrating mapping technologies for local development. An important aspect of learning here, one that goes beyond the formal schooling, is in active participation of school children in community development. The notion of participation takes on a whole new meaning in the activities of the school children. ICTs provide a context for social networking and ongoing conversations among children and adult members of the rural communities.

Commenting on the innovative work, Rumi Mallick and Himanshu Kalra point out "that young people learn about participation and democracy while in school where they not only spend considerable proportion of their lives and undertake a formal education, it is also a place were many of their views and perspectives on life are developed and shaped." Although the idea behind the project is referred to as "an alternative learning experience," the primary intent is to integrate ICTs into formal education. Mallick and Kalra explain that "with an aim to create an enabling context for the youth to live, grow, learn, participate, decide, analyze, and change, the programme empowered the youth of the mountain areas by exposing them to technology tools in this case Geo-ICT tools." These are innovative ideas, extending the traditional community mapping through technologies and bringing school children as stakeholders in the development process. More important, it is aimed at transforming the idea of education from classroom settings to the field. These strategies enable learning, and as Mallick and Kalra rightly point out, provide knowledge as well as raise the consciousness of the school children.

Working Class Neighbourhoods and Community Mapping

The three media labs of Cybermohalla are located in different parts of Delhi – an illegal working class settlement in central part of the city and a poor colony in south Delhi – and provide opportunities to young people to work individually and collectively. The idea of a "mohalla," as a neighbourhood, exceeds the semantic connotations implied by the English term. As a social space, mohalla, with "its sense of alleys and corners," can be conceived as "dense nodes" where young people from economically deprived and marginalized communities negotiate their lives and subjectivities. Formal schooling is out of reach or unaffordable for the youngsters. They visit the lab out of curiosity, but soon get absorbed in the creative possibilities offered by computers and other media. Gradually, the young members, mostly women, begin to express themselves via the computer screens. A bi-monthly magazine "Ibarat" explored various meanings of work in women's lives. The magazine in Hindi and English is made available in digital and printed forms. A series of creative writings as diaries has been published into a book called, "Galiyon Se" (By Lanes). These are a bunch of reflections and thoughts on the everyday life in the city. Here is one such reflection on streets and by lanes:

For the last one year now, I have been in regular conversation with the group of young people in Compughar. Amongst other things streets and lanes were discussed many times, Streets make for great conversations. Streets would lead us to think about the harsh and aggressive behaviour of men towards each other and towards women in particular, the total lack of pedestrian pathways or respect towards them, the absence of street lighting, noisy traffic and its uncaring behaviour, or the near-total inaccessibility for disabled people or elder people. Also being amidst strangers, in crowds and moving with crowds.

This young women's narrative account of the streets of Delhi offer some unique insights into what has become of the public places and spaces. Although this reads as a political critique, there are many more writings that offer some interesting solutions to civic life and public infrastructure in the city. Some participants write about streets, some draw and sketch using graphics software presenting multiple perspectives on the topic. The materials produced become available to all participants and distributed in the neighbourhoods for further commentary and reflections. Shveta Sarda, coordinator at the Cybermohalla project, suggests that linking the broader environments of our digital worlds with the conversational worlds that we live with in our localities is central in understanding "publicness":

The world of the digital surrounds us. In our lanes and by-lanes we live through a dense palimpsest of images, texts and sounds, increasingly accessed and accelerated through the digital – VCDs, CDs, Cable, PCOs, DTP operations (pamphlets, stickers, sign boards), etc. Through our own practice, we are trying to work out an interface between this density and our concerns. We use the digital to create for us a networked platform in our own explorations with texts, images and sounds.

Sixty young participants from three different labs – 20 from each – have been involved in sketching ideas around "publicness." Working with a range of multimedia forms like animations, booklets, broadsheets, HTML, typed and formatted texts, sound scape, photo stories, written word, audio and visual juxtapositions or narratives, storyboards, etc. members develop innovative perspectives on alleys, corners, mohallas, and locality – important metaphors for "publicness." Visiting the city alleys and corners, meeting disadvantaged children and other dwellers in the poor and working class neighbourhoods, young participant begin conversations with a young girl child working in a factory, an old woman sweeping the streets of Delhi, to a middle aged man who runs a photo studio, a shop keeper, a tea stall owner, etc. Several young members have produced a collage called "Hamari Dilli" (Our Delhi) texts.

The "Walls" project draws upon ideas of publicness and locality to talk about how walls interact with and shape human experience. The experimental multimedia work being carried-out by young participants connect ideas of dwelling and experience. "Dwellings are made of walls. Our lived experience shows these walls are testimonies of fractured, fragile, contested stories of the everyday struggle to make life in the city. Walls are demolished. Walls get hardened. Fragile lives build themselves and reside along walls. Women gather around walls to share experience, youngsters lean against them to recount the day's stories from other parts of the city, infants rest in their shade." The Cybermohalla project provides opportunities of self-expression and exploration for the young under privileged people from Delhi. The new and old ICTs not only enable an enhanced participation in media, but also allow young participants a creative range of possibilities for commentary, critique, and dialogue.

In recognition of the contributions in media education through ICTs for young people, Sarai, the parent organisation of Cybermohalla was awarded the UNESCO Digital Art Award in 2004. The approach to cyberspace and the new media as open-ended and globalised forms of communication with the ability to connect with localised forms of communication as embodied in the "mohalla" is an innovative feature that provided inspiration to several groups in different parts of the world. Several youth members from Cybermohalla were invited to Hamburg, Germany for a workshop on innovative uses of new media.

Although the Cybermohalla project is organised around a set of inter-related objectives, its main focus is in making available ICTs, and the emerging technologies to poor working class youngsters. Consequently, the long-term new media explorations undertaken by these youngsters lead to some interesting and unexpected outcomes. The individual diaries, commonly known as "Compughar Diaries," as a record of creative and critical ideas in several formats that include written texts, still and moving images, graphics, and audio bytes, contain mundane observations on the flow of the city life to the serious social and political reflections. These begin to take on new meanings as the conversation proceeds among the members via hyperlink notes. The juxtaposition of personal experiences with the social and political realities produces a series of questions. Thus, what begins as an individual idea evolves into a collective engagement. The ideas, observations, questions, generated in the media labs are taken into the neigbourhoods, the "bastis," to which these young members belong for an extended dialogue with the community.

In important ways, then, the computers and the new media function as more that mere technological artifacts: rather these ICTs are "demystified" and provide a context for the young participants from the poor neighbourhoods to express and explore their creative and interpretative ideas. Although the urban areas in India (as well as the many other developing and underdeveloped regions of the world) have a high density of information and communication-based technologies in the form of the presence of printing presses (old and new), photographic studios, radio, cinema, television, cable television operator's, internet kiosks, etc., these have not been made particularly relevant to youth development or as enablers of media education. Commenting on the dynamics of the urban public culture, within which the old and new ICTs are embedded, Shuddhabrata Sengupta articulates the general idea behind the project: "We were interested in the way in which we could see the urban space we were located in, begin to reveal itself to us as a dense communicative network. As a matrix (as crowded as the streets of the old quarters of our city) within which, new and old technologies and the practices of communication, ranging from print to photography to film and the Internet were able to constantly renew a dynamic media ecology." It is precisely this "media ecology" – constituted by the co-presence of the old and new ICTs – that offers a context for developing innovative media education models that not only overcome the deficiencies of traditional approaches to education, but also shift the focus of media from commercial considerations to its pedagogic role. As discussed in chapter one, some of the emerging media education models, drawing insights from the work of Dewey and Freire, have identified the innovative uses of ICTs. Both the Cybermohalla and Mapping the Neighbourhood projects serve as good examples of these emerging models of media education.

The main goal of Mapping the Neighbourhood is to make computer-based education attractive to young learners. Although ICTs are understood to enhance learning and participation, the project integrated the uses of several technologies like personal digital assistants and global positioning systems to local developmental needs. This itself is an innovative approach. The involvement of school students makes it a unique exercise. First, it seeks to transform the traditional education process with learning that now takes place in the community, outside the classroom. It is through "doing" that students acquire knowledge. Second, the idea of development itself is transformed. Community participation provides the student learners opportunities and training in citizenship. The convergence of ICTs, development and education can be glimpsed in the work being carried out by students in Almora and Nainital area in Hawalbag. Here community mapping goes beyond territories and landscape; rather, the visual representations of their regions gives the people knowledge and understanding of how communities live in the social and material world. Mullick, Dhar, and Satyaprakash (2004) conclude that, "the use of ICT as an alternative form of education in rural and urban areas has demonstrated that this form of education can have a positive affect on the community at large… Innovative use of technology change the way development takes place and ensures that the issues of general public are addressed. Taking the children as 'agents of change', this project has tried to evolve an alternative form of education as well as developmental process."

The creation of community maps – of basic socio-economic, cultural, and ecological resources – by the school children in their respective neighbourhoods provides a new learning experience that is not only free from the formalized classroom education, but takes them into the 'real' world where learning and knowledge become complementary. In other words, as Siva Kumar asserts, "instead of learning geography, history, and environmental sciences and the textbooks, the children will learn by producing knowledge of relevance for their community." Further, referring to the feasibility of the project, Siva Kumar points out that the initial fears about the ability of rural school children to adapt to technologies like GIS, GPS, and PDA's proved wrong as these experiments became successful. Gradually the concept of community mapping has been integrated into the curriculum of several schools. An excerpt from "Mapping of Water Resources with PDA and GPS," provides a concrete example on why school children find these experiments challenging and useful:

With the help of PDA coupled with GPS (running on an indigeneously developed GIS software called Todermal) the students with assistance from the community created base maps for villages. Other than the patwari maps [traditional revenue maps in India, outdated and unavailable to the community], no village map exists. The students generated the village maps, collected and marked GPS locations of all water resource points (natural and man-made). The location of each house was marked and linked to GIS in order to be able to reassess the water need and supply situation. Other built structures (temples, roads and pathways, shops, community centers, health centers, other infrastructures etc) were also mapped. This involvement of the students in community mapping, the ongoing conversations with rural citizens, the engagement with their environment, the coming together of local forms of knowledge and modern information and communication technologies, points to an innovative exercise in social development that can be adapted and replicated in other underdeveloped and developing regions of the world. This form of the local-global engagement is more productive than the one that is visible in commercial and popular media around the world, and is an interesting social communication and development model articulated by young people. The conversations between student teams and local community members is an exercise in decentralized planning and rural development. As a form of "direct education" it emulates what Paulo Freire had outlined through his philosophy of education: dialogical education through interaction with a focus on practice (or praxis). The ICTs also open up "spaces of dialogue" for the young participants: conversations and discussions lead to collective participation in a variety of multimedia experimental work.

References

Buckingham, David (2003) *Media Education: Literacy, Learning, and Contemporary Culture*. Cambridge: Polity Press in association with Blackwell.

Dewey, J. (1966) *Democracy and Education: An Introduction to the Philosophy of Education*. New York: The Macmillan Company.

von Feilitzen, Cecilia and Ulla Carlsson (2002) *Children, Young People and Media Globalization*. Göteborg: Nordicom, The UNESCO International Clearinghouse on Children, Youth and Media.

Freire, P. (1972) *Pedagogy of the Oppressed*. London: Penguin.

Goodman, Steven and Maxine Greene (2003) *Teaching Youth Media: A Critical Guide to Literacy, Video Production, and Social Change* (Series on School Reform, 36). New York: Teacher's College Press.

Kumar, Siva (2004) 'Technology at Local Level: Mapping the Neighbourhood with School Children', paper presented to the Cambridge Conference, United Kingdom.

Lankshear, Colin and Peter McLaren (ed.) (1993) *Critical Literacy: Politics, Praxis, and the Postmodern*. Albany, NY: State University of New York Press.

Livingstone, Sonia (2001) *Children and Their Changing Media Environment: A European Comparative Study*. Mahwah, N.J: L. Erlbaum Associates.

Mullick, Rumi, Anuradha Dhar and Satyaprakash (2004) 'An Alternative Learning Experience'. *I4d Journal*.

Sefton-Green, Julian (ed.) (1998) *Digital Diversions: Youth Culture in the Age of Multimedia*. London: UCL Press.

Sholle, David and Stan Denski (1993) 'Reading and Writing the Media: Critical Media Literacy and postmodernism', in Colin Lankshear and Peter McLaren (eds.) *Critical Literacy*. Albany, NY: State University of New York Press

United Nations (2005) *World Youth Report: Young People Today, and in 2015*.

Educational Television and School

Susanne Krucsay

When I began working in the Ministry of Education – more than 20 years ago – the department I joined focused on the so-called qualification of educational media to be used in class. Austrian school law provides that media (books and audio-visual media) used in schools be in accordance with certain didactical-methodical requirements. Thus media are submitted to the ministry for qualification, which is granted or rejected depending on the result of a thorough examination by expert commissions. This all sounds extremely bureaucratic, in practice it works quite well as the criteria of the qualifying process are clearly and exhaustively defined. The most important indispensable property of an educational medium is whether it corresponds to the syllabus of the specific discipline. Another criterion is essential correctness; another important one especially for audio-visual media is the so-called media adequacy. Media adequacy addresses the question of inter-dependency between content and form: Thus there is no point in presenting a written text on an elaborate technical carrier such as a DVD without exploiting the complex chances a versatile medium offers to teachers and students. So much to the legal provision and now I am turning to the segments of the teaching/learning process with media.

The Teaching/Learning Process with Media:
On the whole we can distinguish between 5 main parts:

- Structure   "What are we going to deal with?"
- Research   "I am getting closer to the point"
- Co-operate   "We are going to work together"
- Produce   "I am going to make something"
- Present   "I am going to explain to you something"

These methods used according to the situation in class and the nature of the media are a challenge as well as a profit for interacting with media.

What Should Didactic Media Be Like?

When using media we are often guided by euphoria for what technical development can accomplish. The question, however, should rather be if and in what ways the quality of teaching/learning is improved. So it is always the combination between the methodical considerations and the technical aspects which enhances the quality of the teaching/learning. To sum up, educational media should

- contribute to improving the quality

- make possible a systematic planning and processing of the contents

- stimulate action-oriented learning

- support open learning methods

- activate the student to construct his/her own knowledge

- promote autonomous and discovering learning

- put the students in the centre making possible individual learning within a group

- support cooperative learning

- promote sustainable, lifelong learning

How Do Students Become Media Literate (media competent)?

- They develop their media skills by:

- using media equipment (hardware)

- procuring information

- using standard programmes

- using learning programmes

- decoding media texts and negotiating meanings

- visualizing and presenting contents

- producing media

Which Parts of the Process Can Educational Media Cover?

Audio-visual media are always a part of the whole didactic process alongside with the other media. 'Other media' also include the personal medium, namely the teacher. He/she plans methodically by which teaching aids the targeted goals of the teaching unit or subject matter respectively can be attained. Once a rough plan is made it becomes evident in which parts of the process the use of audio-visual media is an absolute **MUST**.

Educational media help us

- to enlarge the scope we perceive the world through our senses (e.g. biology)

- to facilitate communication over space and time (e.g. history)

- to present dangerous and/or risky experiments and inaccessible events (e.g. science, geography)

- open up contents through generated images and other technological devices

How (when) Do We Use Educational Media?

- We would like to introduce a topic, not necessarily in a linear systematic way – rather we want to raise the curiosity of our students by presenting them one side of the coin. We intend to challenge them by a pointed presentation and hope to get numerous controversial responses. This category we call *impulse medium* – a kind of a pointed introduction to new contents.

- The medium covers areas which no other medium could accomplish – it is – as already mentioned before – an indispensable part of the teaching/learning process. This type is called an *integrative medium*, as is an integral part of the entire unit.

- The medium covers areas which may be a bit outside the core of the curriculum – *enrichment medium*

- The medium serves as a systematic summary (conclusion) of a unit – a *synoptic medium*.

Integrative Media Use

For all their didactic elements as teaching aids educational media should simultaneously regarded as texts to be analyzed. A simplified text analysis model asking for the 3 pillars of any communication process is if great use. Thus we ask for the communicator (producer), the medium (contents) and the recipient (impact, perception).

School and Educational TV – Phases of a Relationship

Back in the last decades in the 20th century School TV had a fixed place in the programme schedule on public television in Austria. This meant until 1991 15 minutes films, aired in the morning and repeated in the afternoon ("Schulfernsehen" – School TV). The films were produced and financed under the auspices of the Austrian Ministry of Education, the topics selected by a committee consisting of ministry and television people, the project accompanied from the beginning to the end by expert pedagogues. By the way the same scheme was true of radio broadcasts, called "Schulfunk" (School Radio).

There is no need here to go into detail what happened with the advent of Internet, together with the overall media revolution. In brief, fixed time schedules became obsolete and so the cooperation between public television and radio and the educational authority had to be put on an entirely new basis. Let me describe in a few words what this means:

For about 12 years TV and the media department of the ministry have been co-producers, the ministry's financial contribution making a rather small part of the entire production, which is planned for the prime time programme on TV for a programme slot of 50 minutes. The producers submit their projects (culture, science, history, religion) to a small working group made up of TV and ministry people (6 persons altogether). The representatives of the ministry then decide which projects are appropriate for use in class. These decisions are naturally based on the accordance with the curricular requirements mentioned formerly. So the ministry has its financial share in a high-class professional production and gets for it the copyrights for use in the non-commercial sphere and the rights to use the material in special Intranets. In most cases school versions are made, which are usually shortened spin-offs, with accompanying didactic material.

The films together with the didactic material are digitalized and offered to educational institutions on a Video on Demand scheme as Streaming and Digital TV. The technology is a so-called Edu-Box, which streams the media on 25 monitors. This allows the students to work independently and interactively. Thus using educational TV is becoming an important ingredient of Blended Learning.

Conclusion

Looking back at this resume it is clear that educational TV has undergone substantial changes during the last 20-30 years. What has not changed and will probably always be needed is the contribution of audio-visual elements to the didactic process, which – naturally – differs a great deal from what it was a short time ago. To my mind, the most important change concerns the acquisition of knowledge, which is grounded in a moderate version of an "instructional constructivism" (cf.Blömeke http://www.medienpaed.com/00/blomeke1.pdf) – students are active learners who construct their own understanding on the basis of what they already know, so that they "cannot be simply presented with prescriptions for new instructional practices and be expected to 'receive' them and use them as is" (Putnam/Borko 1997, p.1224 and p. 1236).

References

Blömeke, Sigrid (2001) Zur medienpädagogischen Ausbildung von Lehrerinnen und Lehrern. In: *Medienpädagogik. Online-Zeitschrift für Theorie und Praxis der Medienbildung* (http://www.medienpaed.com/00-2/bloemeke.pdf).

Putnam, Ralph T./Borko, Hilda (1997) Teacher Learning. Implications of New Views of Cognition. In: Biddle, Bruce J./Good, Thomas L./Goodson, Ivor F. (eds.) *International Handbook of Teachers and Teaching*, vol.2 Dordrecht/Boston/London: Kluwer Academic Publishers, pp. 1223-1296.

New Educational Needs
Distance Training and Life-long Learning for Teachers

Geneviève Jacquinot-Delaunay

A New Training Model

Until now, throughout the world *"simultaneous collective teaching"* has been practised. This is a model whereby teachers and learners are together all at the same time and in the same spot to teach/learn the same thing.

What is emerging nowadays is a new model more in tune with the changes that are taking place in technology, the economy, and the socio-cultural sphere. This is the distance-learning model (DL) – also termed open distance learning (ODL) or e-learning. These terms are not strictly equivalent; however, they do place *"distance at the centre of the teaching/learning relationship"*. The concept is the opposite of "simultaneous collective teaching" – also termed "face-to-face" or "classroom" instruction – as teacher and learners are no longer together at the same time, in the same place, and to focus on the same thing.

We have still not dropped the old model whereas we must take on the new one; hence the difficulty of this changeover phase.

1- Why "distance" and "lifelong"?

– "lifelong"

because knowledge is evolving fast and must be updated;

because job content is also changing and people need to change jobs;

because school is no longer the only place where knowledge is passed on and training can no longer be confined to what has been termed, until now, "the formative years"; and,

because modern life requires flexibility, adaptability, openness, and re-newal.

What is true of all occupations applies just as much – if not more – to teaching, so that the generation gap does not become too wide, as it is tending to do now.

- *"distance"*

because training requirements are rising throughout the world, are more and more diversified and specialised, and no traditional education system can keep up economically speaking;

because both time (no travel, no time off work to undergo training etc.) and money must be spared (new skills must be acquired without attending a separate training centre);

because nowadays the technology is available for information and knowledge to be stored, distributed, accessed, and exchanged by "remote" learners.

It is becoming ever more common for things to be done "remotely": shopping, entertainment, banking... everything can be done "from a distance", under certain conditions of course.

It 2- What are the underlying principles of this new training mode?

The teaching/learning process has become fragmented in time and space; so the question is how to rebuild unity and logic for the learner. How can he/she be approached, engaged, guided, and helped to learn?

- *designing training as a system* that factors in learners and teachers but also the instructional materials and media that serve to establish pupil/teacher and pupil/pupil communication; but also the processes of enrolment, monitoring, and assessment of both distance learners and the organisation as a whole.

- *building an environment conducive to training*: it is not enough to merely "put courses on line" – as is often propounded when it comes to distance learning (DL) or ODL that emphasises flexible learning, focuses on the needs of the individual, and seeks to cater to all the features of the various groups. The question is: who are the would-be learners and what do they know already? It must be explained to them how they will learn in the new system. They must be approached in a certain way so that they do not feel "distance" is "absence". Where will they be working? Which resources will they have? What will be their pace? Which constraints will they face?

- *anticipate the learner's self-reliance* or set yourself the goal of making him/her gradually more self-reliant, **because self-reliance does not come on command: it must be built up**. The successful self-paced students are those who are self-reliant enough to learn by themselves or who have acquired such self-reliance due to their strong motivation to learn. Not everyone has the same learning capability and often those who have had the least schooling find it hard to get organised and manage their personal work: they need guidance and monitoring so as to acquire greater self-reliance.

- indeed, all this amounts to *factoring in distance so as to better master it*; but which distance are we talking about? Distance can be geographic or **spatial** – as when would-be learners are disabled or far away from the training centre; *temporal* because with distance training the learner can freely choose when to study and his/her own pace of study; furthermore, learners do not have to wait too long for responses to any requests they may have; *technical* by way of the different types of mediation but there is often a great difference in the equipment used by the learner and that available in the training institution.

social, cultural and economic – the hardest to control, it is said that thanks to the Internet knowledge is available to one and all (a slogan of the information society); however, there are real access disparities not only between but even within countries and continents – hence the increasing recognition of the importance of peer learning and the social dimension of learning.

2- What role for the media and ICTs? Both all and nothing

- **All**. ICTs are everything as they have become indispensable to overcome spatial distance: they serve to link various groups to knowledge of all types as evidenced; furthermore, they can be connected in real time or off line to other learners. The whole history of distance education has stuck to the development of the communication media. The first distance courses began in London in 1840 – the same year that the postage stamp was introduced (with the same rate applied all over the UK (stenography course offered by its inventor Isaac Pitman); other media came to be used (telephone, radio, cinema, television, the Internet and Internet-related media such as blogs, mobile phones, etc. ; that is, everything that serves to facilitate and/or present knowledge differently and help share information and communicate). However, they did not squeeze paper out.

- *Nothing*: because the media and the various technologies can be used for any purpose and type of education. This is because technologies cannot give meaning to the acquisition of knowledge. "Technicist" approaches that advocate providing ever more sophisticated equipment to boost access to knowledge should be viewed with caution.

The accessibility of instruments must be factored in as must the specificity and complementarity of the media used: new digital technologies are enabling multimedia, multimodal, interactive systems as long as the old Socrates-style teacher-to-pupil dialogue is not transposed mechanically. *The* prerequisite of all these

ICTs and various media is the ability to be self-reliant: *"By requiring self-reliance ICTs are revolutionising the world of work and knowledge and consequently the spheres of adult training and education."* They require major changes of teachers in the way they do things and in their thinking.

Conclusion

In this changeover phase, how can teachers be led to change the way they see and do things?

All this can serve anyone wishing to embark on distance training – if, that is, the resources are available are accessible in the fields of knowledge and know-how. It is also useful to the person designing distance training for pupils and students. It can prove useful for those working in institutions that specialise in distance training but also more "local" less "professional" settings to meet particular needs.

Naturally, the implementation of all these mechanisms – especially on a large scale – is far more complicated than the description just given: when the real work begins difficulties emerge at all levels (technical, institutional, organisational, pedagogical, relational) both human and non-human! But many of such difficulties are caused by non-preparation, an unawareness of the implications of this new training mode, and a clinging to familiar representations (it is well known that people teach the way they have been taught).

Clearly, there can be no question of "replacing the teacher" by machines or all sorts of media. Under no circumstances should teaching be downgraded or students neglected. What is needed is a new "professionality" that meshes with the new conditions of knowledge transmission and acquisition – and teachers in tune with the 21st century. A long experience with distance training suggests that: *"the good thing about distance training is that it makes teacher presence the essence"*.

The Authors

Hanan Ashi

Dr., Head of the Communication Department for
the Women Section
King Abdulaziz University
Jeddah
Saudi Arabia
hashi@kau.edu.sa

Sanjay Asthana

Dr., Assistant Professor
College of Mass Communication
School of Journalism
Middle Tennessee State University
Murfreesboro
USA
sasthana@mtsu.cdu

Cary Bazalgette

Education Policy Adviser, and
General Secretary of the 8-nation Steering Group
for the European Charter for Media Literacy
British Film Institute
London
UK
cary.bazalgette@blueyonder.co.uk

Evelyne Bevort

Deputy Director, international activities
CLEMI – Centre for liaison between teaching and
information media
Paris
France
e.bevort@clemi.org

Ulla Carlsson

Dr., Professor and Director
Nordicom/The International Clearinghouse on
Children, Youth and Media
Göteborg University
Göteborg
Sweden
ulla.carlsson@nordicom.gu.se

Divina Frau-Meigs

Dr., Professor of American Studies and Mass
Media Sociology
Paris 3-Sorbonne Nouvelle
Institut du Monde Anglophone
Paris
France
divina.meigs@orange.fr

Saeed Abdallah Hareb

Dr., Professor
Department of Sociology
University of the Emirates
Al Ain
The United Arab Emirates
drhareb@gmail.com

Geneviève Jacquinot-Delaunay

Dr., Professor
University of Paris 8, and
MediaMorphoses INA/A.Colin
Paris
France
gjacq@noos.fr

Abdul Waheed Khan

Dr., Assistant Director-General
Communication and Information Sector
UNESCO
Paris
France

Muhammed El-Khateeb

Dr., Director of Al Riyadh School
Riyadh
Saudi Arabia
mohammed@kfs.sch.sa

Susanne Krucsay

Head of Department
Media Pedagogy/Educational Media/Media Service
Federal Ministry of Education, Science and Culture
Vienna
Austria
susanne.krucsay@bmbwk.gv.at

Fathia Al Qurashy

Dr., Assistant Professor
Department of Sociology
King Abdel Aziz University
Jeddah
Saudi Arabia
falqurashi@hotmail.com

Vito Reia-Baptista

Dr., Professor of Communication, Media and Film
Studies
University of Algarve
Faro
Portugal
vreia@ualg.pt

Pier Cesare Rivoltella

Dr., Professor
Director of CREMIT (Research Centre on Media,
Information and Technology Education)
Università Catolica del Sacro Cuore
Milano
Italy
piercesare.rivoltella@unicatt.it

Catherine Souyri

Advisor for Communication
French National Commission for UNESCO
Paris
France
catherine.souyri@diplomatie.gouv.fr

Essmat Sweedan

Dr., Professor
Centre for Languages and Scientific Development
International Islamic University of Malaysia
Kuala Lampur
Malaysia
sweedan8_w2@hotmail.com

Samy Tayie

Dr., Professor and President of Mentor Association
Faculty of Mass Communication
Cairo University
Cairo
Egypt
stayie@link.net

José Manuel Pérez Tornero

Dr., Professor
Universidad Autónoma de Barcelona
Barcelona
Spain
jmtornero@gammamedia.e.telefonica.net

Philippos Vardakas

Trainee (between March and July 2007)
Unit A2 "Media literacy and MEDIA Programme"
DG Information Society and Media
European Commission
Brussels
Belgium

Patrick Verniers

Director Média Animation npo
Membre of the Media Education Council (CEM)
and Higher Audiovisual Board (CSA)
Lecturer at University of Louvain-la-neuve
Brussells
Belgium
p.verniers@media-animation.be

271

Matteo Zacchetti   Responsible for the Media Literacy Initiative
Unit A2 "Media Literacy and MEDIA Programme"
DG Information Society and Media
European Commission
Brussels
Belgium
matteo.zacchetti@ec.europa.eu